Policy Measures for Low-Wage Employment in Europe

Policy Measures for Low-Wage Employment in Europe

Edited by

Wiemer Salverda

University of Amsterdam, The Netherlands

Claudio Lucifora

Università Cattolica, Milan, Italy

Brian Nolan

Economic and Social Research Institute, Dublin, Ireland

In Assiociation with the European Low-Wage Employment Research Network (LoWER)

Edward Elgar
Cheltenham, UK • Northampton, MA, USA

Published by
Edward Elgar Publishing Limited
Glensanda House
Montpellier Parade
Cheltenham
Glos GL50 1UA
UK

Edward Elgar Publishing, Inc.
136 West Street
Suite 202
Northampton
Massachusetts 01060
USA

A catalogue record for this book
is available from the British Library

Library of Congress Cataloguing in Publication Data

Policy measures for low-wage employment in Europe / edited by Wiemer Salverda, Claudio Lucifora, Brian Nolan.
    "In association with the European Low-wage Employment Research Network (LoWER)"—data sheet.
    "These essays result from the conference on 'Policies for low-wage employment and social exclusion in Europe' . . . at the U. Groningen in November 1998"—Introd.
    Includes index.
    1. Wages—Government policy—Europe—Congresses. 2. Labor policy—Europe—Congresses. 3. Income maintenance programs—Europe—Congresses. 4. Labor economics—Europe—Congresses. I. Salverda, Wiemer. II. Lucifora, Claudio. III. Nolan, Brian, 1953–

HD5014 .P65 2000
331.2'94—dc21

00–039397

ISBN 1 84064 410 9

Printed and bound in Great Britain by Biddles Ltd, *www.biddles.co.uk*

Contents

Figures

Tables

Contributors

Donna Brown
School of Management, Royal Holloway, University of London.
E-mail: Donna.Brown@rhbnc.ac.uk

Marco Doudeijns
Organisation for Economic Co-operation and Development (OECD), Paris

Marcel Einerhand
Ministry of Social Affairs and Employment, The Hague.
E-mail: MEinerhand@minszw.nl

Jonathan E. Haskel
Queen Mary and Westfield College and CEPR.
E-mail: J.E.Haskel@qmw.ac.uk

Gerard Hughes
Economic and Social Research Institute, Dublin.
E-mail: Gerry.Hughes@esri.ie

Bruno Van der Linden
Fonds National de la Recherche Scientifique and Institut de Recherches Economiques et Sociales, Département des Sciences Economiques, Université Catholique de Louvain.
E-mail: VanDerLinden@ires.ucl.ac.be

Claudio Lucifora
Istituto di Economia dell'Impresa e del Lavoro, Università Cattolica, Milan.
E-mail: Lucifora@mi.unicatt.it

Steven McIntosh
Centre for Economic Performance, London School of Economics.
E-mail: S.McIntosh@lse.ac.uk

Abigail McKnight
Centre for Analysis of Social Exclusion (CASE), London School of Economics. E-mail: A.A.McKnight@lse.ac.uk

Arthur van de Meerendonk
Ministry of Social Affairs and Employment, The Hague.
E-mail: AMeerendonk@MINSZW.nl

Robert Mohr
University of Texas at Austin.

Peter Mühlau
Amsterdam Institute for Advanced Labour Studies, University of Amsterdam. E-mail: Muehlau@fee.uva.nl

Brian Nolan
Economic and Social Research Institute, Dublin.
E-mail: BNolan@esri.ie

Cathal O'Donoghue
University of Cambridge.
E-mail: Cathal@econ.cam.ac.uk

Wiemer Salverda
Amsterdam Institute for Advanced Labour Studies, University of Amsterdam. E-mail: Salverda@fee.uva.nl

Viktor Steiner
Zentrum für Europäische Wirtschaftsforschung, Mannheim.
E-mail: Steiner@zew.de

Francesca Utili
University of Rome 'Tor Vergata'.
E-mail: Francesca.Utili@tesoro.it

Claudia Weinkopf
Institut Arbeit und Technik, Gelsenkirchen.
E-mail: Weinkopf@iatge.de

The LoWER Network

Members of the *European Low-Wage Employment Research* network
Wiemer Salverda (co-ordinator) and *Peter Mühlau*, University of Amsterdam; *Mary Gregory, Andrew Glyn* (Oxford University); *Ronald Schettkat* (Utrecht University), *Jonathan Wadsworth, Stephen Machin, Abigail McKnight* (London School of Economics); *Gerard Hughes, Brian Nolan* (Economic and Social Research Institute, Dublin); *Andries de Grip, Maarten Wolbers* (University of Maastricht); *Thomas Zwick, Viktor Steiner* (Zentrum für Europäische Wirtschaftsforschung, Mannheim); *Rita Asplund* (Research Institute for the Finnish Economy, Helsinki); *Ioannis Theodossiou, Peter Sloane* (University of Aberdeen); *Ive Marx* (Centre for Social Policy UFSIA, Antwerp); *Nicholas Burkitt* (Low Pay Unit, London); *Stephen Bazen* (Université Montesquieu, Bordeaux); *Claudio Lucifora* (Università Cattolica, Milan); *Ana Cardoso* (Universidade do Minho, Braga); *Juan Dolado* (Universidad Carlos III, Madrid); *Juan Jimeno* (Universidad de Alcalá, Fundación de Estudios de Economía Aplicada, Madrid); *Florentino Felgueroso* (Universidad de Oviedo); *Antje Mertens* (Max Planck Institute for Human Development, Berlin); *Sophie Ponthieux* (INSEE, Paris).

Other publications of the network
Statistical Data Available on Low-Wage Employment in the European Union and its Member States, Special Report to the European Commission, LoWER, Groningen, April 1997; *Low Pay and Earnings Mobility in Europe* R. Asplund, P. Sloane and I. Theodossiou (eds), Edward Elgar, July 1998; *Low-Wage Employment in Europe,* S. Bazen, M. Gregory and W. Salverda (eds), Edward Elgar, December 1998; *Policies for Low-Wage Employment and Social Exclusion in Europe,* C. Lucifora and W. Salverda (eds), Francoangeli, Milan, October 1998; *The Overeducated Worker? The Economics of Underutilization of Skills,* A. de Grip and L. Borghans (eds), Edward Elgar, March 2000; *Low-Wage Employment: A European Perspective,* M. Gregory, W. Salverda and S. Bazen (eds), Oxford University Press (forthcoming).

Further network information on website: *http://www.uva.nl/aias/lower*

1. Introduction

Wiemer Salverda, Claudio Lucifora and Brian Nolan

Policies for the low paid and low skilled have come centre-stage. Every government, in Europe and North America, has some kind of policy for the lower end of the labour market, or seems to think it should have one. Despite this recent popularity, however, policies directed at the less advantaged and marginal workers in the labour market are still a 'black box' in many respects. The ten contributions collected in this book take a fresh look at policymaking for the lower end of the labour market. Chapters 2 to 5 critically review some existing policy instruments and measures. Chapters 6 and 7 discuss neglected long-run issues relating to low pay and exclusion. Chapters 8 to 11 consider the role of demand and policy measures to affect it, which have played little role in the European policy debate with its concentration on the supply side. In each case, the contributions are either directly focused on policy or have significant implications for its formulation.

These essays result from the conference on *Policies for Low-Wage Employment and Social Exclusion in Europe* that was staged by the European Low-Wage Employment Research network, LoWER, at the University of Groningen in November 1998. The present book is the final product of the first, very productive phase (1996–98) of network activities. During its new phase (2000–2003), the network plans to build on this, particularly making further forays into the issue of product demand for low-skilled services. More information on the network and its output can be found on page xii. We gratefully acknowledge the financial support given to the network activities by the European Commission under the Targeted Socio-Economic Research programme (Fourth Framework) and the Key Action Improving the Socio-Economic Knowledge Base (Fifth Framework) respectively. We also like to thank Arthur de Boer for his important assistance to readying the manuscript for publication.

THE ISSUES

Over the last twenty years, the European labour market situation has been characterised by high levels of unemployment. It is only very recently that the average rate of unemployment has shown some tendency to decrease from a level well above 10 per cent of the active population to somewhat less than that. Unemployment rates are particularly high for the low skilled but this is not unique to Europe. It also applies to the US, and to those European countries with unemployment rates well below the European average such as Austria, Denmark, the Netherlands and the UK. Typically, those in the labour force with less than secondary education have an unemployment rate 2.5 times that of the best educated. Therefore, the difficult labour market situation at the lower end of the educational spectrum is not something that will automatically disappear even with a decline in overall unemployment and the general improvement of the labour market.

It is important to note that it is not always inequality *per se* which is worrying government and policymakers, but the existence of imperfections and distortions in the working of market forces (such as monopoly or monopsony power) which at the lower end of the distribution of earnings may result in increasing poverty and social exclusion. These key issues are receiving the attention of policymakers in various EU countries to varying degrees, and certainly merit their continued attention in the coming years. For a long time political attention was primarily fixed on (minimum) wages and unemployment benefits on the one hand and labour market regulations on the other. The former were often thought to be too high, the latter too inflexible, and consequently policy measures in many countries tended to reduce wage and benefit levels and decrease employment protection. The political debate seems to be shifting lately. Increasingly, the question is how employment growth can be furthered without negatively affecting the position of individual workers; how the functioning of the labour market can be improved without increasing poverty and social exclusion. The new research findings pointing to minimal employment effects of minimum wage hikes have been associated with a growing concern with distributional issues. The issue is how policy measures and the working of the labour market can act together to secure acceptable standards of living for the low skilled and their families. The incapacity of certain segments of the labour market to provide a decent standard of living inspires a widespread desire to provide financial support in the form of transfers, but to the extent that these are 'means-tested' this also increases dependency and reduces the ability of recipients to improve their situation through their own effort and achievements.

The low-paid and low-skilled segment of the labour market is a stage on which the roles played by welfare, taxation and earnings are difficult to disentangle. Taxation and benefits have been playing their roles for a long time and are now increasingly joined by specific subsidies targeted on the low paid. The issues are also intricately linked to the whole system of taxation and social security contributions. Pleas to lend policy measures a (more) permanent character, such as the employer subsidy on low pay proposed by Edmond Malinvaud, seem to underline this. However, measures are often taken ad hoc, creating administrative complications and putting up barriers to the smooth functioning of labour markets. This seems to hold for all industrial countries, albeit with some (interesting) variation. Whilst some countries such as the US or the UK follow an approach favouring in-work subsidies to the employee, such as Family Credit or Earned Income Tax Credit, other countries, mostly from Continental Europe, appear to attach more weight to subsidies paid to employers for creating low-paid jobs. It is as yet unclear which approach works better. Both seem to have significant consequences and limitations, for incomes, for labour supply and for job growth. Is it simply a matter of trading off one effect against the other on the basis of political preferences that differ between countries?

We should not accept such a conclusion without further analysis. The approach of in-work benefits aims at leaving it to the market to create the employment. This may mitigate the risk of artificially creating unsustainable jobs, but at the same time it is no guarantee that jobs are produced in sufficient numbers to alleviate unemployment and poverty. Basically, the scope of in-work benefits is to produce better incomes from jobs that are there and no additional jobs may necessarily be produced. Moral hazard may also be a problem, on both sides of the market. On the one hand, employers may reduce wages speculating that employees will receive additional in-work benefits from government; on the other hand, workers receiving an income supplement may restrain the number of hours supplied to the labour market, taking advantage of in-work benefits to make up for the difference. Depending on its design, in-work benefits are no panacea for poverty as the lowest incomes may still remain very low.

By contrast, Continental subsidy measures focused on firms are more explicit about desirable labour market outcomes, namely increasing employment. The support given to employers seems to rest on the idea that there is a lack of low-skilled low-paid jobs. However, depending on the design of the measure, there is no guarantee that the jobs will go to people from low-income households, who most need the job and the income. Measures focusing narrowly on specific target groups (that is the long-term unemployed, the low-skilled and/or the poor) may have little effect on overall employment, whilst a broad application of subsidies may lead to large dead-weight losses: the subsidy may well be paid for low-paid jobs that are already there or would have been created anyway. They may also have displacement effects.

In addition, both types of measures face problems of intrusiveness and transaction costs. Easy take-up and satisfactory targeting seem to be at odds with workers' privacy and with cost effectiveness. Finally, as previously mentioned, employer subsidies may reinforce 'bumping down' in the labour market more than in-work benefits, as the subsidised jobs may be occupied by the better educated. In addition to their impact on movements between inactivity and employment – the unemployment trap – a comprehensive assessment of these policies should also regard the poverty trap, that is the impact on hours worked and earnings growth for the low-paid once they have managed to enter paid employment.

Basically, taxes, benefits and subsidies are different sides of the same coin – in various national colours. It is helpful that recent theoretical and political debates seem to be moving away from ideological assertion. The contributions for this book aim to continue the debate and assess different policy measures in their own right. If they teach any lesson, it is to emphasise how immensely complicated the state of affairs at the lower end of the labour market is, and that no single measure will be adequate to tackle its problems. A balanced mix should be investigated. The wheel has not yet been invented in any single country and, in Europe at least, monetary unification seems to require joining forces. From a research perspective, this implies the need for international comparisons to be carried out with great care for the details – taking measures in other countries than one's own at face value is an easy source of misunderstanding and policy deadlock as is illustrated by the short-lived popularity of one 'model' after the other, the Swedish model, the German, the American and so on.

The urgency of tackling high rates of unemployment justifies the strong focus of policymaking – and of the above debate – on the present situation. However, it is very important to consider future problems that are already starting to emerge. A lifelong perspective on social exclusion is essential in this context. Earnings in the labour market are of decisive importance – increasingly so as female labour market participation is approaching that of men – not only for those in employment now but also after retirement, and equally for the following generation now still dependent on their parents' earnings. There is more to this than calculating wage inequality on a lifelong basis. Two contributions in this book consider the matter: the provision of pension rights after working life has ended, and intergenerational transmission: youths who start their career in the labour market with a handicap and run an increased risk of being low paid themselves as a consequence of their parents' situation. One of the lessons that we can learn from history is that an unfettered labour market tends to produce widespread poverty among the old aged and to reproduce poverty from one generation to the next. It is extremely important to consider how increasing flexibility and deregulation in the labour market and government policy can complement each other to break such vicious circles or prevent their reappearance on the societal stage.

Over the last two decades European policies have been solidly focused on the labour market's supply side, while relatively little has been heard about the demand side. Naturally, taxation, social security and labour market regulation are important, but sometimes the impression is given that every problem can be solved by some kind of fine-tuning of such measures, also for the range of low earnings and household incomes. However, the magnitude and functioning of demand seem to be particularly important issues for low-paid labour. Present-day trends in the industrialised economy may hit unskilled jobs more than those requiring higher skill levels. The concept of 'globalisation' is almost synonymous with increased international trade and rapid technological change. Both may affect unskilled jobs negatively. The debate that economists have been waging on these issues for some time now is addressed and continued in the present book, with two contributions that focus on the experience of Germany and Britain respectively. These point in different directions, technology in the former and trade in the latter. They show that at best trade and technology are only part of the explanation and that globalisation has no potential to improve the situation of the low-skilled in the short run. In so far as trade does play a role, this may provide additional input to the international debate on trade liberalisation. There seems to be more point, however, in improving the training of the work force than in seeking vainly to curtail technological change.

However, there is more to the demand side than trade and technology. The low-wage labour market appears to be characterised by a higher level of employer power than other sectors, as is suggested by monopsony approaches. Put differently, labour supply and demand may be interacting in a specific way in the low-wage part of the labour market, distinguishing it from the rest of the market. One of the contributions to this volume, a study of employee turnover in two prominent low-paying industries (hotels and supermarkets) serves to illustrate this. In this context, the more employers are dominating the market – that is, the greater the wage setting power of employers and larger the departure from 'fair' competition – the more notorious it is to monitor and investigate wage determination and employer behaviour and, eventually, correct distortions with policy measures.

Finally, 'labour demand' is conventionally and conveniently identified with direct employer demand as it manifests itself in the labour market. Very little attention is ever paid to the role of product demand behind it. It should not be forgotten, however, that labour demand is a 'derived' demand and that the labour input is functional to the production of goods and services. Henceforth, the possible negative pressures of imports on unskilled labour mainly concern the part of low-wage employment that is in the production of goods. There is little role for product demand in this analysis, apart from the fact that it seems to be satisfied by products from a different geographical origin. In services the effects are experienced less directly. The effects of technology are most intensely felt in manufacturing but services are certainly not exempt and increasingly so. However, 'services' is a very broad sector comprising the entire spectrum of pay from the highest levels in finance and ICT to the lowest in cleaning and retailing. There is good reason to take a closer look at the services where most of the low-paid jobs are concentrated. These seem to be closely related to consumer demand. Traditionally, demand is seen to depend on prices, which in turn depend on productivity and (wage) costs. Basically, this reflects the world of goods and goods production. However, in consumer-oriented services other aspects related to the nature of the product itself may be playing an important role.

In a world of asymmetric information, the quality of the service and trust and also perceptions of social status may be important factors determining the size of the market and related employment. By definition, the quality of a service relates more strongly to the person of the provider and is often difficult to determine ex ante. This relates directly to the trust the consumer needs to put in the producer, even in the short run. It concerns the nature of the service itself – for example, good quality food implies the proper respect of hygiene regulations in restaurant kitchens, invisible to the client – particularly in a context where relatively low levels of initial investment are leaving room for all kinds of fly-by-night operations. Often, however, the trust may also be needed for a much broader domain –for example, house cleaning in absence of the owner – and informal markets may (be thought to) be better in providing this (at a limited scale). Finally, on the demand side, considerations of social (in)equality may be at play wherever one person is directly servicing another – for example, shoe-polishing may be 'not done'. 'Professionalisation' may be a potential means to change attitudes. Equally, the 'quality' aspect may be at play on the labour supply side. The types of jobs concerned are often held in low social esteem ('everyone can do this') and may figure as a kind of employment of last resort failing to attract workers who find satisfaction in the nature of the work. In short, the 'image' of the services may be a significant factor determining the size of the market and employment. The two-sided effect implies a potential role for government to try to remove barriers in the market hindering the expansion of low-skilled employment and to create incentives for economic transactions (mostly low-skill–low-wage) that often take place in the informal economy, to emerge in the formal sector. Hesitantly, some initial policy measures are now being taken to stimulate the demand for these services, and create missing markets. In this book a first overview of such measures is given and discussed in an attempt to provide some guidance for their further development.

THE CHAPTERS

In Part One of the book, on *Taxes, Benefits and Subsidies,* the role of a series of well known policy measures is discussed, such as Earned Income Tax Credit (EITC) for low-wage households and subsidies on (employer) contributions to social security for low wages. In the absence of specific interventions targeted at the low skilled, many may find themselves stranded in dead-end jobs or long-term unemployment, or alternate between the two in low-pay–no-pay cycles.

In Chapter 2, Cathal O'Donoghue and Francesca Utili use a prototype microsimulation model to assess the impact of tax-benefit policy on this group and evaluate a number of proposals for improvement. The model is one result of EUROMOD, which like LoWER began as a research network under the TSER programme. It draws a comparison between five EU countries: France, Germany, Ireland, Italy and the UK. Monetary union strongly adds to the importance of making such comparisons, whilst the implied fiscal competition underlines the need to co-ordinate the introduction of new policy measures. There is already a lot to learn even if, in the model, the number of countries covered is still limited and the approach partial and static.

The authors investigate at first the possibility of a reduction in labour costs for the low waged aimed at increasing the demand for this type of workers, in the spirit of the Malinvaud–Drèze proposal to subsidise employer contributions to social insurance for the low paid. Second, O'Donoghue and Utili explore the impact of an Earned Income Tax Credit scheme offering income protection to the low waged and at the same time offsetting disincentives to work. They find that both measures benefit many in the middle of the income distribution. The subsidies aimed at boosting labour demand can be very expensive, and poorly targeted in terms of poverty alleviation. A better targeting may diminish expenditure but cannot solve all the problems (dead-weight loss, displacement effects, stigmatisation). Studying the alternative of an EITC in a European context, they also find a trade-off between cost and the achievement of various objectives. To improve the incentive to work, less emphasis is placed on poverty alleviation. To take those with the lowest incomes out of poverty an EITC should also provide a minimum income to those in work (as does the new Working Families Tax Credit in Britain) but such generosity will again be more expensive. As the authors state, there are good reasons to consider inclusion in the labour market as a priority but then, if work appears not to guarantee a minimum standard of living, one may expect society to sustain incomes from work, even if it implies some spill over effects.

Marco Doudeijns, Marcel Einerhand and Arthur van de Meerendonk (Chapter 3) meticulously shine a new spotlight on the difference between net earnings and net out-of-work benefit levels for a range of OECD countries, with some surprising results. Focused on household labour supply at first-decile level earnings, the authors extend the replacement-rate type calculations to present unemployment and poverty traps in a new manner. One of the startling results is, for example, that contrary to common conception, financial incentives (at the household level) to take up low-paid employment do not differ greatly between Continental European countries and the US or UK. This occurs in spite of the distinctive difference in welfare provisions, which are much more focused on in-work assistance in the latter than in Europe. Although employment-conditional benefits, earnings disregards and the tapering of means-tested benefits significantly improve work incentives, households whose net income includes means-tested benefits appear to face serious financial disincentives to start a job over a wide range of earnings up to the level of the first-decile wage.

A more detailed comparison of the Netherlands and the US shows that there appears to be a trade-off in terms of marginal effective tax rates. Their reduction, in the US, up to the first-decile level comes at the price of high rates in the range above the first-decile level. On the other hand, the Netherlands appears to claw back all earnings up to first-decile level, but has relatively modest marginal rates in the subsequent earnings range. Consequently, in-work benefits are an important source of disincentive to raise one's earnings above low levels. The dilemma this entails is of great significance for countries yet to design and implement in-work benefits.

In Chapter 4, Peter Mühlau and Wiemer Salverda study an important specimen of real-time policy measures to lower gross labour costs for low-paid jobs, exempting employers from social security contributions. It is a good example of the type of approach advocated by Malinvaud and others. In 1996, the Netherlands introduced a new scheme (SPAK) to subsidise low-paid jobs, which has been very successful in terms of take-up and large amounts of money have been spent. The authors focus on the scheme's employment effects. At the macroeconomic level and for low-paying industries, they find no convincing evidence that the subsidy has boosted low-wage employment growth. At the microeconomic level, the employment response of individual enterprise to the subsidy is studied for two consecutive years. Results of a cross-section comparison of two categories of firms with eligible employees: either making use of SPAK or not, appear to contradict any positive employment effect of the subsidy. Mühlau and Salverda conclude that changing relative wages – the aim of such wage subsidies – may not be an effective means to further the employment position of the low-skilled.

Bruno van der Linden pursues the debate on the proposals brought forward by Jacques Drèze and others concerning the beneficial effect on low-skilled (un)employment of a reduction of social security contributions on low wages. It is particularly advocated to exempt the minimum wage from employer contributions. Van der Linden considers this in a dynamic general equilibrium framework with imperfect competition on the labour market, thus adopting the influential wage-setting–price-setting model used by the critics of such proposals. It is applied to a typical Continental European economy (strongly unionised and regulated), distinguishing skilled and unskilled labour, with a focus on the long-run effects. The very fact that the reduction is restricted to low wages, making the change in contributions non-linear, appears to render it effective also in this framework. In addition, a highly interesting comparison is drawn in the same framework with the introduction of a basic income (or the equivalent negative income tax) as an alternative to the reduction of social security contributions. It turns out that, if appropriately designed both policies have a positive long-run effect on the unemployment rate of the low skilled. In the case of two types of skills relative wages should be rigid and the supply of skills not perfectly elastic, which both seem fairly plausible assumptions. It is argued that it is insufficient to focus on the unemployment rate effects only as wage adjustments will occur. A welfare analysis shows that introducing either of these measures can, conditionally on an appropriate design, induce a Pareto improvement. In Van der Linden's view, a basic income should be restricted to the labour force. Surprisingly, it leads to an outcome that is remarkably close to the concluding observations of O'Donoghue and Utili.

Long-Run Issues

Under the tension of the very high levels of unemployment in Europe, one can appreciate that the attention of policymakers is primarily focused on creating jobs now, particularly in the low-skill segment. Nevertheless, it seems necessary to take the long-run effects into account in designing policies, to avoid solving one problem with another – foresight is the essence of government. In Part Two, on *Long-Run Policy Issues of Low Pay*, two important but rather neglected long-run effects of low earnings are treated.

First, in Chapter 6, Gerard Hughes and Brian Nolan discuss the risks of poverty after retirement. Population ageing and reductions in social security benefits could lead to the re-emergence of poverty rates in Europe and the United States among the elderly which have not been seen since the 1950s or 1960s. Many employees have no employer-provided pension and therefore depend on state pension benefits, which have not been indexed in line with increases in earnings in recent years. The withdrawal of the state that underlies this trend can only be successful if it is replaced by an improved private provision, which is still uncertain.

The authors investigate what factors determine private pension entitlement, comparing two competing views. First, the (mainstream) theory of compensating pay differentials suggests that employees with a preference for future over present consumption can trade off lower wages in return for deferred pay in the form of a pension in the future. Lacking pensions reflect individual choice. By contrast, the theory of segmented labour markets suggests that differences in rates of time preference have limited influence on membership of occupational pension schemes, because employees are constrained in the exercise of their preferences by the structural characteristics of the industry in which they work and its employment practices. Segmentation theory predicts that it is the kind of jobs which employers offer that will determine membership of occupational pension schemes.

Hughes and Nolan carefully show, for Irish data, the relevance of the latter approach. In Ireland in the 1990s poverty rates among households headed by a pensioner are increasing. Efforts to push private sector coverage well above 50 per cent – also in other countries – have not been successful, largely due to the existence of segmentation in the labour market. Low pay and a low coverage of private pension schemes go together and cumulate in certain industries. The rapidly increasing role of women and of part-time labour in the labour market, and the concomitant growth in importance of 'economic independence', combined with the strong concentration of female labour in exactly these industries, make this a worrying phenomenon on which action should be taken to prevent future problems of social exclusion from arising. The authors conclude that an adequate level and indexation for state pensions will be more effective than introducing tax exemptions on saving for pensions, which usually benefit the better paid.

The other contribution (Chapter 7), by Abigail McKnight, starts at the opposite (younger) end of the age distribution. It has often been observed that children growing up in low-income households can suffer from many forms of deprivation concerning, for example, diet, health, housing and education. McKnight's study of the intergenerational transmission of exclusion in the labour market adopts an economic perspective. She examines the extent to which childhood circumstances influence adult outcomes by comparing the economic status and earnings of young adults who grew up in low-income households with those who grew up in higher income households.

The degree to which disadvantage is transmitted across generations is clearly of interest due to equity issues. However, the author goes one interesting step further assessing the extent to which the transmission has changed over time. She analyses the experience of two British birth cohorts, one born in 1958 and the other in 1970, to investigate whether the penalty associated with growing up in poverty has changed over time. Particularly, employment outcomes are compared for young adults in relation to their childhood situation, controlling for other characteristics. The uneasy outcome is, first, that household poverty has an independent effect and, second, that the 1970 cohort appears to be worse off than that of 1958, implying that the negative effects of growing up in a low-income household have increased over time. As to the consequences for policymaking the author concludes that income-sustaining measures such as EITC must be accompanied by additional services which help recipients move from 'poverty in work' to full economic independence.

Demand for Low-Paid Labour

Part Three, brings together four chapters that consider different aspects of the demand for low-wage labour. First, Viktor Steiner and Robert Mohr (Chapter 8) analyse the dramatic decline in the employment share of unskilled workers in the (West) German economy in comparison to skilled employment. They investigate whether the decline relates to the relatively rigid earnings structure. The analysis covers the (West) German economy as a whole including services and is supported by a more detailed study of the manufacturing sector.

The authors find that the substitution elasticity between unskilled and skilled labour is rather low in most sectors of the economy. Exceptions are men working in construction and women in personal services, where reductions in the relative earnings of the unskilled could have contributed to a stabilisation of their relative employment level. In fact, unskilled relative earnings have even increased in these sectors – but, in absolute terms, unskilled female earnings in personal services are still low. In the rest of the economy the decline in the employment share of unskilled relative to skilled workers that can be attributed to an inflexible earnings structure seems to have been modest compared to the trend decline in the skills ratio. It has fallen by about 3 per cent per year for men (6 per cent for women), at a relatively uniform rate across sectors of the economy and, within the manufacturing sector, between industries with different levels of trade integration. From this uniformity, irrespective of sectoral exposure to international trade, Steiner and Mohr conclude that increased international competition has had little direct effects on the relative employment of unskilled labour. The uniform decline across all sectors and the much stronger decline in manufacturing industries with rapid productivity growth do seem to be compatible with the hypothesis of technological bias against unskilled labour. However, this does not explain the much faster decline in the skills ratio for women than for men across all sectors of the German economy, which suggests that the general increase in educational and vocational qualifications is also playing an important role for the trend decline of the skills ratio. Thus, there is little reason for policies to worry about international trade. More attention should be paid, however, to the effects on the least skilled of the increased levels of qualification produced by the system of training and education.

Jonathan Haskel elaborates on the same topic of trade and technology for British wage inequality (Chapter 9), putting a new step in a vivid debate. The skilled–unskilled ratio rose very sharply over the 1980s more than undoing the fall over the preceding decades. Haskel examines the contributions to these relative wage movements of changes in prices and technology, using the production side of the Heckscher–Ohlin model. On the theory side, he advocates better empirical modelling to make assumptions more adequate and incorporate institutions. Also, a better understanding of the determinants of industry product-price changes seems to be vital.

He carefully considers the crucial assumptions of earlier studies and concludes that one should look, in a multi-sector model with labour mobility, for the sector bias of changes in prices and all types of technology. Following the method applied by Leamer to American data, the author finds significant Stolper–Samuelson effects on UK relative wages in the 1980s. That is, international trade is putting downward pressure on product prices of sectors with a relatively high employment share of the unskilled. By contrast, he finds that UK technical change in the 1980s had no clear sector bias and hence did not contribute to wage inequality.

These results contrast with the German outcomes found by Steiner and Mohr. Further research should find out whether this is a matter of method or of national circumstances, including the training of the work force. As for policy, to the extent that price changes are driven by policies such as tariffs future falls in tariffs are likely to raise wage inequality. This suggests that inequality is likely to remain on the policy agenda and it could explain some of the opposition to tariff reform.

Claudia Weinkopf, in Chapter 10, presents an international inventory of policy measures such as *chèques emploi-service* (FR), *Haushaltschecks* (DE), *HomeService* (DK) or *SchoonmaakSter* (NL) which is breaking new grounds. These are subsidies aimed at stimulating product demand for low-skilled labour to increase employment opportunities, centred on the provision of services to private households. The measures show a great variety over the four countries covered: Denmark, France, Germany and the Netherlands, and are in different stages of development. The anticipated, or at least hoped-for, employment effects have not yet been achieved. This may be disappointing, but a comparison of the problems attached to such approaches can help improvement (and application in other countries such as Austria, Belgium, Finland, and Italy that intend to proceed along similar lines).

Weinkopf lays great weight on the interrelated augmentation of the quality of services on the one hand and that of the quantity of employment on the other. A better quality will be needed to improve the low regard in which both customers and workers hold services to private households. Thus the boundaries of the black economy, which generally abounds in household services, may be forced back in favour of regular employment. On the demand side, households seem unwilling to pay for the services on offer, but a superior quality may help. Also, on the side of labour supply, services to private households have a poor image, still shaped by the traditional character of housework as unpaid work of women. Improving qualifications, a corollary of improving quality, can ameliorate the situation. This seems to imply a professional organisation of the services, guaranteeing an undisturbed good-quality provision to households and adequate training and increased job security to employees. In a similar vein, the LoWER network plans to continue its activities over the next years, investigating the jobs potential of professionalising low-skill services supplied to consumers.

Last not least, Donna Brown and Steven McIntosh consider the workings of the low-wage labour market itself in Chapter 11. They look at the link between satisfaction and job separations of individual workers in two national service sector chains, one in retail and one in hotels, both in the British low-wage service sector. Such workers are generally low paid and their demographic characteristics would lead one to anticipate some constraints on their labour market mobility.

In contrast to previous research the authors find no significant link between satisfaction and separations for any demographic group. Dissatisfied workers may not necessarily leave the firm. Instead, ease of mobility and availability of outside alternatives appear to determine the turnover. Brown and McIntosh relate these findings to the dynamic monopsony view of the labour market: those with a degree of labour market power, particularly better-educated young men, are more likely to exit whilst those in a weaker bargaining position show a lower propensity to leave their jobs irrespective of dissatisfaction levels. On the basis of this, various policies emerge. Government could stimulate mobility, by, for example, improved training of the individuals or provision of childcare. Another implication is that increasing the minimum wage could be welfare-enhancing. At the company level, appointing applicants with education levels that exceed requirements seems to be counterproductive as it increases turnover. Instead, a good job match with persons previously unemployed seems to benefit the firm. Finally, Weinkopf's quality option may also help to improve situations of dissatisfaction.

PART ONE

Taxes, Benefits and Subsidies

2. Micro-Level Impacts of Low-Wage Policies in Europe

Cathal O'Donoghue and Francesca Utili[1]

2.1 INTRODUCTION

The general rise of unemployment in Europe during the last ten years has received much attention in recent research. While the severity of the problem varies considerably among and within the European countries, a worrying feature of contemporary unemployment is that a high proportion of the unemployed are low skilled. The proportion of workers in marginal employment with low wages and high mobility into and out of unemployment is also a concern.[2] It is argued that many of these problems result from disincentives implicit in the tax-benefit system, both in terms of the cost to employers of hiring the low skilled and of the barriers to work faced by those on low incomes. In addition, public policy mechanisms often fail to adequately address poverty amongst this group. This paper uses a prototype five-country microsimulation tax-benefit model, EUR5, to assess the impact of tax-benefit policy on this group and evaluate a number of proposed reforms.

Table 2.1
Unemployment by educational status (1995) in EUR5 countries (%)

Educational level:	< Upper Secondary	Upper Secondary	All
France	14.1	9.1	10.2
Germany	14.2	8.1	8.2
Ireland	16.9	7.5	10.8
Italy	9.6	7.6	8.6
UK	9.8	7.2	7.5

Sources: EUROSTAT, *EU Labour Force Statistics 1995* (1997).

Recently unemployment rates have reached very high levels at 10 per cent or more in four of the five countries we deal with (the UK being the exception).

Unemployment particularly appears to be associated with low skill, evidenced by Table 2.1 which classifies unemployment rates in EUR5 countries by both observed skill and the highest level of education attained.[3] The unemployment rate of those with less than upper secondary education level is a good deal higher than those with upper secondary level or above, as much as 75 per cent higher in Germany and Ireland.

Table 2.2 shows a common tendency for the ratio of unskilled to skilled unemployment rates to increase, often attributed to shifts in demand towards the more highly-skilled due to skill-biased technological change. The fear in Europe is that because of institutional constraints, real wages are more rigid and thus unemployment may be more persistent than in the US, leading to the 'disenfranchisement of the unskilled'. Snower (1997), for example, underlines how the response to competitive pressure has differed according to the different institutional frameworks, producing increasing wage differentials in the US and rising unemployment of unskilled in Europe.

Table 2.2
Ratios of unskilled to skilled unemployment rates by gender

Year	France M	France F	Germany M	Germany F	Italy M	Italy F	UK M	UK F	US M	US F
Upper secondary to below upper secondary[1]										
1979	1.4	1.3	2.3	1.2	0.5	0.9	2.5	1.4	2.1	2.0
1990	2.0	1.8	2.9	1.5	1.0	1.1	2.7	1.6	2.5	2.4
Manual to non-manual[2]										
1980	1.9		2.9		0.8		2.2		3.1	
1992	3.5		3.4		1.3		3.8		3.2	

Sources: 1. OECD (1994, table 1.16, 40); 2. Alogoskoufis et al. (1995, 50 and table 2.1, 7).

However the explanation may not be that simple. Nickell and Bell (1996) estimate that only 10 to 15 per cent of the increase in European unemployment can be attributed to the collapse in demand for the unskilled. Atkinson (1997, 1998a) describes three empirical facts which do not fit with the traditional explanation: (1) the widening of earnings differentials has not been accompanied by a significant movement at the top of the wages distribution that should have risen if the demand for skilled workers had increased; (2) the bottom decile in the US has in fact been rising in the last ten years (albeit at a slower rate than top earners); and (3) the rise in dispersion in UK affects nearly all occupational sectors.[4] Also, since technology can only be analysed as a residual, there is no *direct* evidence that technological progress has been especially biased against the low skilled. For example, the computer revolution may substitute for the medium skilled labour rather than unskilled. The trend of increased unemployment amongst the low skilled has tended mainly to occur in countries with smaller increases in unemployment.

Even if they cannot be definitively attributed to demand shifts, high unemployment rates among the low skilled may be a more difficult problem to handle than general unemployment. In particular, without a specifically targeted intervention it could be more difficult to reintegrate low-skilled workers in the labour market.

This chapter uses prototype models built as part of EUROMOD, a project investigating the construction of an integrated Europe-wide tax-benefit microsimulation model. The next section briefly describes the model and the data used. Section 2.3 assesses the impact of the tax-benefit system on the low skilled. Sections 2.4 and 2.5 then examine a number of proposed reforms, including the reduction of employer's social contributions on low wages and the introduction of an Earned Income Tax Credit scheme. Section 6 draws some conclusions.

2.2   MODEL AND DATA

Numerous studies have made proposals to reform tax-benefit systems in order to improve the chances of employment of the low skilled and to prevent poverty amongst the low waged (see for example Snower and de la Dehesa 1997; OECD 1997; Haveman 1996). Evaluations of the impact of such policy reforms have generally been based on either macroeconomic models, theoretical models, or the micro-level analysis of hypothetical households. However, in order to evaluate in detail the impact of policy at the micro level, one needs micro-models based on representative samples of the population. Microsimulation models are valuable tools to help design policies and to evaluate their impacts. Although national tax-benefit microsimulation models have been available for many years to examine country-specific issues, cross-country comparisons have been difficult because of lack of comparability between the available datasets and differences in the assumptions built into the existing models.

The main output from a tax-benefit model is a measure of disposable income at the household level, and is a combination of incomes taken from micro-databases with taxes and transfers simulated by the model. Changes in policy may be specified and disposable incomes recalculated, so that for each household the change in income following a policy change can be measured. Once weighted up to the population level and aggregated, the overall revenue cost of the change, and the scale of gains and losses for different groups of households, can be derived (see O'Donoghue et al. 1998).

This chapter uses a prototype model built as part of a preparatory study for

EUROMOD, a project which is building an integrated tax-benefit model covering all 15 European Union countries. The model is focused on social and integration policies and their implications for the economic resources of people who are at risk of social exclusion. Illustrations of the effect of policy reforms are provided here, by applying them using the prototype model. This is based on micro-data from five countries: France (FR), Germany (DE), Ireland (IE), Italy (IT) and the UK.[5] In each of the five countries the following tax-benefit instruments are simulated in EUR5: social insurance contributions on wages (paid by employers or employees), on self-employment income and on other incomes; income tax and other taxes on labour incomes; family benefits: child benefits, housing benefits, and out of work and in-work social assistance.

2.3   TAX-BENEFIT SYSTEMS AND THE LOW SKILLED

The primary interest of this chapter is how tax-benefit systems interact with low-skilled/low-paid individuals. This section examines the impact of the tax-benefit system under a number of headings including the impact on labour costs, the incentive to participate in the labour market and poverty alleviation.

Tax-Benefits and Labour Costs: the Tax Wedge

Given the high unemployment rates described above for low-skilled individuals, the extent to which taxes and contributions add to labour costs, thus reducing labour demand for this group, is of concern to policy makers. Here we examine the tax wedge which measures the gap between what employers pay and what employees receive, defined as the ratio of the net payment of taxes, contributions and benefits to total income, where total income is the sum of market incomes including payments made by employers such as social insurance contributions and non-market investment and savings incomes. Thus the higher the tax wedge, the more taxes and benefits add to labour costs.

Table 2.3 shows the tax wedge rate for each earnings decile for the five countries examined.[6] Negative values imply that benefits received are higher than taxes and contributions paid in that earnings decile. The size of the tax wedge on low earnings is of interest to us. This depends in part on the size of taxes and transfers to those in work and also on the degree of progressivity within the system. Although generally progressive across the earnings distribution, the level of progressivity varies substantially by country. Italy in particular has the least progressive system.[7] Even on earnings in the 3rd earnings decile, the tax wedge there is as high as 46 per cent. Although slightly more progressive, France too has a very significant tax wedge on lower earnings. In both cases this high and mildly progressive tax wedge results from the reliance on mainly flat rate social insurance contributions. In France and Italy over 50 per cent of government revenues from income result from employer social insurance contributions compared with about a third in Germany and about a fifth in Ireland and the UK (described in Table 2.4). The existence of social transfers such as child benefits ensure lower net tax wedges at the bottom. The remaining three countries, which rely to a greater extent on both income tax and income related social benefits, have similar degrees of progressivity. The extent of the tax wedge in these cases relates primarily to the net size of the fiscal system.

Table 2.3
Tax wedge rate by earnings decile

	1	2	3	4	5	6	7	8	9	10
FR	−65	34	39	40	39	42	42	44	45	48
DE	−220	−9	24	37	41	43	44	44	46	44
IE	2	17	30	32	33	35	36	39	38	39
IT	34	43	46	47	45	47	48	48	48	51
UK	−36	−6	14	21	25	27	29	32	32	35

Source: EUR5.

Table 2.4
Ratio of charges on labour

Type of charge	France	Germany	Ireland	Italy	UK
Employer's SIC	54	35	22	54	22
Employee's SIC	31	35	15	12	19
Income taxation (direct)	15	31	64	34	59
Total	100	100	100	100	100
% of Disposable income	58.9	53.5	39.5	49.2	31.5

Source: EUR5.

What can be done to reduce the tax wedge faced by low earners and improve labour demand for this group? The tax wedge will be reduced if either taxes and contributions are reduced or in-work benefits are increased. As Snower and de la Dehesa (1997) point out, across the board reductions in the tax wedge may contribute to increased disposable incomes but do little to reduce labour costs and thus increase labour demand. Reductions in the tax wedge may have some effect where wage rates are set outside the labour market, as a result of floors set by minimum wages or unemployment benefits. However, if minimum wages are set in terms of pre-tax wages, then reducing income taxes or employee contributions will tend to increase disposable income for this group, but again may not reduce labour costs. Reducing employer contributions for this group may achieve this aim as they lower the cost of jobs provided at the minimum wage. Section 2.4 below thus considers in particular reductions in the employer element of social contributions.

Tax-Benefits and Unemployment Traps: Replacement Rates

In addition to labour demand for low-skilled workers, there is some evidence of lower labour supply for low-skilled workers. One of the obstacles to the participation of individuals in the labour market described in OECD (1997) is the existence of unemployment traps which occur when out-of-work incomes in the form of social transfers are high relative to expected in-work earnings, thus giving little incentive to take up work.

The extent of the unemployment trap is measured through the use of net out-of-work replacement rates,[8] the ratio of out-of-work household disposable income to disposable income in work. In particular, we consider the population aged 18 to 65 who have no earned income and who are not retired. This is a wider definition than often used, because in fact many of those who enter employment come from states other than unemployment.[9] In our simulations we assume that all single people and all married men[10] moving into employment receive a hypothetical wage. This definition of a replacement rate does not take into account in-work expenses, such as travel and childcare costs, which can be quite significant. Nor does it take into consideration the cost of losing any non-cash benefits such as free health care when entering employment.[11] This implies that high cash replacement rates, even if below 100 per cent, may still have a considerable discouraging effect.

The results of our analysis are shown in Table 2.5. Simulations use a hypothetical wage equivalent to the standard often employed for low pay, namely 66 per cent of male median wages. Using a microsimulation model, we are able to look at disaggregated data and take into account the variety of disincentives that different individuals and households may face as a result of differences in income, composition, eligibility to benefits and so on. We can then look at the distribution of replacement rates and quantify how many people face different work incentives.

Replacement rates higher than 100 per cent imply that there is no economic incentive to enter work. This is very infrequent in Italy and the UK but affects about 5 per cent in France and in Germany. However, given the additional costs of taking up work not explicitly included, replacement rates of above 80 per cent can be considered very discouraging as well. Between 15 and 27 per cent face this level of disincentive in the countries being studied. All countries show a concentration of replacement rates between 40 and 80 per cent.

Table 2.5
Replacement rates with two-thirds of median male wage

%	France	Germany	Ireland	Italy	UK
<20	1.0	0.3	0.3	1.7	1.0
20–40	6.7	10.5	10.7	6.5	6.0
40–60	28.4	28.7	23.5	19.6	28.0
60–80	37.9	40.1	44.6	44.9	45.7
80–100	21.5	15.3	19.1	27.2	18.7
100+	4.5	5.2	1.8	0.2	0.6
Total	100.0	100.0	100.0	100.0	100.0

Source: EUR5.

High replacement rates exist for a number of reasons.[12] Non-means-tested earnings-related benefits or high benefits resulting from the existence of dependent children can be important factors. For example, families with children in receipt of the *RMI* in France tend to have higher replacement rates than others. In the UK, high replacement rates can reflect the interaction between housing benefits and income support (rent paid in full) and family credit (rent means-tested) when individuals move over 16 hours work per week. This interaction is also important in Germany when *Sozialhilfe* is removed. Replacement rates in Italy are low primarily because of the small size of the social transfer system and because earnings-replacement benefits are on average low. Finally, the fact that we are measuring income at household level tends to increase replacement rates especially for large households, which is particularly important in Ireland and Italy. In many cases young unemployed people there live at home with employed parents, and if they enter work the household income may not be greatly affected so the household replacement rate remains high.[13] This raises the question of the level at which work incentives should best be studied. We measure household-level replacement rates for comparative purposes because instruments in many of the countries are determined at the household level, but it may also be interesting to carry out a more disaggregated analysis.

Although high replacement rates can indicate a high degree of income protection, in the long run they may provide a disincentive to work. We thus consider policies to reduce the replacement rate. To do this, either in-work incomes must increase or out-of-work incomes decrease. One approach therefore is to *cut benefits,* a policy pursued by a number of countries recently. Methods used include the direct reduction or elimination of earnings-related unemployment and illness benefits, and indirectly by restricting eligibility conditions or enforcing stricter job search requirements.

These measures, however, reduce the incomes of those in the bottom of the income distribution and thus place the cost of improving labour supply incentives on groups who are already disadvantaged.

Alternatively in-work incomes can be increased. This is a policy often applied to families with children, as the unemployment trap can be particularly pronounced for this group since benefits are often provided only in the absence of in-work incomes. Examples include assistance with childcare costs and the provision of universal child benefits. In addition a number of countries have targeted child-related payments for low-wage workers. An example in the case of Ireland is where families can retain means-tested child payments for a limited time upon entering employment. Another option used in mainly English-speaking countries (Canada, Ireland, New Zealand, the UK and the US[14]) is the use of work-related *refundable tax-credits* for families with children.[15] Increasing the amount of in-work income relative to out-of-work income for those on low earnings, these both improve work incentives and provide a measure of income protection. In Section 2.5 we shall simulate the impact of introducing a variant of the US Earned Income Tax Credit (EITC) in the EUR5 countries.

Tax-Benefits and Poverty Alleviation

In this section we explore the relationship between low pay/low skill and poverty risk. Table 2.6 looks at poverty risk as measured by 60 per cent of median household equivalised disposable income, using the square root of household size equivalence scale. Poverty is primarily related to not working (see columns A and B). For each country except Italy, households with individuals of working age but without any labour market income have about three times the average poverty risk. Column C illustrates that poverty rates amongst households containing low-wage earners are actually very close to the average. This is primarily because low-paid workers tend to be secondary earners in richer households, but it does not apply to all households with low-paid individuals. Households whose only income comes from low-paid employment tend to have poverty rates much higher than average (Ireland being the exception). Generally those with lower skills tend to have higher poverty risks (see Table 2.7).

When considering anti-poverty measures for those of working age, we should consider the low skilled both in and out of work together. There may in fact be little distinction between the two as many of those currently in low-paid employment may have recent unemployment experience and vice versa (see Pissarides 1991). This point is highlighted by the fact that poverty rates for households with only low earnings in Germany and Italy approach or surpass the poverty rates of out-of-work households.[16] This is because many in this group have some employment income for a short period in the year, but are otherwise unemployed. Because of their short employment spells they are less likely to qualify for unemployment insurance benefits, and marginal employment for this low-skilled/low-paid group is generally more vulnerable to macroeconomic fluctuations. In addition, these jobs very often offer little opportunity for enhancement of human capital and thus provide low chances of mobility into more regular employment.

Table 2.6
Poverty risk of households [a]

	A. No labour market income [b]	**B.** All households	**C.** Low-paid earner in household	**D.** Only low-paid earner in household
FR	49.0 (18.6)	17.1 (100)	20.1 (18.8)	37.7 (9.5)
DE	46.0 (14.4)	16.3 (100)	19.9 (27.1)	40.5 (12.9)
IE	63.5 (17.7)	19.3 (100)	13.3 (29.9)	22.4 (17.6)
IT	34.7 (12.1)	21.8 (100)	26.5 (26.7)	44.1 (15.2)
UK	64.5 (15.9)	24.0 (100)	12.7 (28.6)	35.5 (9.7)

Notes:
a. Numbers in brackets are the proportion of households of this type in the dataset. b. Refers to only those households with individuals of working age (that is aged below 65).

Source: EUR5.

Table 2.7
Percentage of adults living in households in poverty by education

	10 years of education or less	More than 10 years of education
FR	17.9	16.5
DE	15.7	13.2
IE	18.8	5.8
IT	27.5	9.5
UK	27.6	7.8

Source: EUR5.

The policies outlined above aiming at the reduction of replacement rates relate mainly to incentives both for job creation and labour supply for those with low potential wages. Aiming to increase the numbers employed is a valid and important objective, but may not do much to reduce poverty if pay levels are too low to bring families above the poverty line. This has been the experience recently in the US where high levels of economic growth have not had much of an impact in reducing poverty rates (see Blank 1997). It is plausible, therefore, if low-skilled work became more attractive as a result of policies described above that the result would be more low-paid jobs with little impact on poverty rates. It is beyond the scope of this chapter to examine detailed anti-poverty measures for those in and out of work, so here we focus on policies which reduce the poverty risk for families reliant on low earnings. In particular, we examine in Section 2.5 an EITC which, in addition to improving labour force participation incentives by reducing replacement rates, also increases the income levels of in-work families on low earnings. First, though, we look at the impact of reducing employers' social insurance contributions.

2.4   THE DRÈZE–MALINVAUD REFORM PROPOSAL[17]

In this section we examine a proposal to reduce work disincentives created by tax-benefit systems, put forward by Drèze and Malinvaud (1994) and others, to reduce employer payroll taxes in Europe which account for a significant proportion of the tax wedge of low-wage workers. Box 2.1 briefly describes the main features of these contributions in the EUR5 countries.

According to the proposal, minimum wages should be exempt from employer social insurance contributions (ERSICs). In order to reduce the cost of the reform this reduction in ERSICs is diminished as earnings rise, so that by twice the minimum wage, the reduction is zero (described in equations 2.1 and 2.2, where w_{50} is the median wage).

$$\delta \, (\text{ERSIC}) = - \, \text{ERSIC if } w \leq 0.6^* w_{50} \tag{2.1}$$

$$\delta \, (\text{ERSIC}) = - \, \text{ERSIC}^*(w - 0.6^* w_{50} \,)/(0.6^* w_{50}) \text{ if } w_{50} < w < 1.20^* w_{50} \tag{2.2}$$

Table 2.8 shows the cost of reducing ERSICs as a proportion of household disposable income. Eliminating ERSICs for wages below 60 per cent of the median would cost an amount equivalent to 6 per cent of disposable household income in France, 3 per cent in Germany, 2 per cent in Ireland, 6 per cent in Italy and 1 per cent in the UK.

The cost of the reduction is a function of the relative importance of employer's social insurance contributions in the country, and of its structure. The reform costs the most in France and Italy because ERSICs in these countries have the highest revenue share combined with high effective tax rates. The reform costs least in Ireland and the UK for two reasons. First, employers' contributions tend to be lower due to private pensions and health care being primarily funded from other sources including employees' contributions and the general budget rather than by social insurance contributions in France, Germany and Italy. Second, since in the UK the bottom 10 per cent of workers are already exempt, the cost is lower there.

Box 2.1
Employer's social insurance contributions by country, 1994

France
French social contributions are levied on gross earnings, are contingency dependent and vary according to work status. The regime varies according to the contribution's purpose and the level of gross earnings: some (for example sickness, housing contributions and accident) are proportional to gross earnings, family contributions are progressive, old age and unemployment contributions have a progressive structure on earnings up to an upper earnings limit, having a zero or lower rate on incomes above this limit.[18] The rate structure is very complex; interested readers are referred to Bourguignon et al. (1998).

Germany
Employers in Germany pay social contributions for pensions (at a rate of 9.3 per cent), unemployment (6.3 per cent), health (about 6.9 per cent) and accident insurance (1 per cent).[29] Contributions are levied on all earnings up to an upper earnings limit which varies by insurance type.

Ireland
Employer social insurance contributions in Ireland levied on gross earnings vary by sector of employment, with the public sector in 1994 having lower contributions than the private sector.[20] For private sector workers, employers in 1994 paid a rate of 8.5 per cent on all earnings for workers earning below an lower earnings limit at around the average wage (APW) and 12.5 per cent on all earnings for workers earning more than this and with earnings below a maximum earnings limit of about twice APW.

Italy
Social contributions vary according to type of income, working status and sector of activity and is levied on gross earnings. Average rates in 1994 are about 42 per cent for employers contributions but they vary considerably according to the size of the firm, to the work status of the dependent worker and to the sector of activity. The effective rate of contributions is lower then the nominal one because of state intervention to reduce labour costs in deprived areas. This support takes the form of contribution holidays and reliefs.

United Kingdom
Employer's national insurance contributions are paid for employees who are below the pension age and who have earnings above the lower earnings limit. There are four different bands of employer social insurance, ranging from 3 to 10.2 per cent, with no upper earnings limit. If an employees earned income falls into a band then all earnings are charged the contribution rate associated with the band.

Standard labour market literature assumes that payroll taxes such as ERSICs are fully incident in the long run on employees. However, it can be argued that because of unemployment benefits, minimum wages and unions, wages at the bottom of the earnings distribution are not flexible and therefore payroll taxes are not borne entirely by labour. Therefore, if it is assumed that low wages in most European countries are essentially administered wages – that is minimum wages and wages just above the minimum level – a change in ERSICs should not affect the wage received by these workers.[21] It should, at least in the short run, only modify the cost of labour for employers. Under this assumption, a cut in ERSICs for low wages should have no effect on household incomes. The financing mechanism may, however, have a more important role to play. We do not consider financing mechanisms here, preferring to focus on the direct impact of the reforms themselves. Bourguignon et al. (1997) considered a similar ERSIC reduction financed by an increase in income tax levels or alternatively making ERSIC rates more progressive and found both methods to have similar distributional impacts.

Even if the reduction of ERSICs on low wages does not have direct effects on household incomes, it may have indirect effects through employment creation. Macroeconomic models have found that reductions in labour costs, offset by an increase in other non-labour related charges, would have a significant positive effect on employment. For example, a reduction in ERSICs valued at 1 per cent of GDP was expected to lead to a reduction in the unemployment rate of 2.5 per cent in the 1994 White Paper (CEC 1994). This effect, however, is rather hard to model in a microsimulation context since that would involve identifying not only the number of new jobs created because of the drop in labour costs but also the individuals who would be the beneficiaries of these jobs and the households they belong to. It is logical for tax-benefit models to consider these effects as purely exogenous and therefore outside of the scope of the model.

Microsimulation models can, however, look at the impact of reforms on behavioural pressures such as the tax wedge described above. Table 2.8 describes the impact on the tax wedge when implementing the Drèze–Malinvaud initiative. Comparing with Table 2.3, we find as expected that the countries with the highest levels of employer social insurance contributions have the largest reductions, so that Italy, France and Germany have the highest reductions with Ireland and the UK having very small changes. The UK has particularly small changes given the existing exemption for those in the bottom earnings decile.

Another potential impact of reduced ERSICs is the impact on the black economy, since it may give an incentive to many employers to regularise the position of their employees. Ferrera (1998) stresses the *crowding out effect* that very high ERSICs currently have on regular employment, resulting in a sizeable informal sector of the economy in many countries. This would be particularly important for low-skilled workers who comprise much of the labour in this sector. Such an effect may have been seen in France where a reduction of 50 per cent in CSG social contributions for domestic-service workers contributed to a substantial increase in the number of workers in this sector (see Piketty 1997). It is likely that much of this increase resulted from the regularisation of former workers in the black economy.

Table 2.8
Tax wedge rate by earnings decile as a result of ERSIC reform

	1	2	3	4	5	6	7	8	9	10
FR	−110	15	25	29	32	38	41	44	45	48
DE	−271	−29	9	27	36	41	44	44	46	44
IE	−5	11	24	28	31	34	36	39	38	39
IT	7	15	23	33	36	43	48	48	48	51
UK	−36	−8	10	17	22	26	29	32	32	35

Source: EUR5.

Table 2.9
Percentage of cost of ERSIC reform by household income decile*

	1	2	3	4	5	6	7	8	9	10	Total
FR	3	4	8	9	14	14	12	13	9	14	100
DE	3	7	10	10	11	13	12	12	12	9	100
IE	2	3	7	7	7	9	9	11	17	28	100
IT	7	6	10	12	9	16	14	13	6	6	100
UK	0	2	5	10	11	16	16	17	15	7	100

Note: * Equivalised household disposable income with a square root of household size equivalence scale.

Source: EUR5.

One of the principle aims of the reform is to lower employment costs of low-skilled individuals because of their high unemployment and poverty risk. However as ERSICs relate solely to individual employment income, it treats equally a second earner doing some part-time work in a rich household and a full-time primary earner on low income in a poor household. Table 2.9 highlights this effect, classifying the proportion of costs by household equivalent disposable income decile. We find that rather than concentrating resources at the bottom of the income distribution, the reform concentrates expenditure on the top half, varying from 70 per cent of all expenditure in Ireland and the UK to about 60 per cent in France and Germany and over half in Italy. Although expenditure would tend to be concentrated on individuals in the top of the income distribution, it is hoped that because the employment of low-skilled workers is cheaper, labour demand will increase for this group. However, given the large sums of money involved in reducing employer social insurance contributions, it can be argued that a more targeted reform may be more cost effective and indeed more effective at increasing the numbers of low skilled in employment.

2.5 THE EARNED INCOME TAX CREDIT

In this section we consider the introduction of an Earned Income Tax Credit (EITC) in Europe. The EITC is a tax credit currently given to working families on low income in the United States.[22] Recipients must have employment incomes (both employee and self-employment income) and are excluded if non-employment incomes exceed a certain amount. It was originally introduced in the US in 1975 as a mechanism to relieve the cost of payroll taxes on low-wage workers (Scholz 1996), and aims to ensure that in-work incomes are higher than out of work incomes. It is also now one of the main transfer payments in the US and thus has a significant poverty alleviation role.

The credit is dependent on the number of children up to a maximum of two and is valued at a percentage of gross earnings. It increases with earnings in the *phase-in period* (see Figure 2.1) and once earnings reach a lower earnings limit, the value of the credit remains constant until the upper earnings limit is reached. At this point, the *phase-out* period begins as the credit is gradually reduced until fully withdrawn. For example, the credit was valued at 40 per cent of earned income in 1996 for a family with two children up to $8938, remains at $3575 up to $11,670, and was then phased out until eventually totally withdrawn at $28,645 per annum (see Table 2.10).

Figure 2.1
The value of the Earned Income Tax Credit by gross income for single-earner couples with two children or no children

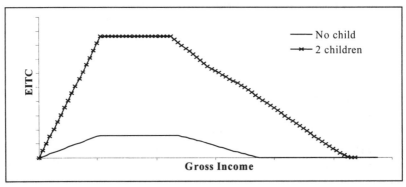

Source: EUR5.

In terms of labour supply incentives, the EITC encourages increased labour participation because in-work incomes are raised compared with out-of-work incomes. Also, in the phase-in region marginal tax rates will tend to fall, providing increased work incentives for those already in work. However, income taxes and thus the EITC are often paid only at the end of the year and therefore the EITC may be seen more as reward for work rather than a work incentive (see Walker and Wiseman 1997). Even if it is regarded as a work incentive, the labour supply position is not unambiguously positive. Because the phase-out region of the Credit is wider than the phase-in region, and therefore more people may in fact have increased rather than reduced marginal tax rates, on aggregate work incentives of workers may be reduced. Nevertheless, Scholz (1996) found that the expansion of the EITC in the US would lead to a greater labour participation effect than the estimated decreased hours worked by workers, and thus the overall effect is positive.

Because the tax system is used as a means of redistribution, take-up rates will tend to be higher than if the scheme were implemented through the benefits code. Also, because the incidence of the tax credit depends on a broader income base (family rather than individual) the instrument is better targeted than individual based measures such as employers' social insurance contribution reductions.

Table 2.10
Parameters of the Earned Income Tax Credit (1996 in US$)

	No child	1 child	2+ children
Credit Rate	7.65	34.0	40.0
Lower Earnings Limit	4,244	6,365	8,938
Upper Earnings Limit	5,305	11,670	11,670
Maximum Credit	325	2,164	3,575
Withdrawal Rate	7.65	15.98	15.98
Income Cut-off	9,553	25,212	28,645

Source: Scholz (1996).

We now examine the impact of the reform on the five countries. Because of a number of differences between tax-benefit systems in Europe and the US, we make a number of changes to the structure of the credit. First, as income-related social transfers are more common in Europe than in the US, marginal tax rates over the range of the EITC will tend to be higher. Introducing an EITC based on gross income may therefore result in very high marginal tax rates in the phase-out region. As a result, we simulate an EITC for European countries, where income is based on earnings after taxes, which will result in higher expenditure than if gross earnings were used. Also, because social assistance programs are more important in Europe, we integrate the tax credit with existing systems by setting the end of the phase-in period equal to the level at which social assistance benefits are completely withdrawn.[23] This results in a reduction of the marginal tax rate over a range where in many European countries a marginal rate of 100 per cent is experienced. Where in-work benefits already exist, we assume that families receive the maximum of the existing benefit or the EITC. The width of the constant EITC is kept the same as in the US.

Figures 2.2a–e describes the effect of the introduction of an Earned Income Tax Credit on the budget constraint of single-earner families with two children. These figures highlight the fact that except for certain points in the UK system, families with children are better off over the entire range of the EITC. Importantly, in each country except for Italy (where there is no minimum income) disposable income rises with earnings at low earnings levels as a result of the reform. This is because the lower limit of the EITC is set equal to the end of the social assistance phase-out range and thus families get a positive and increasing EITC over the whole range of the social assistance benefit. Over the next phase, the EITC is kept constant and the new budget constraint is parallel to the existing budget constraint before entering the phase-out stage where the value of the EITC is decreased until the old and new system are equal.

As in the case of the ERSIC reform, we do not consider financing options in detail, as we wish to isolate the direct impact of the EITC on redistribution. The choice of financing could clearly have a major effect on the redistributive effect depending on the instrument used (VAT financing is more regressive than the use of income taxes for example), so here we merely note the aggregate cost of the reform. In terms of a flat rate tax on pre-reform disposable income it varies from 2.6 per cent in Ireland to 2.5 per cent in France to 2.2 per cent in Italy and 1.6 per cent in Germany and the UK. Not surprisingly the introduction of an EITC in Italy and France would have a higher cost relative to the others because of the absence of in-work benefits. Although Ireland already has an in-work benefit, the Family Income Supplement, the reform in Ireland is expensive because at present the instrument is only paid to employees and at a lower rate (see Callan et al. 1995). One might however, expect the cost to be higher in Germany. Smaller family sizes in Germany imply that fewer families are eligible for higher rate payments. In addition, the phase-in period is equal to the phase-out period of social assistance and thus the proportion of the income distribution covered by the EITC depends on this and also social assistance benefits in Germany are less generous relative to the median. As expected the cost is least in the UK, where a substantial in-work benefit, Family Credit, already exists.

In terms of household income, the area of the distribution which is more affected by the reform varies from country to country according to the

Figure 2.2
Earned Income Tax Credit for single-earner couples with two children

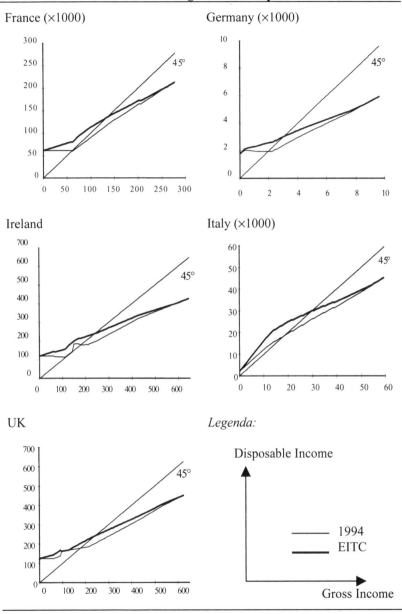

France (×1000)

Germany (×1000)

Ireland

Italy (×1000)

UK

Legenda:

Disposable Income

——— 1994
━━━ EITC

Gross Income

Source: EUR5.

position of the low paid in the distribution and the existing tax-benefit system. For countries like Ireland and the UK, the greatest gains tend to be concentrated in the middle of the income distribution (see Table 2.11). The peaks in the gain from the reform in the middle of the distribution correspond closely to the deciles with the largest family sizes. The limited impact at the bottom of the distribution relates primarily to the fact that households in that part of the income distribution tend not to have employment income, and thus are not eligible for the EITC. Although the instrument is targeted by family income, it is not targeted by household income. Thus it is possible for independent individuals in wealthier households to receive the credit, hence the gainers at the top of the income distribution.

Table 2.11
Percentage change in equivalent disposable income by equivalised disposable income decile resulting from EITC

	1	2	3	4	5	6	7	8	9	10	Tax rate	%A[a]	%P[b]
FR	2.4	3.7	2.9	2.5	2.5	1.5	2.5	2.1	2.5	2.4	2.5	40.0	35.3
DE	2.2	3.0	3.7	3.4	2.2	1.5	0.7	0.4	0.2	0.1	1.6	24.4	33.6
IE	1.3	1.8	5.7	5.7	6.2	4.7	2.8	1.1	0.6	0.1	2.6	39.8	16.6
IT	7.7	5.2	4.3	3.0	3.1	2.5	2.3	1.8	0.6	0.1	2.1	41.9	38.4
UK	0.6	1.7	3.2	5.9	3.9	1.9	1.0	0.5	0.3	0.1	1.6	28.4	29.5

Notes:
a. Percentage affected; b. Poverty rate for households with only low-paid earners.

Source: EUR5.

By improving the incomes of only those in work, the EITC would have a limited direct impact on overall poverty alleviation. One might, however, expect the position of households reliant on low pay to be improved. The effect is in fact quite limited though, as is illustrated in Table 2.11. Here we see that the poverty rates of this group are only partially reduced by about 25 per cent in the case of Ireland to less than 10 per cent in France. This is as a result of the design of the EITC giving more benefit to those with relatively higher earnings.

Although not simulating labour supply behaviour in this chapter, using the microsimulation model we can estimate some of the pressures on labour supply created by the tax transfer system. Here we consider the impact of the EITC reform on the incentive to enter the labour market by improving in-work income relative to out-of-work income (replacement rates) and the incentive to alter the number of hours worked as a result of changes in marginal tax rates. Comparing replacement rates before and after the reform, we find that the incidence of high replacement rates (80 per cent or higher) in each country falls substantially (Table 2.5 versus 2.12). Considering two-thirds median earnings as the replacement income, we note that high replacement rates fall between a fifth and a third in France, Germany, Ireland and Italy. Of course, the method of financing the EITC may have an effect on the distribution of replacement rates, varying from no effect if a proportional tax is used, to a reduction of the number of lower replacement rates if a progressive system of taxation is used to fund the reform.

Table 2.12
Replacement rates after EITC reform with 2/3 median male wage

%	France	Germany	Ireland	Italy	UK
<20	1.1	0.3	0.3	2.0	1.0
20–40	7.7	10.9	13.4	6.0	7.3
40–60	32.4	35.0	31.3	25.1	35.0
60–80	38.6	39.3	40.2	49.3	39.9
80–100	16.3	10.9	14.7	17.6	16.7
100+	4.0	3.5	0.1	0.1	0.1
Total	100.0	100.0	100.0	100.0	100.0

Source: EUR5.

We turn now to the impact of the EITC reform on marginal tax rates. Table 2.13 defines marginal tax rates as the ratio of the change in household disposable income to the change in household gross income, where gross income is increased by 1600 PPP-Euro of employee earnings per year for all single people and all married males aged 18 to 65.

Table 2.13
Marginal tax rates under 1994 system and EITC reform

%	France		Germany		Ireland		Italy		UK	
	1994	EITC	1994	EITC	1994	EITC	1994	EITC	1994	EITC
<20	0.2	6.0	8.1	12.4	13.3	15.6	4.6	8.8	6.3	11.0
20–40	59.2	36.6	43.1	29.4	27.7	16.6	6.9	46.8	70.4	56.8
40–60	24.7	37.7	38.9	48.0	39.1	46.6	37.3	39.5	9.3	25.2
60–80	4.1	9.8	2.2	4.8	8.4	12.7	42.2	4.5	10.0	5.9
80–100	1.3	6.4	0.7	2.1	2.0	6.8	8.9	0.1	1.8	1.0
100+	10.5	3.4	7.1	3.2	9.6	1.6	0.0	0.3	2.2	0.1
Total	100.0	100.0	100.0	100.0	100.0	100.0	100.0	100.0	100.0	100.0

Source: EUR5.

The impact of the phase-in period of the EITC is visible through the reduction of very high marginal tax rates (over 80 per cent) for each country, accompanied by an increase in the number with zero or negative marginal tax rates. This effect is particularly noticeable for the UK and Italy. The impact of the phase-out region, meanwhile, is noticeable in the shift in most countries from the 20–40 per cent range to the 40–80 per cent range.

2.6   DISCUSSION AND CONCLUSIONS

With deteriorating long-term employment prospects for low-skilled workers, European labour markets are facing a situation whereby growing numbers of people are becoming marginalised. Lower demand for the low-skilled, resulting in falling relative wages, means that households reliant only on low-wage jobs are often not earning enough to stay out of poverty. In addition, the sectors employing these low-skilled workers tend to be more prone to macroeconomic fluctuations and also provide little opportunity for human capital enhancement. The result is employment spells too short for entitlement to unemployment insurance benefits to be built up, and in the long term individuals are trapped in a cycle of low pay and unemployment. In Europe much of the brunt of the changes to labour markets has been borne in the shape of rising unemployment rates. In the absence of specific interventions targeted at the low skilled, many may find themselves stranded in dead-end jobs or long-term unemployment. Therefore it has been argued that European tax-benefit systems need to be adapted to cope with these labour market changes.

This chapter explored the impact of the tax-benefit system in five European countries on labour costs, work incentives and poverty alleviation, and examined a number of tax-benefit reforms targeted at low-wage workers. These include policies which aim to reduce the cost to employers of hiring low-skilled workers, such as targeted reductions in employer social insurance contributions suggested by Drèze and Malinvaud. Such reforms can have significant impacts on the employment levels of the low skilled which are constrained by a wage floor set at a level higher than the market-clearing one. In the longer run, especially when such policies explicitly include training programmes, workers will benefit because of increased human capital which in turn will permit them to aim at better-quality/higher-paid jobs.

However, we found that reforms aimed at boosting labour demand can be very expensive, and poorly targeted in terms of poverty alleviation because most low-wage workers tend to be secondary workers in richer households. A more targeted reform aimed primarily at those in poverty or at risk of poverty may be more cost effective. More focused policies include labour cost reductions aimed at individuals or regions with particularly high unemployment rates. For example, Ireland now has an exemption on employers' social insurance contributions for unemployed people recruited into jobs. In France, employers' family allowance contributions have been eliminated for the low-paid, while in Germany low-wage part-time (marginal) workers do not pay social insurance. After the time covered by the research in the UK, ERSICs – which were already progressive – were reduced again for low-paid employees, and Italy plans to reduce ERSICs for young workers and for those recently unemployed.

Another current proposal is to allow the unemployed to use part of their unemployment benefit as a subsidy for employers (see Snower and de la Dehesa 1997). Although less expensive, there are a number of potential problems associated with targeted labour cost reductions, including dead-weight losses if the worker would have been hired anyway; displacement if the worker favoured by the tax relief is hired at the place of another one not entitled to the benefit; reduction of the returns to training if aimed at the low skilled; and the stigma associated with being part of an employment scheme.[24]

In the last section we examined the introduction of an in-work benefit (EITC) aimed at those on low pay, which has achieved a certain degree of success in the US in fighting poverty and unemployment traps. In the European context, we again find a trade-off between cost and the achievement of various objectives. In attempting to improve the incentive to work, less emphasis is placed on poverty alleviation. We find that the incidence of high replacement rates in each country falls substantially as a result of in-work incomes increasing, with the greatest gains concentrated in the middle of the income distribution. In terms of poverty alleviation, the policy has limited impact on the working poor as a result of the phase-in region where individuals receive a credit proportional to their incomes, so those with the lowest in-work incomes receive less.

Although the EITC cannot directly reduce poverty levels of those not in work, in the long run by improving work incentives it may be able to remove barriers to work and thus indirectly alleviate poverty. However, the design of the EITC as it stands does not greatly assist in this as those with the lowest incomes are not taken out of poverty. An instrument such as the former Family Credit (FC) in the UK, which gives those families with someone working more than 15 hours a minimum income dependent on family size, may be more effective in this respect.[25] It operates in the same way as the EITC by making in-work incomes higher than out-of-work incomes, but also provides a minimum income to those in work. We again, however, face the trade-off of cost versus generosity, since a FC of similar maximum value to the EITC will be more expensive. One concern about FC was that it gave individuals little incentive to work more hours than the threshold level, which is why recently a higher amount is paid to those who work 30 hours or more. Also the FC payable as a social benefit has the problem of take-up, where only about two-thirds of recipients actually apply for the benefits they are entitled to. As a result, the UK has opted to replace FC by a refundable tax credit, the Working Families Tax Credit (WFTC), paid through the tax system. This instrument is also more generous than FC, and reduces another barrier to employment by providing a childcare subsidy.

How should we interpret the high cost of the proposed reforms and the fact that they benefit many individuals in the middle of the distribution? In general, employment strategies can have two possible goals. The first is an income goal that aims at increasing employment among the poor to assure them a higher income. Policies like this are mainly concerned about the risk of poverty and thus have the objective that work will result in a net gain. Policies that are more oriented towards the employment goal aim at replacing benefits with income from work even at a one-to-one replacement rate since the ultimate focus is on the integrating role of work in people's life (Blank, 1997). However significant the disincentive effects are, they all arise from an unfavourable relation between the benefits received and the prospective salary. In the end, the judgement of whether benefits are too high or the salary too low is a political decision that will depend on overall societal attitudes towards poverty. A society very concerned about poverty may give priority to guaranteeing a minimum standard of living, independently from the attachment to the labour market. In other contexts this link may be required as part of a wider notion of citizenship. There are good reasons to consider inclusion in the labour market as a priority. At the very least, however, we may want to live in a society where work guarantees a minimum standard of living. If we find that this is not the case then there is a need for intervention to sustain incomes from work, even if it implies some spillover effects.

A concluding remark relates to the European dimension of the proposal. This European dimension is not only reflected in the fact that our analysis covers a number of different countries in a comparative way. It also relates to the fact that these types of reforms are often only possible if they are the outcome of co-ordinated action by countries. The reduction in labour costs, for example, has a very different impact if it is implemented only in a subset of countries, since it implies a comparative advantage for them given by cheaper labour. For this reason, implementation in only some of the countries will not be accepted by the community of the member states, as evidenced by the difficulties experienced by the Italian government in providing contribution relief in the South. A scheme like the EITC is in principle only constrained by the financial situation of the country that implements it. But these constraints are more binding in a context of fiscal competition where governments are generally afraid that raising taxes may negatively affect the tax base. Even in the absence (so far) of clear evidence of 'welfare migration' across countries (see Atkinson 1998b), implementing such a scheme will encounter particular resistance if it is felt that it may be more costly than anticipated because of the risk of subsidising unemployed or low paid coming from the neighbouring countries. In this latter case co-ordination appears not indispensable but it certainly contributes to the chances of implementation and success of the scheme.

NOTES

1. This chapter draws on a prototype model constructed by 'EUROMOD: an integrated European tax-benefit model' which was financed by the Targeted Socio-Economic Research programme of the European Commission (CT95-3009) (see Sutherland 1997). The EUROMOD project involves 35 individuals in 18 institutions from 15 countries. Thanks are due to the whole team for advice and helpful comments. Particular thanks are due to François Bourguignon, Jose Sastre-Descals, Amedeo Spadaro and Isabelle Terraz for initial discussions, to Brian Nolan for his detailed comments and to conference participants at the LoWER conference in Groningen. The views that are expressed, as well as any remaining errors, are the responsibilities of the authors alone. Data from the 1989 French *Enquête sur le Budget des Familles*, from the 1995 German *Socio-Economic Panel*, for Ireland from the 1987 *Survey on Income Distribution, Poverty and the Usage of State Services*, from the 1993 Italian *Survey of Household Income and Wealth* have been made available by INSEE, the Deutsches Institut fur Wirtschaftforschung, the Economic and Social Research Institute, the Bank of Italy respectively. Data from the 1991 UK *Family Expenditure Survey* are Crown Copyright. They have been made available by the Office for National Statistics (ONS) through the Data Archive and are used by permission. Neither the ONS nor the Data Archive bear any responsibility for the analysis or interpretation of the data reported here. The same disclaimer applies for INSEE, the DIW, the ESRI and the Bank of Italy for the French, German, Irish and Italian data respectively.
2. Thus this chapter concentrates on those who are low paid or those unemployed with low skills who would have potentially low pay if in employment.
3. For an explanation of the rationale of using educational attainments as a proxy of skills and competencies see, for example, OECD *Jobs Study* 1994, p. 114.
4. In general he stresses that the explanation usually provided – the transatlantic consensus – actually looks at only one part of the story. The critique is based on the fact that no account is taken of the rise in the cost of capital that may have affected the dispersion of wages through effects on supply (costs and decision of investing in training) and demand through the degree of complementarity between factors. See Atkinson (1998a).
5. For more information see Bourguignon et al. (1998) and O'Donoghue (1998).
6. These figures are reported at the individual level. Note however that many tax-benefit instruments apply at the family or household levels. In this case, benefits are divided equally between adults, while taxes are assigned at the average tax rates in proportion to the individual's component of the tax base.
7. It must however be noted that tax liabilities are calculated on an estimate of the income declared to the fiscal authorities which is smaller than gross income from survey data (used for the denominator of the tax-wedge ratio). See Bourguignon et al. (1998) for a description.
8. The model does not simulate in-work replacement rates as the model database does not contain information about contributions which are important for simulating out-of-work insurance benefits.
9. Anyway much of the increase in benefit recipients over the last two decades has occurred in categories other than unemployment, for example lone parents and those in receipt of

disability and early retirement benefits, reflecting more the design of instruments rather than the availability for work.

10. Here we make the simplifying assumption that only the husband in an out-of-work married couple would enter the workforce. Further work is necessary to examine the impact of either the wife or both spouses entering employment.

11. Because of concern about this disincentive effect, the long-term unemployed in Ireland have recently been allowed to keep their free health benefits for the first months of employment. This issue is still particularly a problem in the US.

12. The existence of high replacement rates do not necessarily imply low participation rates as unemployment benefits often contain strong job search conditions. Failure to accept work even if less than benefit levels can result in the loss of benefits. Also in the short term, individuals may take up work despite high replacement rates, for reasons of self-esteem or the desire to get a better job (such as apprenticeships) (OECD 1997). In the long run, however, high replacement rates will tend to reduce participation rates.

13. The percentage of unemployed living with their parents in Italy is 56.3 per cent, compared to France and United Kingdom around 20 per cent, West Germany 10 per cent and below 10 per cent in Nordic countries (see Gallie 1997).

14. Although in Italy some family benefits are also in the form of refundable tax credits, they are not only payable to employees but also to those on unemployment insurance or in receipt of pensions, and thus are not fully in-work benefits of the types used in other countries.

15. Recently, however, a number of programmes have been extended to families without children as in the case of the US and through a pilot scheme in the UK.

16. This point applies only to Germany and Italy as in the other countries current rather than annual income is used and thus data does not capture the intra-annual mobility reflected here.

17. This section partially draws on work done on a previous paper, Bourguignon et al. (1997).

18. Employers also make contributions to complementary pension schemes. Contribution rates again vary by work status, company size and income.

19. These are 1994 figures. In 1995 long-term care insurance was introduced (an extra 0.9 per cent of earnings).

20. This has subsequently changed, with new public servants having private-sector employer contributions.

21. Of course, this is debatable for the UK and Ireland where no minimum wage legislation was in force at the time of the research.

22. The instrument was originally aimed at working families with children, but since 1994 was extended to those without children. Recipients without children must however be aged between 25 and 65.

23. The EITC is also integrated with housing benefit in the countries where it exists.

24. Studies on the efficacy of the US Targeted Jobs Tax Credits which reduced contributions for employers hiring individuals from disadvantaged categories show that the workers involved in the scheme were less attractive to employers because of the impression on their part that such workers had lower productivity (see Haveman 1996).

25. One point worth mentioning is that in the absence of a minimum wage there is an incentive for employers and employees to collude. The Family Credit can thus be used to subsidise bad employers who give hours but not pay to employees knowing that the state will bring up the minimum.

REFERENCES

Alogoskoufis, G., C. Bean, G. Bertola, D. Cohen, J. Dolado and G. Saint-Paul (1995), *Unemployment: Choices For Europe*, Monitoring European Integration 5, CEPR, London.

Atkinson, A.B. (1997), 'Bringing Income Distribution from the Cold', *Economic*

Journal, **107**, 297–321.

Atkinson, A.B. (1998a), *The Changing Distribution of Income: Evidence and Explanations*, Lecture in Honour of Professor K. Rothschild, University of Linz, October 1998, mimeo.

Atkinson, A.B. (1998b), *Poverty in Europe*, Blackwell Publishers, Oxford.

Blank, R.M. (1997), 'Why has Economic Growth Been Such an Ineffective Tool Against Poverty in Recent Years?', in J. Neill (ed.), *Poverty and Inequality: the Political Economy of Redistribution*, W.E. Upjohn Institute for Employment Research, Kalamazoo, Michigan.

Bourguignon, F., C. O'Donoghue, J. Sastre-Descals, A. Spadaro and F. Utili (1997), *Eur3: a Prototype European Tax-Benefit Model*, Microsimulation Unit Working Paper, MU9703.

Bourguignon, F., C. O'Donoghue, J. Sastre-Descals, A. Spadaro and F. Utili (1998), *A Technical Description of Eur3, a Prototype European Tax-Benefit Model*, Microsimulation Unit Research Note No. 9801.

Callan T., C. O'Neill and C. O'Donoghue (1995), *Supplementing Family Income*, Dublin ESRI Policy Research Series Paper No. 23.

CEC (1994), *White Paper on Growth, Competitiveness, Employment: The challenges and ways forward into the 21st century*, European Commission, Brussels.

Drèze, J. and E. Malinvaud (1994), 'Growth and Employment: The Scope of a European Initiative', *European Economy*, No. 1, European Commission, Directorate-General for Economic and Financial Affairs, Brussels.

Ferrera, M. (1998), *Le Trappole del Welfare*, Il Mulino, Bologna.

Gallie, D. (1997), *Unemployment and Social Exclusion*, paper presented at a Seminar in Nuffield College, Oxford.

Haveman, R. (1996), 'Reducing Poverty while Increasing Employment: a Primer on Alternative Strategies, and a Blueprint', *OECD Economic Studies*, No. 26.

Nickell, S. and B. Bell (1996), *'Would Cutting Payroll Taxes on the Unskilled have a Significant Impact on Unemployment?'*, Discussion Paper No. 276, Centre for Economic Performance, LSE, London.

O'Donoghue, C. (1998), *'Simulating the Irish Tax-transfer System in Eur6, Micro-simulation Unit Research Note'*, MU/RN/25, DAE, Cambridge.

O'Donoghue, C., H. Sutherland and F. Utili (1998), *'Integrating Output in EUROMOD: An Assessment of the Sensitivity of Multi-country Microsimulation'*, paper presented at the Cambridge Workshop: Microsimulation in the New Millennium: Challenges and Innovations.

OECD (1994), 'Evidence and Explanations. Part II: The Adjustment Potential of the Labour Market', *The OECD Jobs Study*, Paris.

OECD (1997), *Making Work Pay. Taxation, Benefits, Employment and Unemployment*, OECD, Paris.

Piketty, T. (1997), 'La Redistribution fiscale face au chômage', *Revue Française d'Economie*.

Pissarides, C.A. (1991), 'Macroeconomic Adjustment and Poverty in Selected Industrial Countries', *World Bank Economic Review*, **5**, 207–29.

Scholz, J.K. (1996), 'In-Work Benefits in the United States: the Earned Income Tax Credit', *Economic Journal*, **106**, 156–69.

Snower, D. (1997), 'Challenges to Social Cohesion and Approaches to Policy Reform', in *Societal Cohesion and the Globalising Economy: What Does the Future Hold?*, OECD, Paris, 39–60.

Snower, D. and G. de la Dehesa (1997), *Unemployment Policy: Government Options for the Labour Market,* CEPR, Cambridge University Press, Cambridge.

Sutherland, H. (ed.) (1997), 'The EUROMOD Preparatory Study: a Summary Report', Microsimulation Unit Discussion Paper, MU9705, DAE, Cambridge.

Walker, R. and M. Wiseman (1997), 'The Possibility of a British Earned Income Tax Credit', *Fiscal Studies,* **18** (4).

3. Financial Incentives to Take up Low-Paid Work: An International Comparison of the Role of Tax and Benefit Systems

Marco Doudeijns, Marcel Einerhand and Arthur van de Meerendonk[1]

3.1 INTRODUCTION

A paid job is still the best route to avoid social exclusion. However, high unemployment and poor labour market prospects, especially for low-skilled people, make it hard for the long-term unemployed to remain motivated to continue looking for work. It is often alleged that the knowledge or perception that there is little or no financial gain from work compared with benefit income causes unemployed job-seekers to hesitate before accepting a low-paid job. Work-related expenses, welfare benefits that begin to be taxed back when earnings start to come in, tax liability and social security taxes that are levied on salary income can work together to make paid employment unrewarding for those on long-term unemployment benefits.

The income security which is provided by unemployment insurance and related welfare benefits serves to prevent the beneficiaries from slipping into poverty. A difficult choice which social policy has to make is trading-off income security and financial incentives to work. The lower the expected earnings are for persons depent upon benefits, the more severe this problem becomes. The endemic tension between socially acceptable benefit levels and work incentives is one of the main dilemmas of modern social policy. Resolving this dilemma calls for a clear understanding of the complex relationship between benefits, taxes and incentives.

There is a vast amount of literature on the adverse incentive effects of taxes and benefits (see for example Ljungqvist and Sargent 1998; Lindbeck 1997; Feldstein 1995; Moffitt 1992). High unemployment benefits are considered to diminish the incentive to look for a job, hence creating an unemployment trap. Increasing the difference between incomes out-of-work and in-work, for instance through the introduction of 'work-conditional benefits', seems a straightforward solution to this unemployment trap. However, the high marginal effective tax rates that arise through the gradual phasing out of such benefits may affect efforts to work more hours or increase earnings, hence creating a poverty trap.

Heckman (1993) points to the distinction between labour supply decisions at the 'extensive margin' (the decision to participate or not) and at the 'intensive margin' (the decision to work full time or part time). Furthermore, there is evidence that men and women have different labour supply elasticities. Elasticities for men, for example, are found to be zero or even negative reflecting their primary-earning status (Leibfritz et al. 1997). On the other end of the scale, the elasticities for married women are found to be high (Bingley and Walker 1997; Blundell 1993) and this is a case in point that not so much the individual, but the household is the relevant decision unit (Atkinson 1993, 31–2).

The first step in resolving the issue how tax-benefit schemes impact on incentives is to map how they operate on gross earnings. What does the net income schedule as a function of gross earnings look like? Haveman (1996), for instance, has listed several instruments that all more or less aim at encouraging employment and earnings simultaneously. Two of these, the earned income tax credit or earnings supplement and wage rate subsidies, top up earnings for those in work. These instruments effectively increase the net income from work and hence increase the difference between in-work and out-of-work income. Additional earnings are subsidised up to some gross earnings level. Below this level a negative marginal tax rate exists. Above this level the earnings supplements are phased out. The point, however, is that marginal effective tax rates are higher in this phase-out range than would have been the case without the earnings supplement plan. In order to assess whether there is scope for introducing an earnings supplement plan its impact on the existing tax-benefit structure needs to be revealed. Family Credit in the United Kingdom is an example of a plan designed to make work attractive for low-income families with children. But, as marginal effective tax rates for families receiving the credit in combination with housing benefit and community charge benefit were near to 100 per cent in the early 1990s, it had the effect of introducing an enormous poverty trap (Atkinson 1993, 172–3).

This chapter will compare effective tax rates focusing on the lower half of the earnings distribution, specifically quantifying the (dis-)incentives the tax-benefit system entails for accepting low-paid work and highlighting the social policy trade-offs at the lower side of the labour market. The first-decile earnings level is used as a benchmark. Throughout this chapter the situation of a one-earner couple with children is taken as the reference case. The results therefore will be different for other households, such as singles and lone-parent families. Three indicators will be used subsequently in this chapter reflecting three different dimensions of the incentives issue. The first is net replacement rates (NRRs), reflecting the decision to start a job for the primary earner. The second is net retained income (NRI), reflecting the decision to take up employment for the secondary earner. And the third is marginal effective tax rates (METRs), reflecting the net household income gain from increasing one of both partners' gross earnings (either through working more hours or putting more effort in). NRRs and marginal tax rates have been calculated in previous studies (CPB 1995; OECD 1998a; Salomäki and Munzi 1999). NRIs, however, are a novel indicator and, as far as the authors are concerned, indispensible in studies of the impact of tax-benefit schemes on household work incentives.

The chapter is structured as follows. Section 3.2 discusses different concepts of low pay. Section 3.3 concentrates on the financial rewards of the decision whether to take a low-paid job, or to remain out of employment. Because of the increasing focus on work incentives for persons in (long-term) unemployment or low-income families, particular attention will be paid to the incentives faced by persons in households with children. A detailed analysis will be presented on the incentives for partners of persons working (Section 3.4) or receiving short-term unemployment or long-term social assistance benefits (Section 3.5). This analysis will cover part-time and full-time, breadwinner and two-earner employment options. Section 3.6 will focus on the effect of employment-conditional benefits on incentives for people with low-pay expectations to de-/increase hours or effort. This section presents an initial comparison between the Netherlands and the United States. The final section provides conclusions.

3.2   INDICATORS OF LOW-PAID WORK

A frequently used indicator for low pay is the income level of two-thirds of the wage of the Average Production Worker (APW; see, for example, the OECD *Employment Outlook 1997*). It is used for instance to calculate replacement rates for the long-term unemployed. However, in seeking to quantify work incentives at the lower side of the labour market, there are some drawbacks to using two-thirds of the APW earnings. The most serious disadvantage is that two-thirds of APW represents different points in the income distribution in different OECD countries. In some – mostly European countries – two-thirds of the APW earnings may be close to the legal minimum wage. Only few people will have to rely on jobs paying less. In

Taxes, Benefits and Subsidies

other countries where the distribution of wages is more skewed – such as the Anglo-Saxon countries – the level of two-thirds of APW may not be a good indicator of the work incentives faced by persons needing to rely on a low-paid job,[2] as a much larger proportion of the work force earns less than this level.

Figure 3.1
Average earnings and low earnings (gross) by country
APW earnings and 2/3 APW earnings as % of first-decile earnings

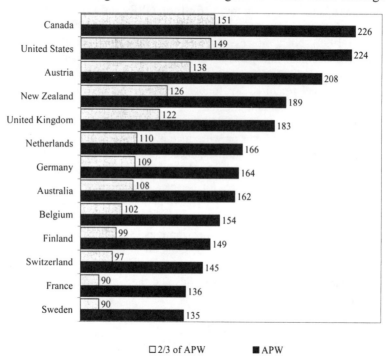

□ 2/3 of APW   ■ APW

A more appealing approach is to take a fixed point on the earnings distribution. This also facilitates the comparability of the outcomes across countries. The wage level at the top of the first decile of the earnings distribution represents an 'empirical' indication of low pay in a country. It indicates that 10 per cent of all full-time workers in a country earn less than the indicated amount. For persons who have only limited earnings capacity, for example, because of low educational attainment or long-term benefit dependency, the empirical demarcation of low pay by the first decile is much more relevant.[3] Exactly because of the empirical relevance of the first-decile indicator we will use this benchmark in the following sections.

Figure 3.1 shows that there is a large difference between two-thirds of the APW earnings and the earnings level at the first decile (D1) in many OECD countries.[4] The bars in the graph represent the gross APW earnings, and two-thirds of that level, as a percentage of the annual gross first-decile earnings. From this figure the following picture emerges. For most European countries, there is not a large difference between D1 earnings and two-thirds of APW earnings (the difference is 10 percentage points at most). In most Anglo-Saxon countries, on the other hand, D1 earnings are generally much lower (more than 20 percentage points) than two-thirds of APW. The exceptions are Australia and Austria. In Australia the gross earnings distribution is relatively compressed, whereas in Austria the difference between two-thirds of APW and D1 earnings appears to be relatively large. Hence, using two-thirds of the APW earnings to calculate net replacement rates gives a biased indicator of the incentives for those persons who have to rely on low wages.

3.3   LONG-TERM BENEFITS AND THE DISTANCE TO NET LOW PAY

The gross wages which are used in Figure 3.1 can give a quick impression of relative dispersion, but will not serve very well as indicators of the actual financial incentives to find work. Including the effects of income taxes and (means-tested) benefits gives a narrower – net – earnings distribution (see OECD 1996). These relative differences, between net benefits and the net income at the first-decile wage level may have an impact on the incentives to take up work: the smaller the difference the less likely beneficiaries are to realise an income gain from starting to work. The – net – wage distribution may influence the push to make a career and to try to increase earnings.

In Table 3.1 we present – for families with children – two different levels of net income. The reference income is the net income at the first decile (= 100). The income when unemployed in the 60th month is included. For almost all countries social assistance is the main benefit available in that situation. In Austria, Belgium, Denmark, Germany and Sweden a person may still receive unemployment benefits.[5] In case these benefits are shown the reference earnings for which unemployment insurance benefits are calculated is a previous wage equal to the first decile.

The table displays two different situations in which incentives matter. First of all it shows the financial effect of taking up low-paid work (first decile) by leaving long term-social assistance benefits. Second, it shows the financial effect of moving up the ladder from a low wage to APW level.

Taxes, Benefits and Subsidies

Table 3.1
Net income relative to first-decile income (D1 = 100), 1995

| | Social assistance relative to... | | APW relative to |
	D1 excluding additional benefits	D1 including additional benefits[a]	D1 including additional benefits
Australia	78	78	119
Austria[b, c]	80	80	174
Belgium[b]	86	89	166
Canada	95	62	131
Finland	107	100	112
France	74	68	113
Germany[b]	90	90	135
Ireland	117	87	120
Japan	105	87	122
Netherlands	94	94	137
New Zealand	84	84	147
Sweden[b]	111	100	109
Switzerland	78	78	136
United Kingdom	97	81	128
United States	97	63	131

Notes:

a: 'additional benefits': temporary income subsidies to increase work incentives, they can take the form of earnings/income exemptions in the SA means test (Canada, France, Japan, Sweden), in-work benefits (Ireland, UK, US) or both (Canada).

b: In Austria, Belgium, Germany and Sweden unemployment benefits are payable for very long time periods. For Austria the unemployment benefit at 60 months is listed, for the other countries SA is displayed in the table.

c In case unemployment benefits are shown the reference earnings for which unemployment insurance benefits are calculated is a previous wage equal to the first decile.

Source: OECD (1998a).

With respect to social assistance, the benefit levels (the net replacement rates) taking the first-decile level as a benchmark, are not widely apart across the different countries in the table: no straightforward pattern is visible in the first column of Table 3.1. The situation in the United Kingdom and United States, where out-of-work families with children receive social assistance benefits that are close to net first-decile wages if these would not be topped up by allowances, is perhaps the most remarkable. However, the table takes into account the existence of financial measures intended to help people leave the benefit system for a paid job. The bandwidth increases considerably when moving from the first to the second column where work-conditional benefits are taken into account.

Some countries with income assistance benefits allow households who re-enter the labour market to retain part of their employment income through disregards in the benefits' means test. An example is Canada, where bene-ficiaries who start to work may disregard a fixed amount (about 17 per cent of their basic benefit level) plus an additional 25 per cent of gross earned income. Some municipalities in the Netherlands allow recipients to earn about 15 per cent of their social assistance benefit level before the benefit is means-tested. Other countries have benefits that are specifically targeted at people in low-income employment and re-entrants. Family Credit in the United Kingdom and Earned Income Tax Credit (EITC) in the United States are perhaps the best known examples.[6] Topping up work income by supplementary benefits creates a distance between benefit income and in-work income, thereby increasing or creating work incentives. For the United Kingdom the replacement rates at first-decile income for couples with two children decrease from 97 per cent to 81 per cent. This suggests that one of the main reasons behind this measure (introducing Family Credit) is to regain or increase where necessary work incentives. In fact, one of the reasons for the introduction of in-work-benefits has been the relatively limited distance between low pay and benefits for households with children as it appears from Table 3.1. The decrease in replacement rates for the United States due to work-conditional allowances is even larger: from 97 per cent to 63 per cent. Low gross pay levels are possible – thereby creating an incentive for employers to hire – because the effect of gross low pay is compensated by the government. And incomes for those working, even if only part-time, are raised substantially.

What stands out, looking at Table 3.1 compared to Figure 3.1, is the much smaller distinction between the European and Anglo-Saxon countries. The distribution of earnings before-tax (as shown in Figure 3.1) in Anglo-Saxon countries is much wider than in Continental European countries. However, this pattern is not present in the after-tax distribution of income. The difference between gross earnings at the D1 level and at the APW level is much larger in, for example, the United States (124 per cent) than in the Netherlands (66 per cent). After-tax APW income for a couple with two children in the United States, however, is only 31 per cent above after-tax income at the D1 level against 37 per cent for a couple with two children in the Netherlands. The distance between low income (net D1) and net APW income is about the same for Canada, the United Kingdom and United States, but also for Germany and the Netherlands. This shows the substantial impact of taxes and benefits, as these tend to focus on protecting families with children, specifically at the lower end of the income scale.

Summing up, one may argue on the basis of the data that are presented in Table 3.1 that for families who are long-term unemployed the differences between their net benefit income and net first-decile earnings are not much more pronounced in Anglo-Saxon countries than in the European countries. It contradicts much of the existing literature on work incentives and is contrary also to common perception. A further conclusion that can be drawn from the table is that, for families with children, the incentives to move up the job-ladder from a low-wage job to one paying an APW wage in most Anglo-Saxon countries do not exceed those in European countries.

3.4   WORK INCENTIVES IN TWO-EARNER HOUSEHOLDS

The *Employment Outlook 1998* (OECD 1998b) highlighted a simultaneous growth of both two-income earner households and households with no work income. The lack of work incentives to start or stay in work for people who depend (in part) on means-tested benefits could be an important determinant. The focus in this section is on families in which initially one person is working. Subsequently it is assumed that the partner accepts low paid work. The first question then is whether the fact that already one person is working influences the incentives for the partner to take up low paid work. And the second question is: does the level of pay of the person in the household who already works matter?

Panel A in Table 3.2 shows the income gain for a one-earner couple where one partner, say Partner 1, is earning the APW earnings level and the non-employed partner, Partner 2, starts to work part-time or full-time. In fact, four situations are discerned: the partner starts working at a quarter-, half-, three-quarters- and a full-time job earning a first-decile level wage. In the table this corresponds with 25, 50, 75 and 100 per cent of full-time first-decile level (D1) earnings. Panel B differs only in the assumption that Partner 1 is full-time employed and earning D1 (instead of APW level). It is assumed in both panels that Partner 2 will take up work at the level of the first decile. The table should be read as follows: in Australia, in Panel A, partners earning 25 per cent of the first-decile earnings level increase the family income with 99 per cent of their earnings; 1 per cent is taxed or means-tested away (the figures in the table are round numbers: in fact only 0.6 per cent is taxed away). Partners earning a full first-decile level can add 85 per cent of their earnings to the net family income. As there is one working partner earning an average income the family is assumed to be free of social assistance type benefits.

The first observation from Table 3.2 is that the net retained income (NRI) is generally quite high in case a person takes up low-paid work, while the partner earns an APW income. Only few countries still pay means-tested benefits at the APW income level. In the Anglo-Saxon countries and Japan the NRIs are generally higher (Panel A, partner earns APW income) than in the other countries. In Australia, this can be entirely attributed to disregarded earnings in the means test of the partner's individual benefit. In Japan and New Zealand, tax rebates to working people are credit to the partner's high work incentives. In the United States, the employment-conditional benefit for two earner couples with children – the dependent care credit (DCC) – causes high retained income percentages.

Table 3.2
Disincentives in low-income households
(Net percentage of additional earnings which can be retained)

	A. Partner of an employed person earning APW				B. Partner of an employed person earning D1			
	Additional earnings level (as a percentage of D1)							
	25	50	75	100	25	50	75	100
Australia	99	91	87	85	56	58	65	68
Austria	81	75	77	78	82	82	82	82
Belgium	56	36	39	43	75	51	55	56
Canada	71	71	69	67	62	69	69	68
Denmark	53	53	51	51	42	40	44	46
Finland	80	76	72	68	68	64	64	62
France	57	62	64	66	60	61	63	63
Germany	67	48	49	50	66	48	51	49
Ireland	86	79	75	74	40	20	23	34
Japan	89	85	87	87	89	89	89	89
Netherlands	58	59	59	59	55	57	58	58
New Zealand	90	83	78	77	93	76	64	60
Sweden	73	70	71	69	57	62	66	65
Switzerland	73	72	71	71	77	76	75	74
United Kingdom	100	96	89	89	28	50	59	61
United States	100	94	86	82	79	60	53	51
Total	77	72	70	70	64	60	61	62
Anglo-Saxon countries	91	86	82	80	64	60	60	62
European Countries	66	62	61	62	65	60	62	62

Notes:
The numbers are calculated for a two-parent family with two children aged 6 and 4 years, paying a private market house-rent equal to 10 per cent of the APW earnings level. The family is assumed not to receive social assistance benefits. One working partner has earnings at the APW level, or at the D1 earnings level in Panel A and Panel B, respectively. The other partner starts to work at 25, 50, 75 or 100 per cent of the D1 earnings level in either Panel A or Panel B.

Source: OECD Database on Benefit Systems and Work Incentives.

The difference between Panel B and Panel A is that now the working partner, Partner 1, has lower earnings, at the first-decile level. The low income level at the initial situation entails that means-tested welfare benefits are very likely to be part of the initial income and to create work disincentives. For most European countries the net retained income is roughly at the same level if the already working partner, Partner 1, earns only first-decile income (Panel B) or when the working partner earns APW-level income (Panel A). For the Anglo-Saxon countries there is sometimes a sharp decrease going from the NRI in Panel A to Panel B. In Ireland, the initial income level entitles for employment conditional benefits, the 'Family Income Supplement' (FIS). The FIS has a very steep means test that causes strong disincentives for Partner 2 to take a part-time job if the household is already receiving FIS. Note, however, that FIS can only be paid for one year. Family Credit in the United Kingdom causes an extra incentive to work when the partner works two days per week and the full credit is paid. However, as the benefit is means-tested on net household income, the incentive is much less when one partner is already in paid employment. The partner's activities in the United States cause the couple's entitlement to Earned Income Tax Credit to be reduced, however, both EITC and DCC are paid over the whole earnings range covered in Panel B.

The three bottom rows in Table 3.2 show the average NRI for all countries, for the Anglo-Saxon countries and for the European countries, respectively. On the basis of these figures one can conclude that:

- the take-up of low-paid work by other members of a working family does pay off, even in low-income families;
- in European countries, on average, the earnings of the already working partner have little influence on the incentives for the spouse to take up a low-paid job;
- in Anglo-Saxon countries, on average, the incentives for the partner to take up work are much higher when the already working partner earns a higher income;
- the NRI are not homogenous in the two groups of countries; in some countries, NRI are markedly below the (group-) average (Denmark and Germany), in others they are much higher (Austria and Japan)

In the Anglo-Saxon countries the take-up of low-paid work by other members of a working family does pay off. But the reward is much higher when the already working partner earns a higher income. Paradoxically, therefore, the instruments in place that make taking up low-paid work financially rewarding have the opposite effect for partners in households when the already working partner also earns a low wage. Despite this, it should be noted that financial incentives for members of a low-income working family in the Anglo-Saxon countries still are roughly comparable to those in the European countries presented in Table 3.2.

3.5   UNEMPLOYED HOUSEHOLDS AND WORK DECISIONS

We now turn to the situation in which no household member is currently employed so the family receives a benefit income (see Table 3.3). Our assumption is that the unemployed person, say again Partner 1, used to have earnings at the APW level and has worked a sufficiently long time to qualify for unemployment benefits.[7] The family situation is similar to that in Table 3.2. Since the family members are not employed in the starting situation, they receive low incomes and may very well receive means-tested and assistance benefits. Three situations are presented.

Panel A shows the NRI for a situation where there is one unemployment insurance beneficiary and one non-active person.[8] The person receiving unemployment insurance benefits, Partner 1, starts to work at low-wage level and gradually increases earnings from 25, to 50, 75 and, finally, 100 per cent of the D1 earnings level. Panel B shows the NRI for the same situation but now the partner of an unemployment insurance benefit recipient, Partner 2, takes up low-paid work and gradually increases earnings from 25, to 50, 75 and, finally, 100 per cent of the D1 earnings level. Panel C shows the NRI for a situation where the family is dependent on SA benefits. One of the two partners takes up paid work and gradually increases earnings from 25, to 50, 75 and, finally, 100 per cent of the D1 earnings level.

Income Retained for the Unemployed Person Accepting Low-Paid Work

Panel A shows the effect of starting to work part-time or full-time for a D1 wage if one receives unemployment insurance. The insurance benefit is based on previous earnings at APW level. Panel A therefore describes the situation of an unemployed APW worker who takes a low-paid job. For many countries, Panel A shows that leaving unemployment to start low-paid work – even full-time – is hardly financially attractive. Unemployment insurance discourages the take up of part-time work, or work paying less than previous income. In the United States, D1 income exceeds the benefit income only by a few per cent. Hence, there is hardly any financial incentive to work. Starting to work at the D1 income level in the Netherlands, Austria and Denmark would actually result in a drop in net income. In countries where flat-rate benefits are paid (Australia, New Zealand and the United Kingdom),

Taxes, Benefits and Subsidies

the effect of previous income is not relevant for the benefit level. In these countries, an increase in net income of more than 25 per cent relative to the benefit income is indeed possible (to a lesser extent for New Zealand).

Table 3.3

Two-earner couples and work incentives

(Net percentage of additional earnings which can be retained)

	A. Unemployment insurance recipient				**B.** Partner of unemployment insurance recipient				**C.** Long-term benefit recipient			
	\multicolumn{12}{c}{additional earnings level as a percentage of D1}
	25	50	75	100	25	50	75	100	25	50	75	100
Australia	48	39	37	29	48	39	37	29	48	39	37	29
Austria	83	–135	–63	–27	40	49	60	66	42	51	–54	–19
Belgium	–244	–78	–23	4	59	73	78	74	–73	7	34	47
Canada	0	0	0	0	76	76	73	72	99	82	63	52
Denmark	–36	–30	–30	–29	53	53	53	53	42	47	49	39
Finland	21	14	11	3	68	64	62	60	0	0	0	0
France	20	21	20	5	60	61	63	63	17	23	60	52
Germany	59	–67	–22	..	51	58	65	67	60	58	52	51
Ireland	–64	117	34	34	–60	152	108	80	39	68	13	19
Japan	–225	–68	–15	11	88	89	89	89	30	22	17	14
Netherlands	–8	–7	–8	–10	58	59	59	59	0	0	0	2
New Zealand	74	46	36	16	74	46	36	16	74	46	36	16
Sweden	6	3	4	1	60	64	67	66	0	0	0	0
Switzerland	–4	–5	–5	–5	77	75	73	72	0	0	1	21
United Kingdom	-64	53	50	42	–14	111	80	71	38	12	22	21
United States	–98	–31	–10	6	110	108	106	96	79	60	53	51

Notes:

1: Family Resources are excluded from social assistance.

2: In all three panels the employed person earns the first-decile earnings level in full-time employment.

3: Earnings are proportional to the number of hours worked: the benefit system causes discontinuities in Ireland, the United Kingdom and Australia.

Source: OECD database on Benefits and Incentives.

In general therefore, one may conclude that the incentive to take up low-paid work is absent in the situation where earnings-related UI schemes exist. The provisions for working when receiving insurance benefits do not facilitate small jobs or work that is paid very little compared with the reference salary (that is, the salary in last employment that is used in the benefit formula). It is unclear, however, whether the immediate financial incentives play such an important role for someone who has just become unemployed. Unemployment insurance fulfils the need of a temporary income source and most job-seekers may be expected to be re-employed shortly at approximately the last earned wage. But if the average unemployment spell is not short and if unemployment insurance benefits have long payment durations, then the financial incentives are important.

Income Retained for Partner of Unemployed Person when Accepting Low-Paid Work

Panel B in Table 3.3 shows the NRI rates for the partner of an unemployed APW worker. Partner 1 receives unemployment insurance benefits, Partner 2 starts a job for 25, 50, 75 and 100 per cent of D1 earnings. The first observation is that the numbers are much higher than those in Panel A: the work incentives for the partner of someone who has just become unemployed are much stronger than for the unemployed person him- or herself. The main reason is that the benefit unit and the resource unit for insurance benefits are the insured person, the individual as opposed to the family. The amount of benefit is therefore not affected by other household members' incomes. Nevertheless, there still are considerable differences in NRI.

Only if means-tested benefits are paid will there be an effect on Partner 1's benefit when Partner 2 takes up low-paid work. For example, in countries where dependent's allowances – a benefit supplement in recognition of a dependent spouse – are paid, the event of a working partner will affect the benefit amount. This is the case in Ireland and the United Kingdom, where NRI rates in the first columns are negative due to benefit withdrawal. In Ireland, the dependant's allowance is withdrawn as soon as the dependent partner starts to earn. In the United Kingdom, when the partner's earnings reach the level of the dependent allowance, which takes place when the partner's earnings equal around 20 per cent of the first-decile level, the allowance is withdrawn. Housing benefits are usually also means-tested. In the United Kingdom, housing benefits cease when the partner's earnings reach about 20 per cent of the first-decile earnings level. This effect adds to the effect of the withdrawal of the dependant's allowance from the unemployment benefit.

Typical cases are Australia and New Zealand. For these two countries, NRI rates in all three panels are identical. Dependent partners in Australia receive an individual unemployment assistance benefit which is means-tested on individual income. Whether one partner works or the other, the reduction of the benefit amount is the same. In New Zealand, the means test does not come into effect until the earnings of both partners exceed a certain threshold; the percentage of retained income is high in the first column.

Hence, the incentives are strong to earn up to this point and are then strongly reduced because of the withdrawal of the remainder of unemployment benefits if the beneficiary is working full time. Unemployment assistance in New Zealand is paid disregarding employment history, means-tested on income from other sources and after the means-testing is paid in equal amounts to both partners. The numbers in all panels are therefore exactly the same. The family benefits means test in Australia and New Zealand adds to the disincentive to work more at higher earnings levels as these are reduced proportionally with earnings above specified threshold levels (that is the earnings disregards. Because of that disincentives are less present at lower earnings levels which is expressed in all panels as a higher percentage of earnings that can be retained for low-paying jobs).

In-work benefits can give a significant boost to earned income. The jump in NRI for the United Kingdom in the second column of Panel B is the effect of Family Credit; Family Income Supplements in Ireland have a similar effect. In Ireland, Family Income Supplement is paid to a family with children where the partners work more than 20 hours (taking the sum of the hours worked by both partners, which is here where earnings equal 50 per cent of the first-decile level) and then (after a disregard) reduced with 60 per cent of gross family income. Hence, the income supplement gradually reduces when earnings increase. In the United Kingdom, Family Credit is introduced when Partner 2 is working two days, making part-time work very attractive (in fact, the credit offsets the drop caused by social security contributions and causes net income to temporarily increase more than the partner's earnings). In the United States, the Earned Income Tax Credit is payable to the household with one partner working over the whole earnings range covered in Panel B of Table 3.3, lifting the percentage of retained earnings up to around 100 per cent.

Income Retained by Long-Term Unemployed Accepting Low-Paid Work

Panel C in Table 3.3 shows the percentage of earnings (the partner of) a long-term unemployed person can retain. Hence, the difference with Panel B is the duration of unemployment. In Panel B, the single earner has just become unemployed when the partner starts to work. In Panel C, the single earner, Partner 1, has been unemployed for a long period when one of both partners starts to work. Since in most countries unemployment insurance benefits will have been exhausted, assistance benefits are the basic income source.

Because the resource unit of social assistance is the family, it makes no difference which of both partners starts to work. The exception is Belgium where income related unemployment insurance benefits are paid indefinitely. The situation in this country differs from Panel B because the unemployment beneficiary now receives the long-term benefit which is a lot less generous. On top of that, if the inactive partner starts to work the dependant's allowance ceases, causing a disincentive to work small hours. Only if the partner earns 50 per cent of the first-decile earnings a slight increase in net family income is registered. In Germany, the NRI is high in all columns. The beneficiary's partner's income does not affect the benefit amount unless it exceeds the dependant's tax allowance (which equals about one-third of the first-decile earnings level) and the means test on the remainder is tapered.

The means test of social assistance creates severe disincentives to work for either partner. The NRI is remarkably high all across the earnings range in Canada[9] where social assistance is not means-tested unless earnings exceed certain threshold values (the disregards), and the means test on the remainder of income is tapered. In Finland, the Netherlands,[10] Sweden and Switzerland, the means test applies to all earnings without disregards. In these countries, there are no financial incentives to work unless the total earnings level exceeds the assistance benefit amounts (for example, the Netherlands and Switzerland in the last two columns).

Employment-conditional benefits partly offset the means test of food stamps and family benefits in the United States and create a strong incentive to work for one or both partners in a long-term unemployed couple. Family Credit in the United Kingdom reduces the drop in net income which is caused by the withdrawal of Income Support if the combined effort in the household is more than two days per week. The effect of the in-work supplement, which is paid when the partner works 30 hours, translates into a significant increase in the NRI in the third column. In Ireland, the Family Income Supplements lift the NRI up to nearly 70 per cent in the second column but the withdrawal of unemployment assistance when one of both partners works three days or more per week causes the NRI rate to fall in the third column. The EITC in the United States keeps NRI high. The numbers are lower than in Panel B because the family is relying on long-term means-tested benefits. Without the in-work benefit the NRI would be around 20 per cent after the first column (where income disregards play a role).

The key question in this and the previous section has been how one partner's situation affects the other partner's incentives to take up work. Different situations have been examined: two-earner couples with different wage levels in the previous section, and, in this section, unemployed people with benefit entitlements of their own, and unemployed households on long-term unemployment benefits. From Table 3.2 and 3.3, it appears that:

- disincentives are lowest for people in a household with someone already in work or on unemployment insurance benefits;
- households whose net incomes include substantial amounts of means-

tested benefits suffer most from financial disincentives to increase earnings;
- employment-conditional benefits, earnings disregards and tapered means-testing significantly improve work incentives;

These findings suggest that, on the one hand, income taxes and social security contributions are not an important source of disincentives. On the other hand, however, the means-testing of social assistance and housing benefits, when combined with the liability to pay income tax and social security contributions on low incomes, can significantly reduce the financial reward to work.

3.6   INCENTIVES TO WORK MORE HOURS AND TO INCREASE EARNINGS

A well-known dilemma of social policy is that attempts to overcome the unemployment trap inevitably lead to a poverty-trap situation. As long as the family is receiving means-tested in-work benefits every earnings increase results in a reduction of the in-work benefit which limits the increase in net family income. The analysis thus far showed that means-tested benefits can reduce the financial reward to work over a wide earnings range. This section will focus on the effects of in-work benefits on marginal effective tax rates.

Figure 3.2 graphs net income as a function of gross earnings for the Netherlands and the United States. The figure applies to a married couple with two children in long-term benefit receipt.[11] For both countries, net income is expressed as a percentage of the net income at the first-decile earnings level. Gross earnings are re-scaled for both countries as a percentage of the first-decile earnings level. The left part, up to the intersection of both schedules in point (100, 100) corresponds with the last panel, Panel C, in Table 3.3. At earnings level 0, at the left-hand extreme of the X-axis, the couple receives long-term social assistance benefits. The line for each country indicates the net income the couple would have were it to earn a certain percentage of the gross first-decile earnings level. Thus, the figure illustrates how quickly net income increases with the rise in gross earnings for long-term beneficiaries in the Netherlands and the United States.

Long-term beneficiaries in the United States have a much lower net income than those in the Netherlands. The Dutch social security scheme provides relatively generous out-of-work benefits. The flat line for the Netherlands indicates that long-term beneficiaries who start to work will not be able to increase their net income until their earnings begin to exceed the first-decile level. The untapered means test of social assistance takes away all incentives to work for earnings that, after tax, are hardly more than the social assistance payment rates.[12] This was also indicated in Table 3.1, which showed that only 6 per cent of earnings at the first-decile level contribute to a net income increase of social assistance beneficiaries who start to work at this earnings level. The graph also shows, as Panel C in Table 3.3 indicated, that long-term beneficiaries in the United States see their net income increase from the first few hours they start to work.

Figure 3.2
Trade-off between the incentive to accept a low-paid job, and the incentive to move from part-time to full-time
METRs of couples with two children; 1997

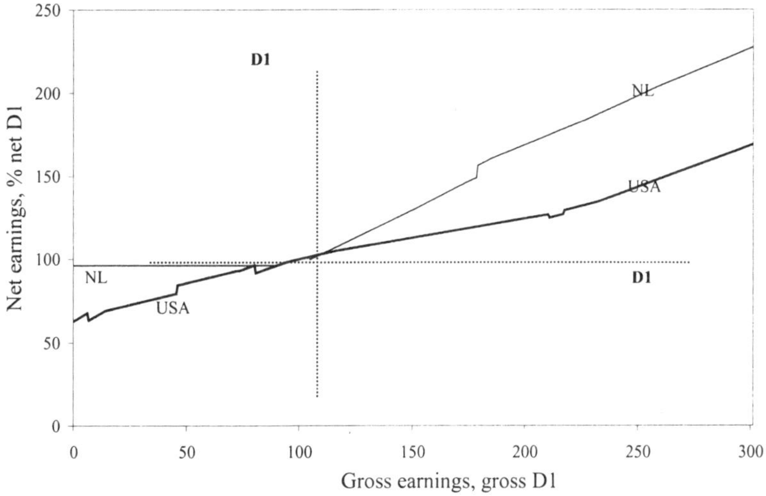

Source: OECD Tax/Benefit

But the figure includes more information. The wider earnings distribution in the United States is reflected by the bigger difference between gross D1 and D5 (the fifth decile or median earnings level) as depicted on the horizontal axis: D5 is 210 per cent of D1 in the US compared with 171 per cent of D1 in the Netherlands. The way in which the tax and benefit system acts to reduce this difference, an observation already made in Section 3, is reflected in the much smaller difference between average and low incomes after tax. As shown in Table 3.1, workers with family responsibilities have 137 per cent of D1 after tax in the Netherlands compared with 131 per cent in the US; this is depicted on the vertical axis.

For the Netherlands, Figure 3.2 shows a much steeper graph than the US between 100 per cent and 200 per cent of D1 gross earnings. Means-tested benefits are no longer paid (although housing benefits can, under certain circumstances, still be paid at these earnings levels), and this means that NRI rates are high. For the United States, the chart shows only little net income improvement while going up the gross income ladder. This reflects the EITC means test. EITC is phased in from zero earnings to just under the minimum wage; the phase-out range starts at the first-decile earnings level and stops (the last annual payment is $14) where there is a small notch in the net income graph.[13]

Figure 3.2 shows some of the important trade-offs inherent in making choices between financial work incentives and avoiding poverty. The Dutch case shows that high social assistance benefits require a beneficiary to find full-time work if he or she is to enjoy financial gains from work. After taking up such work, any additional work effort will generate reasonable increases in net income. The US case show that taking up work – if only for a few hours a week – will result in a substantial income gain, the drawback being limited incentives to move up the income ladder because of the high marginal effective tax rates as a result of the EITC means test. Reducing hours worked, therefore, does not lead to a substantial income loss. A similar effect was noticeable in the UK Family Credit system. In order to maintain work incentives a new additional benefit was introduced if people started to work 30 hours or more. Research for the United States indicates that the positive effects of increased labour supply outweigh the effects of a reduction in hours of those already on the labour market (see for example, Scholz 1996 and OECD 1997b). Similar research for the UK, focusing on lone parents, found weak and potentially negative labour supply responses (see Duncan and Giles 1996).

3.7   CONCLUSIONS

The core aim of social security is to ensure that individuals and households have a decent standard of living it they are for whatever reason unable to provide for themselves. However, the higher the benefit levels are set relative to earnings, the lower is the immediate financial incentive to enter paid employment. High replacement rates are generally taken to affect the incentive to look for a job: this is referred to as the unemployment trap. On the other hand, high marginal tax rates (including social security contributions) and means-tested benefits that are clawed back as additional income is earned, reduce the reward from working more hours or increasing earnings: this is called the poverty trap. Hence, the composite tax and benefit structure has to be taken into account when considering the incentive on labour supply.

In this paper we have used in particular three indicators to measure incentives: the net replacement rate (NRR), net retained income (NRI), and the Marginal Effective Tax Rate (METR). The focus is on quantifying the financial incentives which result for low-paid workers from the interactions of the tax and benefit systems. Our intersection point on the earnings distribution has been the first-decile earnings level. We argued that this is to be preferred compared to the more common measure that takes two-thirds of the gross average production workers' earnings level.

An additional feature of our analysis has been that we have taken households, married couples with children, and several employment/ unemployment situations as point of reference. We concentrated on households and devoted two separate sections to the issue of incentives for partners of low-wage earners and the (long-term) unemployed.

First, we found that the received view that the Anglo-Saxon tax and benefit schemes with respect of their impact on the wage distribution generate outcomes widely distinct from the Continental European and Scandinavian schemes, is in need of modification.

We first compared gross low-pay levels relative to the level of the average production worker (APW) and subsequently compared net earnings levels. The result of taking the impact of tax and benefit schemes into account was that, for households with children, there appears to be much less of a dichotomy between the Anglo-Saxon countries on one hand and the Continental European and Scandinavian countries on the other hand. The differences between net first-decile earnings and net APW earnings is roughly the same in both groups of countries, as was illustrated in Table 3.1. This is to a large extent due to employment-conditional benefits, common in the Anglo-Saxon countries, that raise net earnings and compress the earnings distribution for these households.

Second, disincentives to start a job at a low earnings level are high, in particular for households with children in the majority of OECD countries. Again the Anglo-Saxon countries are no exception to this.

With respect to households with children with a low earnings capacity, the net replacement rates in the majority of OECD countries are as high as 75 per cent and above. This applies to Anglo-Saxon countries as well as to Continental European and Scandinavian countries. Employment-oriented social policies could concentrate on improving the financial consequences of starting to work for families.

Third, employment-conditional benefits, earnings disregards and the tapering of means-tested benefits significantly improve work incentives.

This is because these are all instruments that enlarge the gap between net out-of-work income and net in-work earnings. For example, the employment-conditional benefits in Ireland, the United Kingdom and the United States have large effects on work incentives. Canada and Germany disregard a portion of income in the means-testing of assistance benefits and have markedly higher NRI's than most other countries. Tapered means tests and income disregards are common in Australia and New Zealand which rely heavily on universal means-tested benefits.

Turning from disincentives for single earners to disincentives for partners, the picture with respect to means-tested benefits and employment-conditional benefits changes, however: fourth, households whose net income includes means-tested benefits face serious financial disincentives over a wide range of earnings up to the level of the first-decile wage.

With respect to partners of single earners, we found that disincentives to start a low-paid job are most severe in the situation where the already employed household member earns a first-decile-level wage. The dis-incentives for the partners of APW-level earners to take up low-paid work are generally much less. This points to the impact of means-tested benefits on household work decisions. In general, Anglo-Saxon countries allow a larger share of the low wage received by the second earner to be retained than Continental European and Scandinavian countries. Often more than 80 per cent can be retained in the former countries. With respect to partners of APW earners, this result can be attributed to a large extent to the tax system: the Anglo-Saxon countries in general having relatively modest nominal tax rates. With respect to partners of first-decile earners however, the picture is different. For these households, incentives in Scandinavian countries and in particular in the Anglo-Saxon countries are considerably reduced. These households receive means-tested benefits, for example they may receive housing allowances. And on top of this in the Anglo-Saxon countries they receive in-work benefits, such as the Earned Income Tax Credit in the United States. APW earners generally will not be eligible for these in-work benefits. First-decile earners in most cases will. The moment however, their partners start to work and increase their earnings, this will give rise to a decline in the in-work benefits. A partner of an American APW earner starting a full-time job earning a first-decile wage will retain 82 per cent of these gross earnings. On the other hand, a partner of a first-decile wage earner in the United States will retain only 51 per cent. Means-tested benefits, including in-work benefits, therefore may have the adverse effect of decreasing work incentives for partners of low-wage earners. But it should be noted that incentives for partners of low-wage earners in the US are still of the same magnitude as those in Europe.

Fifth, for households with no member employed, the incentives to start a low-paid job are mixed, depending on whether it concerns the benefit recipient or his/her partner, whether the benefit is determined on an individual basis, and whether in-work benefits apply.

Generally the incentive to accept a low-paid job is limited for unemployment benefit recipients, in particular when (i) it concerns a part-time job, and (ii) the benefit is calculated on the basis of previous earnings, rather than a flat rate. For the partners of these unemployment benefit recipients, however, the incentives to start a lowpaid job are adequate, since they are allowed to retain a considerable share of their gross earnings. This applies in particular when (iii) unemployment benefits are granted on an individual basis, that is, not means-tested against household income. If individual benefits are paid, such as generally is the case in Australia, the incentives to work for each household member are determined by their own individual entitlements. Disincentive effects do not spill over from the beneficiary to the other household members, as is the case when means-testing procedures are based on household income. And the incentive is adequate when (iv) the partner that starts a low-paid job is eligible for in-work benefits, as is the case for example in Ireland, the United Kingdom and the United States.

For long-term unemployed and their partners, the incentives to start a low-paid job are considerably higher in the Anglo-Saxon countries than in the Continental European and Scandinavian countries, excluding Denmark, France and Germany. In the latter three countries individual earnings-related benefits can still be paid after five years of unemployment. In the Anglo-Saxon countries, the higher financial incentives are due largely to in-work benefits. In these countries, in-work benefits again have an incentive-enhancing effect (contrary to the situation referred to in the fourth point where in-work benefits exerted an adverse effect on incentives).

Finally, there appears to be a trade-off in terms of marginal effective tax rates (METRs). We took the situation of a household with two children in the Netherlands and the US as an example. On the one hand, the US tops up earnings, that is, reduces METRs up to the first-decile level; and this comes at the price of high METRs in the range between first-decile and APW earnings. On the other hand, we observe that the Netherlands claws back all earnings up to first-decile level; but has relatively modest METRs in the subsequent earnings range.

We reviewed the financial incentives relating to the decision to increase hours or effort. For two countries (the Netherlands and the United States), an initial analysis was made of the METRs when taking up work starting from social assistance benefits. The analysis showed the trade-offs inherent in the two social protection systems. High social assistance benefits in the Netherlands make work at low pay an option offering only minor financial rewards. Only after taking up low-paid work does increasing wages pay off. For the US work pays both at low pay and if only a few hours a week are worked. Because of the claw-back of the Earned Income Tax Credit, higher wages above the low-wage threshold increase net income less sharply than in the Netherlands. Ironically, therefore, in-work benefits are one of the main sources of disincentives to raise earnings above low levels. This is partly due to complicated interactions between earnings, other benefits and income taxes, but mainly to the gradual reduction of these benefits with increases in earning. The dilemma this entails is of great significance for countries yet to design and implement in-work benefits.[14]

NOTES

1. At the time of writing, the first author worked at the OECD, Paris. The other two authors work in the Ministry of Social Affairs and Employment in the Netherlands. The views expressed are those of the authors and are not to be taken as the views of the OECD or the Dutch Ministry. The authors thank John Martin for his extensive comments on a previous draft.

2. Another indicator that is often used is the minimum wage. To analyse the incentive for persons relying on low-paid work the advantage of this indicator is that theoretically it measures the lowest possible wage at which persons in a country will be legally required to work. However, there may be substantial variation between countries in terms of the groups of workers who are not covered by minimum wages and in the treatment of apprentices and younger workers (see OECD 1997a for more details). At present 17 OECD countries have a minimum wage set by the government unilaterally or following recommendations by a tripartite body. In a number of other OECD countries collective agreements may set minimum wage levels for (unionised) workers. The disadvantage of the minimum wage level is that not all countries use such a concept. To circumvent this problem, sometimes the lowest wages agreed upon in a certain industrial sector are taken as a proxy of low wage. Wage agreements however may differ between countries in scope and coverage. It is therefore difficult to establish the empirical relevance of this indicator.

3. Like two-thirds of APW, the first-decile level represents a point in the earnings distribution. The spread of wages below the first-decile mark is not explored. For Canada, France and the Netherlands, for example, the gross data on the minimum wage suggest that spread below the first decile is limited. In Belgium, Japan, New Zealand and the United States, on the other hand, the minimum wage is significantly lower than the first-decile earnings level.

4. The different wage levels are taken from the OECD database on earnings distribution. Figures are updated from the figures presented in the *Employment Outlook 1996*. For some countries this may lead to differences in the results presented. The distributions do not include income from self-employment.

5. Figures for Denmark are currently not available.

6. We are ignoring the value of in-kind services to job-seekers, of health benefits that may be lost for re-entrants as well as other passport benefits. Tax measures such as an allowance for work-related expenses could also be seen as employment-conditional benefits, especially in Italy where they are quite substantive. However, such allowances have been regarded as an integral part of the tax-schedule and not as specific in-work benefits.

7. The unemployed person is assumed to be 40 years old and to be eligible for the maximum duration of payment of unemployment insurance benefit. These assumptions influence the initial benefit amounts in some countries. (See also OECD 1998.)

8. The person receiving Unemployment Insurance benefit starts to work at a low-wage level and gradually increases the number of hours worked from 25, to 50, 75 and, finally, 100 per cent. Gross earnings are assumed to increase proportional to the number of hours worked so that the person will earn a D1 wage in full employment.

9. The results for Canada reflect the situation in Ontario. As Social Assistance is a provincial responsibility, outcomes may well be different in other provinces.

10. For the Netherlands it should be noted that municipalities may at their own discretion

exempt part of earnings from means-testing. As it is impossible to generate an acceptable estimate of this it was decided not to include this option in the calculations.
11. For other household types other results may be obtained. Specifically in the case of single persons taking up low-paid jobs the graphs may be rather different. First because benefit levels will be much lower relative to low-paid work, which is specifically true for the United States, and second EITC is less generous for singles.
12. See note 6
13. The small upward jump for the Netherlands in net earnings around two times D1 wage is caused by our assumptions about the social security system. Only obligatory taxes and social contributions are included in the analysis. Obligatory public health premiums in the Netherlands stop as from the earnings level of two times D1 wage. Persons on a higher wage income must take out health insurance on the private market. Because private insurance is not included in the calculations net income shows an increase. For the United States premiums to be paid for private health insurance are also excluded. Leaving the benefit system may lead to leaving public health care provisions in the United States. Therefore including this effect of paying private health insurance would flatten the graph for the United States. In cases where private health insurance needs to be taken when starting to work in the US, Figure 3.2 overstates the financial incentives for the United States.
14. One of the shortcomings of the brief analysis that this chapter offers is the issue of child care. Subsidies toward the cost of child care may be crucial to the decision to start work, especially for women and lone parents. However, the treatment of child care costs and subsidies not only is much more complicated than an analysis of in-work benefits, it also calls issues in the discussion that are related to family policy. As such they have determinedly been left out of the present analysis. Another obvious omission is a description of the consequences of losing health benefits for people who contemplate working for low pay. Health-care related benefits, such as pharmaceutical cards in Canada or cheap or free insurance in the US, may be linked to benefit receipt and are thus lost when benefits are no longer paid. The implicit income risk is particularly important for parents with young children who might make the calculation that work is not worthwhile. Other such benefits related to benefit receipt that exist in many countries are free school meals and free dental treatment. The effect on the opportunity to work may be less than caused by the loss of health insurance but may still be significant. These limitations set a possible direction for future work which could draw heavily on an analysis of marginal effective tax rates for different family types.

REFERENCES

Atkinson, A.B. (1993), 'Work Incentives' and 'Have Social-Security Benefits Seriously Damaged Work Incentives in Britain?', in A.B. Atkinson and G.V. Mogensen (eds), *Welfare and Work Incentives: A North European Perspective*, Clarendon Press, Oxford.

Bingley, P. and I. Walker (1997), *Household Unemployment and the Labour Supply of Married Women*, Paper delivered for ninth EALE-Conference, Aarhus.

Blundell, R. (1993), 'Taxation and Labour-Supply Incentives in the UK', in A.B. Atkinson and G.V. Mogensen (eds), *Welfare and Work Incentives: A North European Perspective*, Clarendon Press, Oxford.

CPB (1995), *Replacement Rates: A transatlantic view*, CPB Netherlands Bureau of Economic Policy Analysis, The Hague.

Duncan, A. and C. Giles (1996), 'Labour Supply Incentives and Recent Family Credit Reforms', *The Economic Journal*, **106** (January), 149–55.

Feldstein, M. (1995), 'Behavioral Responses to Tax Rates: Evidence from the Tax Reform Act of 1986', *American Economic Review*, **85** (2), 170–74.

Haveman, R. (1996), *Reducing Poverty While Increasing Increasing Employment: a Primer on Alternative Strategies and a Blueprint,* OECD Economic Studies, No. 26, (1996/1), 7–42.

Heckman, J.J. (1993), 'What Has Been Learned About Labor Supply in the Past Twenty Years?', *American Economic Review*, **83** (2), 116–21.

Leibfritz, W., J. Thornton and A. Bibbee (1997), *Taxation and Economic Performance*, OECD Economics Department Working Papers No. 176, Paris.

Lindbeck, A. 1997, 'The Swedish Experiment', *Journal of Economic Literature*, **XXXV**, 1273–319.

Ljungqvist, L. and Th.J. Sargent (1998), 'The European Unemployment Dilemma', *Journal of Political Economy*, **106**, 514–50.

Moffitt, R.A. (1992), 'Incentive Effects of the US Welfare System: A Review', *Journal of Economic Literature,* **XXX** (1), 1–61.

OECD (1996), *Employment Outlook* June 1996, Paris.

OECD (1997a), *OECD submission to the UK Low Pay Commission*, Economics Department, OECD/GD(97)206, Working Papers No. 185. Paris.

OECD (1997b), *Making Work Pay*, Paris.

OECD (1998a), *Benefit Systems and Work Incentives*, Paris.

OECD (1998b), *Employment Outlook* June 1998, Paris.

Salomäki, A and T. Munzi (1999), *Net Replacement Rates of the Unemployed, Comparisons of Various Approaches*, Economic Papers No. 133, European Commission, DG Economic and Financial Affairs, Brussels, February.

Scholz, J.K. (1996), 'In-Work Benefits in the United States: The Earned Income Tax Credit', *The Economic Journal*, **106** (January), 156–69.

4. Employment Effects of Low-Wage Subsidies: The Case of 'SPAK' in the Netherlands

Peter Mühlau and Wiemer Salverda

4.1 INTRODUCTION

The high incidence of unemployment among the low skilled is considered an important argument that low-wage jobs are severely lacking in the economy. At the same time many observers worry about increased poverty in work when low-paid jobs would be in greater supply. Consequently, much attention is paid to policy measures for increasing the amount of low-paid employment without decreasing the income of low-paid workers. Recently, proposals and measures for subsidising low wages are the entire vogue.

Unsurprisingly, given the diverging aims, such policies come in different shades. The American Earned Income Tax Credit (EITC) and the British Family Credit, or its successor the Working Family Tax Credit (WFTC) (Giles and McCrae 1998), are aimed at raising the income of employees from a low-paid job to socially acceptable standards. By contrast, policy measures such as Malinvaud's (1998) proposal in France to lower employers' contributions to social security, are targeting the employers of the low-paid employees with the aim of lowering wage costs and thus furthering employment with little change to the income level of the persons involved. The former category is sometimes viewed as better suited to the Anglo-Saxon type economies with a wider dispersion of wages, while the second type of policy measures seems to offer an answer to continental-European problems of (un)employment with high rates of taxation.[1]

Employer wage subsidies have been advocated and practised before, for example to stimulate hiring the long-term unemployed, but generally they do not have a ring of great success. Often the take-up is very limited.[2] Also, it seems that more research has been done recently on the in-work type of subsidies, particularly the EITC, than on hiring subsidies. Taken together this substantiates the relevance of taking a fresh look here at an actual specimen of an employer subsidy, the Dutch SPAK measure, which has experienced an amazing take up. SPAK has created a furore in the Netherlands since its start in 1996 and is a success if judged by applications. Without much debate large amounts of subsidy are expended.

In the Netherlands, a wage subsidy was introduced on 1 January 1996, the so-called 'speciale afdrachtskorting' (special reduction of contributions) or 'SPAK'.[3] This essentially does what Malinvaud (1998) advocates for France: provide a permanent subsidy aimed at lowering employers' contributions to social security on low wages. He makes his case arguing that the lower end of the labour market is less equilibrated, having higher unemployment rates, in the presence of the minimum wage. The large annual inflows of unqualified youths from education to the labour market serve to maintain the disequilibrium. Although he thinks that a fully robust theoretical explanation of the effects is lacking, Malinvaud expects lower employer contributions to have a beneficial effect on low-skilled employment in the long run. In addition to the substitution effects benefiting the low skilled on the basis of changing relative wages, economic growth may increase and the management of the social security system may improve. Consequently, he anticipates some direct effects on the hiring of the low skilled and more diffuse but positive effects in the long run. In a similar vein, Nickell (1998) seems rather hesitant about the effects of a subsidy but advocates it in combination with a minimum wage as a means to primarily provide people with work, needed for social self-esteem.

The political and economic need of improving the outcomes of the low-skilled labour market is most eloquently argued also by Phelps (1994). He thinks that the welfare state is the main culprit but claims that, to prevent hardship for the disadvantaged, 'tax credits for use by employers against payroll taxes ... would be a new and extraordinarily effective means to reduce joblessness and poverty' (Phelps, 1997, 230). He has a very large scale subsidy in mind[4] and expects it to 'get results here and now', raising either wages or employment or both for the low skilled in a very few years (p. 233). Naturally, the idea behind all this is that the relative wage of the low skilled will fall inciting increased employer demand for this labour, shifting out the labour demand curve. Phelps may, however, be far too optimistic with his grandiose design while Malinvaud is much more cautious.[5] The latter carefully discusses the repercussions of financing the subsidy but assumes that the consequent job creation will recover a substantial part of this. In his review of US experience with wage subsidies, Katz (1996) draws attention to the uncertainty of labour demand and supply elasticities. The magnitude of the effects and the balance between wage increases and job growth depend on these. At best, he advocates a limited experiment with a non-categorical low-wage subsidy (Katz 1996, 32). As to elasticities, it is important to account for the outcome of the 'modern' minimum wage research (for example, Card and Krueger 1995; Salverda 2000, for an overview of recent Dutch research) which finds hardly any effect on jobs of the most recent US minimum wage hikes. On the basis of this, Freeman (2000, 15) explains the ineffectiveness of the shifting of payroll taxes on low pay from the employer to the state as practised in some European countries.

So far no Dutch research has investigated the stimulus of SPAK on job growth. Evaluation studies (Nes et al. 1998) have focused on the administrative workings of the subsidy, inquiring whether employers with eligible employees have indeed applied for SPAK or not. The widespread use of the subsidy is so impressive that positive employment effects seem to be taken for granted. To establish the effects of the subsidy, this chapter does not aim to develop a formal model determining elasticities, for example using the dynamic monopsony approach of much modern minimum wage research. Instead, it goes on a fact-finding mission at the micro level, regarding ex post the direct effects of the subsidy on the job creation behaviour of companies receiving the subsidy in comparison with other companies. In addition, we take a look at the macroeconomic evolution of the relevant employment. We leave out of account any macro- or microeconomic repercussions of the necessary financing of the subsidy. We also leave the matter of policy efficiency aside as it would necessitate a comparison with other types of measures. The data used cover the first two years of the new subsidy and therefore the study is focused on the short-run effects, the knock on of the establishment of SPAK in 1996 and its first continuation in 1997.

We start by briefly presenting, in Section 4.2, the properties of SPAK, its administrative design and its use. For an answer to the employment question we subsequently take two different roads, at different levels of analysis, one at the national level (macroeconomic) and the other at the level of the firm (microeconomic). The outcomes are mutually reinforcing and present a fuller picture of the effects. We first look at SPAK's employment effects at the macroeconomic level in Section 4.3, but the data at this level are insufficient to reach a solid conclusion on jobs. It underlines the need for a study of microdata to consider firm behaviour in response to the subsidy (Section 4.4). Thereto, we start with an introduction to the dataset containing matched information on firms and employees in the private sector and on the firms' use of SPAK in 1996 and 1997. The data enable a comparison of SPAK use between firms in cross-section, but, unfortunately, they do not allow a comparison of the same firm over time, that is pre- and post-SPAK. It implies that, although the inter-firm comparisons can and do throw an important light on the matter, the determination of behavioural effects in response to the introduction of SPAK remains incomplete also at the microeconomic level.

Taken together, however, the two approaches suggest rather negative conclusions on the employment effects of SPAK at the end of the chapter.

4.2   SPAK: DESIGN AND USE

We will summarily discuss the organisational set-up of SPAK and its use (see Table 4.A1 for some details). As a new policy measure taken by the Dutch government to fight unemployment, particularly among the low paid, SPAK was introduced as a subsidy given to employers for any employee on their payroll earning less than 115 per cent of the full-time statutory minimum wage.[6] In contrast to other wage subsidies which were tried before without much success, SPAK is enjoying great popularity. There seem to be three good reasons for this. First, the scheme is meant to be permanent and not temporary like many similar schemes – but, naturally, the subsidy applies only as long as the employee's pay remains below the threshold level. Second, its administrative design is simple. It is formally a subsidy on employer contributions to social security, but tax authorities deduct it from the payroll taxes, which employers are obliged to withhold from the salaries of their employees and pay to the tax authorities. Consequently, payment to the firm is almost immediate. Third, the only criterion for a worker's eligibility is the wage, and not unemployment duration or any other personal characteristic – with all the administrative burden that accompanies it – as for many other measures. Both the amounts given as a subsidy and the rules governing qualification for SPAK have changed substantially over the three years of its existence. In 1998, the subsidy ranged from 10 to 14 per cent of the relevant gross wage excluding employer contributions.

In all three years, an estimated one-third of all Dutch taxable enterprises and institutions applied for SPAK, receiving a subsidy that grew from almost 800 million guilders to 1.8 billion annually (see Table 4.1). The important low-paying industries are well represented, although their share of the subsidy seems to be lagging somewhat behind their share in low-paid employment, presumably because of the high incidence of part-time work and youth employment in these industries for which less subsidy is given (see Salverda 1998 for more details). Nevertheless, the lowering of their wage bill is substantially higher than for other industries.

Unfortunately, the other side of the measure's administrative ease is the complete lack of administrative data on the employees who are subsidised; the tax authorities know neither their number nor their characteristics. The variation of the subsidy, by age and length of the working week or by the part of the year worked, prevents any plausible approximation to determine their numbers. Fortunately, the annual survey on pay conducted by the

Ministry of Social Affairs and Employment contains information on SPAK use at the firm level. Subsidies appear to have been given for an estimated 16 per cent of all Dutch private-sector employees in both 1996 and 1998, and for some 20 per cent in 1997 (Venema 1998, 28; Venema and Faas 1999, 36). Our calculations indicate that in 1996 this head count number corresponded with some 10 per cent of the labour force measured in full-time equivalents. Even at the lower end of the wage distribution a substantial part of employees remains outside SPAK.[7]

Table 4.1
SPAK wage subsidies on low pay, 1996–98

	1996		1997		1998	
	fl. mln	% Wage sum	fl. mln	% Wage sum	fl. mln	% Wage sum
Total economy	788	0.21	1256	0.34	1795	0.47
Public sector	183	0.18	287	0.27	386	0.35
Private sector	578	0.24	928	0.37	1304	0.50
Retail, hotels and catering[a]	160	0.76	258	1.19	378	1.66
Other services[b]	147	0.33	270	0.54	400	0.73
Other industries	214	0.12	345	0.20	475	0.26

Notes:
[a] Retail trade, hotels and catering; [b] private services excluding banking, insurance and housing (unfortunately no separate data are available for temporary work agencies).

Source: Ministry of Finance.

4.3   MACROECONOMIC EFFECTS OF SPAK

We do a summary scan on the macroeconomic evidence relating to the employment effects of SPAK.[8] First, Table 4.2 pictures the evolution of employment and pay over the last ten years, again distinguishing the most important industries of low pay. Because so many low-paid employees are working part-time[9] one should emphasise hours worked, that is the employment volume, and not rely on a head count to determine the effects. Total employment growth after the introduction of SPAK did indeed increase, but only in 1998 (still provisional) did it exceed earlier growth rates (1990) when no wage subsidy was in place.[10] There is no sign that GDP growth in 1996 and 1997 had a higher employment intensity (hours) than during the previous period of growth (1987–92). Second, SPAK is meant to stimulate general employment growth via low-wage jobs. However, there is no evidence of any exceptional growth here. Minimum wage employment grew from 3.4 per cent of total employment in 1995 to 3.8 in 1996 but subsequently declined to 3.6 per cent in 1997.[11] Up to the SPAK-inspired level of 115 per cent of the minimum wage, the employment share grew from 11.6 per cent in 1995 to 12.3 in 1996 but then fell again to 11.9 per cent in 1997 and 1998.

Table 4.2
Dependent employment: hours worked, 1988–98
Annual change (%)

	1988	1989	1990	1991	1992	1993	1994	1995	1996	1997	1998
Hours worked and paid											
Total economy	1.70	2.11	2.71	1.48	0.92	–0.52	–0.84	1.53	2.26	2.23	3.14
Private sector	2.21	2.92	3.29	1.84	0.82	–1.04	–0.90	2.04	2.96	2.22	3.40
Retail, hotels and catering	3.41	5.00	4.23	4.01	2.56	1.22	1.38	2.41	0.72	1.92	3.29
Temp agencies	8.17	13.26	8.63	–3.86	–3.57	–9.74	13.64	27.11	22.60	10.82	9.04
Other services	4.58	4.05	6.35	6.31	3.30	2.22	4.10	6.25	4.89	1.55	6.12
Other industries	1.72	2.46	2.71	0.86	0.17	–1.92	–2.11	1.23	1.23	1.70	2.61

Note: Unfortunately, no separate data are available for cleaning and personal services.

Sources: CBS, *Arbeidsrekeningen* and *National Accounts* (break 1995 revision).

Another approximation focuses on the evolution of employment in low-paying industries. We saw that these industries are receiving much higher subsidies relative to average wages and therefore one would expect their employment growth to be more favourable. Table 4.2 also pictures job growth for the most important of these industries and for the rest of the economy. The situation is mixed. Retail, hotels and catering experienced increasing growth of employment and some decline in wage growth but this in no way matched earlier job growth (1988–91), which was attained with considerably higher levels of wage growth. Temporary work, which is generally low paid as well, attained very high absolute levels of job growth in comparison to other industries, varying between 9 and 23 per cent. However, these rates fell rapidly over the consecutive SPAK years and also in comparison to 1995 (27 per cent). Also, given that the demand for temporary labour is coming from a vast array of other industries (for which unfortunately no systematic breakdown exists), it is very hard to determine to what extent we have to do here with net job growth or that, instead, it simply reflects the increasing flexibilisation of employment.

More systematically, we studied the relation between employment growth and wage subsidy in a cross-section of 27 industries for which data are available over the three SPAK years (see Table 4.3). There appears to be a (weak) relationship between the relative importance of wage subsidies and employment growth (Model 1). However, this relationship completely vanishes (Model 2) once we take into account a number of factors, such as wage growth, sales growth, long-term productivity growth and the nature of the industry. We conclude that the influence of SPAK on job growth at the level of industries is spurious. The strong dependence of SPAK on factors

Table 4.3

HLM regressions of growth in employment volume[a] on SPAK[b] percentages, 1996–98

(N = 27 industries, n = 3 × 27 industries/year)

	Model 0		Model 1[b]		Model 2[a]	
	γ	(s.e.)	γ	(s.e.)	γ	(s.e.)
1996	0.45	(0.70)	−0.73	(0.93)	0.57	(0.88)
1997	0.88	(0.47)	0.25	(0.62)	1.31	(0.79)
1998	2.14	(0.50)	1.21	(0.65)	1.87	(0.83)
Wage growth[c]					−0.65	(0.11)
Value added[d]					0.14	(0.04)
SPAK × 1996			6.13	(3.36)	0.65	(2.51)
SPAK × 1997			2.06	(1.42)	0.34	(1.22)
SPAK × 1998			2.14	(1.05)	0.40	(0.88)
Productivity[e]					−0.29	(0.14)
Service industries[f]					1.92	(0.66)
τ_0^2	4.11	(1.40)	3.28	(1.18)	1.47	(0.58)
σ_{1996}^2	9.08	(2.71)	9.00	(2.67)	4.39	(1.33)
σ_{1997}^2	1.78	(0.91)	1.93	(0.90)	1.34	(0.55)
σ_{1998}^2	2.55	(1.78)	2.37	(0.98)	1.42	(0.57)
χ^2 value (d.f.) [p][g]			5.1 (3)	[.256]	54.9 (7)	[.000]
χ^2 value (d.f.) [p][h]					0.2 (3)	[.978]

Notes:
Model 0 is the empty model.
[a] hours worked in dependent employment (%); [b] SPAK = % of wage sum; [c] growth of hourly wages (%); [d] 2 years value added growth (%); [e] productivity per labour year, average annual change 1990–95 (%); [f] dummy for service industries; [g] vs. Model 0; [h] marginal χ^2-value for three SPAK dummies. Industries exclude mining (natural gas) because of large price fluctuations.

that appear to have an independent effect on employment growth (industry type, value added, long-term productivity change) may even suggest an inverse causality: the firm is growing and subsequently decides to involve itself with SPAK.

The main drawback of this focus on low-paying industries, or industries more generally, however, is that their work force also comprises higher-paid and better qualified employees on better jobs. Consequently, job growth may be drawing the wrong picture concerning the low-skill jobs for which the subsidy was established. Unfortunately, adequate information about this is lacking. As a rough approximation, for the total economy, Table 4.4 shows, first, the growth of lower-level job as distinguished by Dutch Statistics relative to total job growth. It also shows the evolution of the employment rate of the first quartile of employees ranked by educational qualifications.[12] Compared to earlier years, the subsidy had no positive effect on lower-level job growth and it certainly had no enduring effect, witness the evolution between 1996 and 1998. Although the less qualified do better the recent situation compares fairly well earlier years in spite of the large subsidies that are given now.

Table 4.4
Job growth by job level and educational level, 1988–98
Edge over average annual growth (%)

	1988	1989	1990	1991	1992	1993	1994	1995	1996	1997	1998
Lower-level jobs[a]	2.7	–1.7	–1.7	1.1	–2.7	–3.4	–0.7	–0.2	1.6	0.6	–1.0
Less qualified[b]				–0.2	2.1	–2.1	1.1	1.6	–0.4	1.1	2.4

Notes:
[a] Employment Volume: persons times average hours in three categories of length of the working week: 12–19, 20–34 and 35 or more hours per week. Tentatively corrected for observation problems 1992–95.
[b] Head count employment rate of first educational quartile compared to total employment rate, working at least 12 hours per week.

Source: CBS, *Labour Force Survey*.

So, over its first three years, the macroeconomic data appear not to provide convincing evidence that SPAK has boosted job growth at the lower end of the Dutch labour market in spite of the almost 4000 million guilders spent on the subsidy. Naturally, the use of SPAK can still be advocated arguing that without it things would have been worse. A microeconomic study of how company behaviour responded to the introduction of SPAK can throw more light on the matter.

4.4   FIRM BEHAVIOUR

Turning now to the response of individual firms to the establishment of the wage subsidy, we will first say a few words about the data, then elaborate on the approach to determining the employment effects of SPAK and finally present the results.

The Data

In the study, we make use of two consecutive datasets of the annual survey of employment conditions *Arbeidsvoorwaardenonderzoek* (AVO), kindly made available by the Labour Inspectorate of the Dutch Ministry of Social Affairs and Employment, covering October 1995 – October 1996 (in short: AVO96) and October 1996 – October 1997 (in short: AVO97) respectively (see Venema 1998, Venema and Spijkerman 1998 and Venema and Faas 1999). The AVO surveys provide nested data matching details on the firm and its employees which notably record the firm's use of SPAK. For SPAK, the surveys claim to be representative of the private sector of the Dutch economy but leave out the public sector. Consequently, a full evaluation of the effects of SPAK is not possible but it is adequate for studying firm behaviour in response to SPAK. Table 4.A2 presents a number of characteristics of the datasets.[13]

On the basis of the Labour Inspectorate's questionnaire, the data distinguish between:

- companies that have employees who qualify for SPAK and that also apply for the wage subsidy (APP);
- companies that have employees who qualify for SPAK but that do not apply for this subsidy, for various reasons (NAP);
- companies that have no employees eligible for SPAK and consequently do not apply for the wage subsidy (NTG).

As to the employees, the data discern:

- those who stayed with the firm over each one-year period,
- those who were there at the start but left before the end of the year, and
- those who were newly hired between the two dates.

Each of the sets has a panel character but, unfortunately, this is limited to one calendar year each. Therefore, we are unable to follow the same firm over the years and compare their hiring behaviour to the preceding year, particularly the year before the introduction of SPAK. However, the limited panel nature sufficiently informs us about annual employment growth at the firm level and consequently permits a cross-section comparison between firms which can be used to track the direct response of employment behaviour to SPAK.

How to Trace the Stimulation of Job Creation?

Ideally, what one would like to know is whether companies receiving SPAK have on balance increased their employment by hiring more low-paid workers than they would otherwise have done in the absence of SPAK. It would need an experiment in which companies are randomly assigned the opportunity to apply for SPAK, to answer this question. Unfortunately, SPAK was not instituted on such an experimental basis. We have to make do with a situation in which companies have reacted differently to SPAK and compare their behaviour on the basis of the data available on (low-wage) job growth and a limited number of other firm characteristics. We have formulated a set of hypotheses concerning the behaviour of the three categories of firms mentioned above – APP, NAP and NTG – which would need to be confirmed to establish a positive stimulus from SPAK on the number of jobs.

Jobs of employees who have been newly hired since SPAK became available, are more likely (25 per cent in 1996 and 23 in 1997) to be subsidised than those of employees who were already employed at the start (12 per cent in 1996 and 14 in 1997). Although this fact is consistent with the proposition that low-wage subsidies induce companies to demand additional labour, it is not, on its own, supportive evidence for the 'job-creation hypothesis'. There are three good reasons for this contention. First, it is more likely that recent hires have a wage below the threshold that qualifies for SPAK as, on average, they will be younger, have less work experience, lack employer-specific experience, or they have more likely lost a previous job or experienced difficulties finding one, both signalling 'poor quality' to the employer. Second, companies providing poorly paid jobs are likely on average to have a higher labour turnover and thus a greater need for new hires replacing employees who left the company. Third, a possible positive employment effect of the wage subsidy (which we subsume under the notion of 'job creation') can be to motivate companies not to destruct jobs (in particular jobs at the lower end of the skill hierarchy). This effect cannot be evaluated by the number of recent hires but by the number of forced dismissals and non-replaced 'natural' turnover. Conclusive evidence for the 'job creation' thesis is therefore confined to the net creation of jobs.

However, still it is not clear whether jobs being created in companies that take advantage of the wage subsidy would not also have been on offer without it. Given that people newly hired in relation to job growth are likely to earn less than employees with some accumulated seniority, it seems plausible that companies that create new jobs anyway will be employing more workers eligible for the wage subsidy, which offers them the opportunity to apply for SPAK. Hence, a comparison of companies with similar employment structures is the appropriate level to evaluate the effect of the wage subsidy on employment growth. Stronger support for the 'job-creation' hypothesis is thus expected from the differences between firms that have employees who qualify for the wage-subsidy yet do not apply for it (NAP) on the one hand, and companies that take advantage of SPAK (APP) on the other.

Moreover, there should be a relationship between the number of subsidised employees and the number of newly created jobs. The employment growth of a strongly growing company that employs only a few subsidised employees can hardly be attributed to the wage subsidy. Also, a company that has created hardly more jobs than the average company, yet employs a large number of subsidised workers, is not a good example of the intended employment effects of SPAK. The growth of employment should be stronger the more employees of a company are subsidised. If the relationship between the number of targets and the newly created jobs is weaker for applying companies we must conclude that SPAK subsidises mainly the jobs of incumbents but does not contribute much to the growth of employment.

Summarising, the following two hypotheses should be confirmed:

- H1   Companies that apply for the wage subsidy (APP) have a stronger growth of employment than companies that have employees who qualify for the wage subsidy yet do not apply for it (NAP).
- H2   The relationship between the growth of employment and the number of eligible employees is stronger for APP companies than for NAP companies.

However, given the fact that all companies have the opportunity to apply once they employ eligible workers it is not realistic to assume that there are no systematic differences between APP and NAP companies. First, companies will less likely ignore the wage subsidy or – being aware of its existence – not take advantage of it if they employ eligible workers already at the beginning of the period. Second, and more important, companies that employ only one or a few eligible employees will more likely make the initial 'investments' and get familiar with the procedures if they expect to recruit more employees in this category in the future, and they are less likely to do so if they intend to skip these jobs. Because one may expect that companies 'sort' themselves into APP and NAP companies according to these prospects of growth (which may be 'exogenous' and independent of SPAK), the estimates of the growth effects on APP companies relative to NAP firms will plausibly be overestimated due to selection bias for which, unfortunately, we cannot correct.

Yet, complementary evidence on the job creation hypothesis which will less likely suffer from this bias, can be derived from a comparison of the job creation of companies with no targets and companies qualifying for the wage subsidy across the two one-year periods covered by the surveys. The periods differ in two important aspects. First, the wage subsidy was substantially increased. The amount given per subsidised employee increased by more than 50 per cent. Consequently, their wage costs have fallen and mainstream price theory suggests that the demand for these employees should increase. Also the relative costs of the initial investment of getting acquainted with SPAK will have fallen. Second, the wage subsidy was a new phenomenon in the first period, being introduced during the third month of the period covered by AVO96. It may take some time before employers manage to devise strategies for utilising 'cheap' labour in a profitable way. Possible employment effects of the wage subsidy may therefore be time-lagged and less visible during the first months after the wage subsidy was introduced. For these reasons, we expect the effect on employment to be stronger in the second period than during the first. The same reasons suggest that also the relationship between the number of subsidised jobs and the number of jobs created net should be stronger in the second than in the first. Under 'bounded rationality', companies may predominantly apply for SPAK if they employ eligible workers already in the first period while the employment-creating effects materialise predominately in the second period.

This gives rise to two further hypotheses focused on a comparison across the two one-year periods:

- H3   Companies employing workers qualifying for the wage subsidy create (APP, NAP) relatively more jobs than companies without targets for the wage subsidy (NTG) during the second period, October 1996 to October 1997, than during the first, October 1995 to October 1996.
- H4   Mutatis mutandis, the relationship between number of number of employees who qualify for the wage subsidy and the company's growth of employment is stronger in 1997 than in 1996.

Note that these hypotheses pertain to a comparison between companies qualifying for SPAK and companies that do not qualify, rather than between companies applying or not. The reason for this is that the self-selection process between APP and NAP companies may be more 'advanced' in the second period (see Appendix and Table 4.A3). The share of the companies that are eligible for the wage subsidy and actually apply has significantly increased between October 1996 and October 1997, from 72 per cent of the companies employing at least one eligible worker to 81 per cent (see Table 4.A4). The reason for this increased share is that the relationship between the number of potential targets and the likelihood to apply for the wage subsidy is considerably stronger in the second than in the first period. In 1997, the

NAP companies were more strongly concentrated among the companies with only one or two potential candidates. Over time, the non-users tend to coincide more with NTG firms that have no employees who qualify for the wage subsidy.

Estimation

In principle, we are interested in the net employment growth of a company between October 1995 and October 1996 or between October 1996 and October 1997, measured as the absolute increase in the number of employees.[14] However, the primary aim of the subsidy is to improve employment opportunities for less-qualified jobs, and it is as a consequence of this that total employment growth should be stimulated. It is unlikely that low-wage subsidies significantly affect the dynamics of the labour market for highly qualified workers. Even if we figure that SPAK applied to earnings up to 144 per cent of the minimum wage we are still in the lower half of the wage distribution.[15] If the growth of jobs for the highly qualified on the one hand and for the poorly qualified on the other are not strongly correlated or even negatively correlated at the firm level, the total net growth of employment may be a poor proxy for the direct job creation effect of wage subsidies. Therefore as the most adequate response variable, we will use the growth in employment of low complexity.[16] This is defined as jobs up to 'complexity level 3a' of the LTD job-complexity scale, designed by the Labour Inspectorate of the Ministry of Social Affairs and Employment. This cut-out of the skill distribution comprises very simple, simple and less simple jobs with (predominately) repetitive activities. In both 1996 and 1997, 87 per cent of the employees on the subsidy held such jobs. Conversely, 52 (1996) and 48 (1997) per cent respectively of all such jobs in APP companies were subsidised.[17]

The regression on the net creation of jobs has been specified within a hierarchical linear model (or multilevel model, see, for example, Goldstein 1995). Two levels are specified, 3667 companies as lower-level units nested in 41 two-digit industries as higher-level units. The most important problem of regressing on the net creation of jobs (but also on employment growth rates) is that the variance of the response variables is strongly dependent on the size of the company which may result in biased regression estimates. We avoid this problem by specifying a complex level-1 variance structure. Independent variance components are estimated for the two periods (1996 and 1997) each specified as a linear function of the plant size classes. Another problem is that the employment opportunities created by a company may not be independent of general production growth in the sector or industry. This is taken into account by estimating industry-specific intercepts capturing the 'average' growth in a particular industry ('random intercepts'). It appears that the intercepts of period 1996 and 1997 co-varied very strongly at the industry level. As a consequence, we apply one intercept randomly varying across industries regardless of which period the particular company belongs to. Strong industry-related differences occur, however, for very large (more than 500 employees) and very small (less than 5 employees) companies. For plant-size dummies of these classes, we estimate further random slopes and intercept-slope co-variances. Given the fact that the data are based on a sample stratified according to plant size and industry we further control the regression by seven plant-size dummies.[19]

Results

Before starting to present the answers to these hypotheses it seems worthwhile to stress that causality may as well be running from employment growth to SPAK instead of the other way around. In the Appendix (Table 4.A3) it is shown that recent hires, which we take to indicate employment growth, between companies with eligible employees – to the advantage of applying for SPAK.

Table 4.A6 reports the full results of regressions of the numbers of all newly created jobs and of those of low complexity ('Level') and, for both, how job growth also relates to the number of subsidised employees ('Related'). APP firms are the reference category while NTG and NAP companies are represented by dummies. In addition, Table 4.A7 reports, along the same lines, the results of regressions with period-specific estimates for the relevant predictor variables in order to assess whether the hypotheses hold for both periods, 1996 and 1997 respectively. The most important outcomes are summarised in Table 4.5.

Controlled for company size class, it appears that APP companies did not create more new jobs than NAP companies. The estimates indicate that APP companies created 0.18 less new jobs (Model 1.1) and 0.12 less new jobs of low complexity (Model 2.1). None of these estimates is significant. The period-specific estimates differ considerably for the difference between APP and NAP companies. While APP companies created in general 0.28 less jobs in total than NAP companies in 1996, they created nearly as much (–0.07) jobs in 1997 (Model 1.1a). APP companies created a (weakly significant) 0.30 less jobs of low complexity than NAP companies in 1996, but 0.17 more in 1997 (Model 2.1a). Taken together, the data are inconsistent with the hypothesis H1 that APP companies would create more jobs than NAP companies.

Although there is a strong relationship between the number of potential candidates for the wage subsidy and the number of newly created jobs for

Table 4.5
Summary of fixed effects of HLM-regressions of newly created jobs

Model	All jobs		Low-complexity jobs	
	Level	Related	Level	Related
	1.1 (s.e.)	1.2 (s.e.)	2.1 (s.e.)	2.2 (s.e.)
Pooled Estimates				
NTG	−0.29 * (0.11)	0.23* (0.11)	−0.36* (0.07)	0.01 (0.07)
NAP	0.18 (0.18)	1.74* (0.61)	0.12 (0.11)	1.84* (0.40)
Targets (number)		0.15* (0.01)		0.10* (0.00)
Targets squared × 1000		−0.50* (0.05)		−0.35* (0.04)
Targets × NAP		0.10* (0.04)		0.12* (0.03)
Targets squared × NAP × 1000		−7.20 (3.47)		−8.17* (2.21)

Model	1.1a (s.e.)	1.2a (s.e.)	2.1a (s.e.)	2.2a (s.e.)
Period-Specific Estimates				
NTG	−0.22 (0.17)	−0.21 (0.17)	−0.22 * (0.10)	−0.01 (0.11)
NTG × 1997	−0.11 (0.22)	0.02 (0.23)	−0.15 (0.15)	0.11 (0.15)
NAP	0.28 (0.25)	2.37* (0.73)	0.30* (0.14)	2.20* (0.46)
NAP × 1997	−0.19 (0.36)	−1.78 (1.32)	−0.47* (0.24)	−0.70 (0.94)
Targets (number)		0.13* (0.02)		0.06* (0.01)
Targets × 1997		0.02 (0.02)		0.06* (0.01)
Targets squared × 1000		−0.51 (0.05)		−0.25* (0.03)
Targets squared × 1000 × 1997				−0.17* (0.08)
Targets × NAP		0.15* (0.05)		0.15* (0.03)
Targets × NAP × 1997		−0.14 (0.11)		−0.03 (0.08)
Targets squared × NAP × 1000		−8.67 * (3.70)		−7.90* (2.28)

Notes: Reference group: APP companies; * significant at 5% level, two-tailed.

Source: Tables 4.A6 and 4.A7.

APP companies, this relationship is even stronger for NAP companies. The estimates for the first-order term of the number of potential candidates interacted with the NAP dummy is not negative – as required by H2 – but significantly positive in both specifications.[20] This is mainly due to a much stronger relationship between number of targets and jobs for NAP companies in the first period. But even for the second period the point estimates indicate that the number of targets is for NAP firms more closely related to the number of newly created jobs than for APP firms. Apparently, the data are also inconsistent with hypothesis H2.

Table 4.6 selectively reports the results of regressions which contrast companies that employ no targets for the wage subsidy (NTG) with companies employing employees who qualify for SPAK (APP and NAP) (we present the estimates of interest; the other estimates changed only marginally). The point estimates show that companies with eligible employees created slightly more jobs in comparison with NTG companies. In general, they created 0.38 more jobs than NTG companies in 1997 compared to 0.32 more in 1996. Regarding jobs of low complexity, the figures are 0.37 for 1997 and 0.33 for 1996. The differences between the two periods are, however, so small that the t-ratios for the differences are tiny. Although the point estimates are consistent with H3, the data provide no support for this hypothesis given the low confidence that there really are differences between the two periods. Neither do the data support H4. To the contrary, the relationship between number of targets and the growth of all jobs is slightly less strong for the second period. While for jobs of low complexity the estimate is in the right direction its value is immaterial.

Table 4.6
HLM regressions of newly created jobs, period-specific estimates, selectively

Model	All jobs				Low-complexity jobs			
	1.1		1.2		2.1		2.2	
	γ	(s.e.)	γ	(s.e.)	γ	(s.e.)	γ	(s.e.)
Fixed Effects								
NTG	−0.32	(0.16)	0.24	(0.17)	−0.33*	(0.09)	0.03	(0.10)
NTG × 1997	−0.06	(0.12)	−0.09	(0.22)	−0.04	(0.14)	−0.01	(0.14)
Targets (number)			0.17*	(0.02)			0.10*	(0.01)
Targets × 1997			−0.02	(0.02)			0.01	(0.01)
Targets squared × 1000			−0.41*	(0.07)			−0.23*	(0.05)

Source: Labour Inspectorate, *Employment Conditions Survey 1997, 1998.* Authors' calculations.

4.5   SUMMARY AND CONCLUSION

In order to assess whether the SPAK subsidy has had the effect of inducing companies to create more jobs of the eligible kind, we examined first whether – at the macro-level – there are indications that low-wage jobs have been created at a higher rate since the introduction of SPAK and whether there is an industry-level relationship between the wage subsidy and employment growth. In both respects, we found scant evidence for a job creating effect of the subsidy. Workers in the retail trade, hotels and catering – classical low-wage industries – did not experience stronger employment growth since low-wage jobs have been subsidised in recent years. By contrast, the jobs of temporary help services grew overproportionally during the period between 1995 and 1998 but this happened at a quickly diminishing rate over the years of SPAK. Neither are their indications at the level of industries that the wage subsidy has stimulated the growth of employment. The weak association between the wage subsidy and job growth at the industry level appeared to be a spurious relationship once we controlled for other important factors influencing employment growth.

The main part of the study was situated at the microeconomic level and devoted to differences between companies within industries. We formulated a set of four hypotheses which should find support in firm-level data to substantiate the claim that SPAK has a job-creating effect. The hypotheses concern company responses to the wage subsidy comparing three categories of companies: without eligible employees (NTG), with eligible employees but without the subsidy (NAP) and with such employees as well as the subsidy (APP).

Contrary to the job creation thesis, we first found that NAP companies created more jobs generally and also more jobs of low complexity than APP companies. This was mainly due to the stronger growth of NAP companies during the first year when they created more jobs of all types and even significantly more jobs of low complexity. The result is particularly disturbing for the job creation hypothesis because we also found evidence that companies that expanded their workforce during the preceding year were more likely to apply for SPAK. This can be seen as an indication that companies on a growth path independently from the wage subsidy are more likely to apply for the subsidy than companies that do not expect to grow much in the future (an interpretation which is supported by the industry-level analyses). An implication would be that the growth advantage of NAP companies relative to APP is even under estimated in the first period. The combination of these findings seems to suggest that the increase in applications for SPAK in the second year was mainly due to the fact that the companies that created most jobs in 1995/1996 but at the time ignored the possibility of receiving the subsidy subsequently did take advantage of the wage subsidy in the second year. In turn, this may explain that APP companies created more jobs of low complexity in 1996/1997 than the (remaining) NAP companies.

In addition, we found that the relationship between the number of eligible employees and the number of newly created jobs was much stronger for NAP companies than for APP companies, in fact more than twice as strong for the lower-complexity jobs. This relationship holds for newly created jobs in general, and for jobs of low complexity for both years. This suggests that the NAP companies have a relatively higher share of newly created jobs among eligible jobs than APP companies although the prospects of creating jobs being eligible in the future may motivate companies to apply for the wage subsidy. Again, this is a finding which is strongly at odds with the job creation thesis.

Because of the fact that the amount of the subsidy was strongly increased during the second period and that companies may need time to adapt to the changing circumstances, it was regarded as a further important indication for a job creation effect of SPAK that companies with eligible employees would grow more strongly between October 1996 and October 1997 than in the preceding year, relative to the growth of companies without eligible candidates, and that the relation between the number of subsidised jobs and the number of newly created job would be stronger in the second period than in the first. The data failed to confirm both hypotheses. We found no substantial differences with respect to the relative growth advantage of companies with eligible workers between the two periods. Also, the relation between the number of eligible employees and the total number of new jobs – or the number of new jobs of low complexity – was not substantially stronger in the second period.

Given that none of the four hypotheses found support by the data, we must conclude that the data fail to support the hypothesis that the SPAK wage subsidy induced employers to create more jobs. This conclusion is consistent with the fact that strong employment growth in the preceding period appears to induce firms to apply for the wage subsidy if they have eligible candidates. It is therefore very unlikely that the growth effects of wage subsidy are underestimated due to a self-selection of poorly performing firms (in terms of employment growth) as applicants for the wage subsidy.

Both the macroeconomic enquiry and the firm-level study converge in the finding that the wage subsidy is doing little to promote employment for workers with poor labour market chances. If, as our analyses might indicate, companies do not react strongly on relative prices for disadvantaged workers by their labour demand, wage subsidies may not necessarily be an effective – let alone efficient – way to improve the lot of people who have poor labour market chances.

In the debate, usually, attention is exclusively paid to the employment effects of such measures and, following from that, their efficiency in reaching these results relative to other measures. Other effects, particularly those on employee incomes, are mostly taken for granted. Supposedly, they go to the workers who manage to find employment because of the financial assistance. If, however, the subsidy is spent without much effect on employment, the question as to what the effects on wages are becomes much more important. The smaller the effect on employment creation the more the subsidy effectively is a rent paid by government. This rent can go to either the employer or the employee or be divided between them. On the employee side it does not necessarily go to those for whom the subsidy is given but could potentially also go to other employees in the same firm. The income effects are not necessarily positive – increasing workers' earnings – instead, they may even affect wages negatively – to make or keep them eligible for the subsidy – and primarily benefit employers.[21] Elsewhere, we have considered such effects finding rather negative outcomes for employee earnings, using the same methodology applied here (Mühlau and Salverda, 2000).

The policy implications of these findings clearly are that one should not be too optimistic about the employment and earnings effects that a subsidy on low wages can have. A careful analysis of possible effects should precede the spending of large amounts of subsidy.

NOTES

1. For example Roorda and Vogels (1998). Dickert-Conlin and Holtz-Eakin (1998) for a comparison giving the subsidies to either employers or employees.
2. Mot et al. (1992) evaluated an earlier subsidy, on labour costs at the minimum wage level.
3. Formally 'afdrachtvermindering *lage lonen*'. It is by far the most important part of a broader package of measures (Wet Vermindering Afdrachten) which includes a separate subsidy for hiring long-term unemployed.
4. With 1990 figures, totalling about 100 billion dollars for full-time employees alone. This would amount to 8 per cent of the wage bill in Phelps' own example or 3 per cent of the US wage bill according to OECD *National Accounts*.
5. Malinvaud (1998, 62) hopes that a 10 per cent lowering of the labour costs of the least-paid quintile will entail a 10 per cent increase of low-paid employment in ten years time.
6. Since 1997 SPAK has been topped with a 'flow-SPAK' to cope with the wage increase received by employees under SPAK. To prevent an abrupt stop of the subsidy when an employee crosses the 115 per cent limit, the employer receives half of the full SPAK amount during a period of two years for adult employees who stay with the same enterprise and have a wage that is still below 130 per cent of the minimum wage. Flow-SPAK is included in the general SPAK data for 1997 and 1998 used here.
7. A wage that is low in absolute terms does not necessarily mean that an employee qualifies for SPAK. Youths may earn little in nominal terms, but their earnings can easily exceed the threshhold wage which is defined on the basis of the applicable youth minimum wage. At a 36-hours working week, the adult minimum wage was about 14 guilders per hour in 1996 while that of, for example, a 20-year old was 8.65 guilders.
8. We focus on dependent employment leaving out any repercussions on the self-employed, who do not receive SPAK and may suffer in competition, for example, with super markets.
9. For example 74 per cent of all minimum wage jobs in 1997 were part-time (Ackermann 1998, II)
10. The 1995 revision of National and Labour Accounts makes a substantial difference. Unfortunately no revised figures are available before 1995.
11. CBS, *Sociaal-economische Maandstatistiek,* 1999/2 (authors' estimation of full-time equivalents). Also, up to 110 per cent of the minimum wage there was hardly any growth.
12. Glyn and Salverda (2000) argue that the quartile is a better measure than the categorisation by diplomas, as it corrects for sorting problems.
13. The datasets tell us about the incidence of SPAK at firm and employee level in terms of cases over the one-year period. Unfortunately, they do not contain information on the duration of this use. The firm may have applied in the course of the year, or eligible workers may have been hired later, or their wage may have increased causing the subsidy to stop.
14. An alternative measure for the growth in employment is the rate of growth $[100*(\text{jobs (t1)} - \text{jobs(t0))}/\text{jobs(t0)}]$. The disadvantage of using this is that for newly established firms it is not defined (jobs(t0) = 0). Unsurprisingly, newly founded companies are more likely to ignore

the wage subsidy even if they have employees who are eligible. Both variables have the disadvantage that their variance is dependent on the size of the company (in t0), positively in the case of net employment growth and negatively in the case of growth rate.

15. In 1997, an estimated one-third of employees earned less.
16. Estimates for jobs of very low complexity (first two LTD levels), tend to be similar.
17. The number of newly created jobs in category k has been estimated on the basis of the individual-level data on the complexity level of the job and the firm-level data on employment $[(\Sigma k_{ij})/n_j(t)*\text{jobs}(t)]$.
18. As reference class, plants between 20 and 49 employees at the start of the period are used. For these companies the general variance components apply (1996: σ^2 (1996); 1997: σ^2 (1997)). For the other seven plants classes the level-1 variance is $\sigma^2(\text{year}) + 2 \times \sigma$ (year/plant size class).
19. ps4 = 1–4 employees; ps9 = 5–9; ps19 = 10–19, ps99 = 50–99; ps199 = 100–199; ps499 = 200–499 employees; finally, ps500 = 500 or more employees.
20. Although the estimate for the second-order term is also significantly smaller for these companies, the point estimates show that the relationship between the number of targets and the newly created jobs is stronger for NAP companies up to about 12 (all jobs) or 15 (low-complexity jobs) employees being eligible for the wage subsidy. The latter comprise almost 100 per cent of all NAP and APP companies.
21. An example is the Dutch Minimum Wage Subsidy given between 1976 and 1979. Minimum wage employment grew considerably but soon after the abolition of the subsidy it fell back to the previous level (Projektgroep 1979).

REFERENCES

Ackermann, C.H. (1998), *Toepassing Wet minimumloon en minimumvakantiebijslag in 1997*, SZW/VUGA Uitgeverij, The Hague.

Card, D. and A. Krueger (1995), *Myth and Measurement. The New Economics of the Minimum Wage*, Princeton UP.

Dickert-Conlin, S. and D. Holtz-Eakin (1998), *Employee-Based versus Employer-Based Subsidies to Low-Wage Workers: A Public Finance Perspective*, Paper Joint Center for Poverty Research Conference on 'The Labor Market and Less-Skilled Workers', Washington DC, 5–6 November.

Freeman, R.B. (2000), 'Overview of the Minimum Wage Debate', in Low Pay Commission 2000 (forthcoming).

Giles, G. and J. McCrae (1998), 'Reforms to In-Work Transfer Payments in the UK', in Lucifora and Salverda (eds), 148–56.

Glyn, A. and W. Salverda (2000), 'Employment Inequalities', in M. Gregory et al. (eds), *Labour Market Inequalities: Problems and Policies in International Perspective*, Oxford University Press (forthcoming).

Goldstein, H. (1995), *Multilevel statistical models*, Arnold, London.

Katz, L.F. (1996), *Wage Subsidies for the Disadvantaged*, Working Paper 5679, NBER, Cambridge MA.

Low Pay Commission (2000), *International Symposium on Minimum Wages*, Occasional Paper 4, London.

Lucifora, C. and W. Salverda (eds) (1998), *Policies for Low-Wage Employment and Social Exclusion*, FrancoAngeli, Milan.

Malinvaud. E. (1998), *Les cotisations sociales à la charge des employeurs: analyse économique. Rapport au Premier Ministre, Conseil d'Analyse Economique*, Paris.

Mot, E., A. Paape, F. van Puffelen and B. Schumacher (1992), *Werking van de Wet Lookostenreductie op Minimumloonniveau, een evaluatie-onderzoek*, Ministry of

Social Affairs and Employment SZW, The Hague.

Mühlau, P. and W. Salverda (2000), *Employment and Wage Effects of Low-Wage Subsidies: The Case of 'SPAK' in the Netherlands*, Research Report Graduate School SOM, University of Groningen (submitted).

Nes, P.J. van, E.A.M. Stotijn and J.J.M. van Velden (1998), *Evaluatie van het gebruik van de afdrachtskorting lage lonen, Eindrapport*, SZW/VUGA, The Hague.

Nickell, S. (1998), 'The Collapse in Demand for the Unskilled: What Can Be Done?', in R.B. Freeman and P. Gottschalk (eds), *Generating Jobs. How to Increase Demand for Less-Skilled Workers*, Russel Sage, New York.

Phelps, E.S. (1994), 'Low-wage Employment Subsidies versus the Welfare State', *American Economic Review*, **84** (2), 54–8.

Phelps, E.S. (1997), 'Wage Subsidy Programmes: Alternative Designs', in D. Snower and G. de la Dehesa, *Unemployment Policies*, CEPR/Cambridge University Press, 206–49.

Projektgroep Ekonomie Groningen (1979), *Jeugdwerkloosheid & subsidies; verslag van een falend beleid*, Faculty of Economics, University of Groningen.

Roorda, W. and E. Vogels (1998), 'Werknemerstoeslagen versus loonkostensubsidies', *Economisch-Statistische Berichten*, 13 February, 126–9.

Salverda, W. (1998), 'Vergroting van de onderkant van de arbeidsmarkt? Een overzicht en eerste beoordeling van beleidsmaatregelen', *Tijdschrift voor Politieke Ekonomie*, **21** (1), 24–57.

Salverda, W. (2000), 'The Design and Effects of Minimum Wages in the Netherlands: Issues for the UK debate', in Low Pay Commission (2000) (forthcoming).

Venema, P.M. (1998), *Arbeidsvoorwaardenontwikkeling in 1996*, Arbeidsinspectie SZW/VUGA, The Hague.

Venema, P.M. and A. Faas (1999), *Arbeidsvoorwaardenontwikkeling in 1998*, Arbeidsinspectie SZW/Elsevier, The Hague.

Venema, P.M. and R. Spijkerman (1998), *Arbeidsvoorwaardenontwikkeling in 1997*, Arbeidsinspectie SZW/VUGA, The Hague.

APPENDIX

Table 4.A1
Some details of SPAK

	1996	1997	1998
full adult (23+) amount (NLG/year)	1185	1830	3660
youth amounts	% according to youth minimum wage system; unchanged in 1997–98		
qualifying working week	32 hours	32 hours	36 hours
upper earnings threshold at 38 hour week as percentage of minimum wage:			
SPAK	137%	137%	121%
flow SPAK	n.a.	n.a.	137%

Table 4.A2
Dataset characteristics
October 1995–October 1996 and October 1996–October 1997

	Firms		Employees		
	Records	Extrapo-lated	Records	Extrapo-lated	Extrapo-lated (FTE)
Number 96	1834	336103	42481	5093417	4574321
Number 97	1843	372509	43471	5147618	4693114
Job Growth					
Oct95–Oct96, number	2.71	0.63	207714	159140	
(%)	(9.8)	(11.7)	(4.4)	(3.6)	
Oct96–Oct97, number	2.14	0.59	219705	138960	
(%)	(9.0)	(9.9)	(4.5)	(3.1)	
Avg. no. of employees 96	117	15			
(97)	(98)	(14)			
Shares 96 (97), %					
APP firms	39 (44)	35 (38)	45 (50)	51 (55)	48 (50)
NAP firms	13 (9)	14 (9)	12 (8)	10 (8)	10 (9)
NTG firms	48 (47)	51 (53)	43 (43)	39 (37)	42 (41)
Exiting employees	10 (10)	11 (12)	13 (13)	11 (12)	10 (12)
Staying employees	75 (78)	73 (71)	71 (70)	74 (72)	76 (73)
New entrants	15 (12)	16 (16)	16 (17)	15 (16)	13 (15)
Female			30 (31)	41 (41)	33 (32)
Part-time (<35hr/wk)			13 (24)	27 (33)	10 (19)
Low job-complexity level			41 (40)	43 (42)	36 (36)
Retail trade	7 (8)	17 (14)	6 (5)	11 (10)	9 (9)
Hotels & catering	4 (5)	10 (11)	2 (2)	4 (4)	3 (3)
Laundries etc.	1 (2)	3 (2)	1 (1)	1 (1)	1 (1)
New Entrants and Staying Employees					
Avg. Age 96 (97), years			36.2 (36.4)	36.1 (36.3)	36.3 (36.4)
Avg. Monthly Wage 96 (97), NLG			3711 (3896)	3416 (3742)	3891 (4016)

Source: Labour Inspectorate, *Employment Conditions Survey 1997, 1998*. Authors' calculations.

Company Self-Selection

We consider how the three categories of companies differ in other respects than SPAK behaviour. The most important question appears to be whether there are indications that companies with high growth prospects independently of the wage subsidy are more likely to apply for the wage subsidy, naturally when they have eligible candidates for SPAK. As the closest indicator for the growth prospects (independently from the realised growth that is used as the dependent variable below) available we chose the share of employees with less than one year of tenure (TEN < 1) at the beginning of the period. This is not a perfect measure, first, because companies that expanded their work force in the preceding period are not necessarily companies expanding their work force in the present period (although the number of employees hired in the previous period appears to be strongly significantly and very robustly related to net employment growth), and, second, because the share of hires recruited in the previous period is – lacking information about the quits and dismissals in that period – not a direct proof of expansion of employment in the period.

Table 4.A3
Logistic HLM-regressions of being a no-target or a not-applying firm

Dependent	NTG vs. APP/NAP		NAP vs. APP	
Constant	0.127	(0.123)	–0.283	(0.178)
1997	0.044	(0.119)	–0.553*	(0.115)
CAO	0.129	(0.086)	–0.182	(0.132)
LNSZ	–0.213*	(0.027)	0.188*	(0.032)
LCOM	–1.252*	(0.107)	–0.192	(0.174)
TEN < 1	–0.148	(0.136)	–0.648*	(0.248)
τ_0^2	0.202		0.083	
δ_0^2	1.000		1.000	
N , n	41 , 3667		41 , 1920	

Table 4.A3 informs about the results of a two-level regression, first, on the logged odds of being a company that does not qualify for the wage subsidy, having no eligible employees (NTG). As predictors we used, beside TEN < 1, whether the company is covered by a collective agreement (CAO), the logged number of employees (LNSZ) at the beginning of the period, and the proportion of employees holding jobs of low complexity (LCOM) at the start. Large companies are more likely to employ workers qualifying for SPAK. Unsurprisingly, there is also a strongly significant negative relationship between the share of low-complexity jobs in a company's employment and being a NTG company. The results indicate that the strongly negative relationship to the share of employees on low-complexity jobs holds for both periods and they show hardly any effect of the share of employees hired in the previous period for 1996 and a small effect for 1997. Consequently, companies that employ no potential SPAK employees are mainly smaller and have less simple jobs than other companies.

The exercise was repeated for companies that do not apply for the wage subsidy although they employ 'targets' (NAP) contrasted with companies that do receive the subsidy (APP). The share of low-complexity jobs is negatively related to the logits of being a NAP company but the relation is very weak compared to the NTG companies. By contrast, the share of employees hired in the previous period discriminates much more strongly and significantly between APP and NAP companies. Apparently, companies that grew strongly in the preceding period are more likely to apply for SPAK in the following period given that they have eligible employees. This is consistent with the possibility that companies with good exogenously determined growth prospects are more likely to select themselves as applying for SPAK. Finally, the share of NAP companies lacking knowledge of the wage subsidy was not much smaller in the second period (see Table 4.A5). Such companies are less likely to be systematically different from APP companies for reasons to do with SPAK itself.

Table 4.A4
Firm-incidence of SPAK applications by number of potential and actual SPAK employees, 1996

Classes by no of targets	Percentage of companies not applying NAP/(APP+NAP)		Average number of targets (employees)		Average number of applications (employees)	
	1996	1997	1996	1997	1996	1996
1	40	28	1.0	1.0	0.6	0.7
2	31	15	2.0	2.0	1.3	1.7
3–5	18	11	3.5	3.6	2.7	3.2
6–10	24	15	7.4	7.5	5.4	6.4
11–20	14	7	14.1	15.1	11.6	13.4
21–50	5	5	29.4	31.1	26.8	29.4
50+	4	0	270.3	290.8	263.3	262.2
Total	28	19	1036158	1192729	897021	1053332
			100%	100%	87%	88%

Source: Labour Inspectorate, *Employment Conditions Survey 1997, 1998*. Authors' calculations.

Table 4.A5
Reasons for companies with targets not to apply for SPAK

Reason	Percentage of companies		Average number of targets	
	1996	1997	1996	1997
Administrative costs	11.4	20.3	2.25	1.29
Only few targets	13.9	13.5	1.54	2.54
No targets	5.6	–	1.32	–
Lack of information	64.0	56.1	2.87	2.30
Other	5.2	10.0	3.67	2.12
All NAP companies	100	100	2.57	2.10
APP companies			7.60	7.86
All companies			3.10	3.20

Source: Labour Inspectorate, *Employment Conditions Survey 1997, 1998*. Authors' calculations.

Table 4.A6
HLM regressions of newly created jobs

Model	All jobs		Low-complexity jobs	
	Level	Related	Level	Related
	1.1 (s.e.)	1.2 (s.e.)	2.1 (s.e.)	2.2 (s.e.)
Fixed Effects				
1997	1.59 (0.24)	2.77 (0.26)	1.36 (0.19)	2.10 (0.19)
1996	1.51 (0.24)	2.68 (0.26)	1.23 (0.19)	1.96 (0.19)
PS4	−0.70 (0.25)	−0.15 (0.25)	−0.56 (0.18)	−0.17 (0.17)
PS9	−0.83 (0.23)	−0.32 (0.23)	−0.71 (0.17)	−0.36 (0.16)
PS19	−0.64 (0.25)	−0.30 (0.24)	−0.59 (0.17)	−0.37 (0.17)
PS99	0.35 (0.57)	−0.44 (0.57)	0.22 (0.41)	−0.31 (0.40)
PS199	1.87 (0.89)	−0.06 (0.90)	1.65 (0.58)	0.43 (0.58)
PS499	3.69 (1.93)	−0.68 (2.06)	1.78 (1.18)	−0.97 (1.28)
PS500	12.58 (8.07)	3.16 (7.52)	0.50 (3.28)	−5.66 (3.09)
Jobs number (T0 = Oct95; Oct96)			−0.17 (0.08)	−0.15 (0.08)
NTG	−0.29 (0.11)	0.23 (0.11)	−0.36 (0.07)	0.01 (0.07)
NAP	0.18 (0.18)	1.74 (0.61)	0.12 (0.11)	1.84 (0.40)
Targets (number)		0.15 (0.01)		0.10 (0.00)
Targets squared × 1000		−0.50 (0.05)		−0.35 (0.04)
Targets × NAP		0.10 (0.04)		0.12 (0.03)
Targets squared × NAP × 1000		−7.20 (3.47)		−8.17 (2.21)
Variance Components, Industry-Level				
τ_{CONS}^2	0.21	0.37	0	0.013
τ_{PS4}^2	0.23	0.36	0.011	0.06
τ_{PS500}^2	1044	849	90.1	35.69
$\tau_{CONS/PS4}$	−0.25	−0.39		−0.036
$\tau_{CONS/PS500}$	11.24	17.13		0.43
$\tau_{PS4/PS500}$	−7.96	−14	0.44	−0.87
Variance Components, Firm-Level				
σ_{1997}^2	21.3	21.3	14.1	13.5
σ_{1996}^2	27.0	26.2	12.2	11.8
$\sigma_{PS4/1997}$	−5.58	−6.22	−4.39	−4.43
$\sigma_{PS4/1996}$	−8.5	−8.34	−4.12	−4.09
$\sigma_{PS9/1997}$	−9.02	−9.15	−5.99	−5.76
$\sigma_{PS9/1996}$	−11.0	−10.8	−5.44	−5.29
$\sigma_{PS19/1997}$	−7.52	−7.82	−5.52	−5.32
$\sigma_{PS19/1996}$	−8.05	−8.57	−4.41	−4.26
$\sigma_{PS99/1997}$	48.9	41.2	21.9	17.7
$\sigma_{PS99/1996}$	16.4	19.0	10.1	10.9
$\sigma_{PS199/1997}$	57.1	56.0	29.1	24.3
$\sigma_{PS199/1996}$	121.6	126.6	35.0	38.4
$\sigma_{PS499/1997}$	402.5	448.6	136.4	163.4
$\sigma_{PS499/1996}$	430.2	472.2	173.2	188.8
$\sigma_{PS500/1997}$	2044	1952	1338	1363
$\sigma_{PS500/1996}$	2197	2728	303.7	370.3

Note: Reference group: APP companies.
Source: Labour Inspectorate, *Employment Conditions Survey 1997, 1998*. Authors' calculations.

Table 4.A7
HLM regressions of newly created jobs, period-specific estimates

Model	All jobs		Low-complexity jobs	
	Level 1.1a (s.e.)	Related 1.2a (s.e.)	Level 2.1a (s.e.)	Related 2.2a (s.e.)
Fixed Effects				
1997	1.63 (0.24)	2.9 (0.27)	1.26 (0.17)	2.31 (0.19)
1996	1.54 (0.25)	2.48 (0.29)	1.02 (0.17)	1.40 (0.19)
PS4	−0.69 (0.25)	0.16 (0.25)	−0.44 (0.18)	−0.13 (0.17)
PS9	−0.83 (0.23)	−0.32 (0.23)	−0.66 (0.17)	−0.34 (0.16)
PS19	−0.64 (0.25)	−0.30 (0.24)	−0.57 (0.17)	−0.34 (0.17)
PS99	0.35 (0.57)	−0.43 (0.56)	0.22 (0.41)	−0.35 (0.40)
PS199	1.86 (0.89)	−0.09 (0.90)	1.63 (0.58)	0.31 (0.58)
PS499	3.68 (1.93)	−0.47 (2.06)	1.76 (1.18)	−0.74 (1.28)
PS500	12.46 (8.07)	2.77 (7.53)	0.44 (3.27)	−5.15 (3.09)
NTG	−0.22 (0.17)	−0.21 (0.17)	−0.22 (0.10)	−0.01 (0.11)
NTG × 1997	−0.11 0.22	0.02 (0.23)	−0.15 (0.15)	0.11 (0.15)
NAP	0.28 0.25	2.37 (0.73)	0.30 (0.14)	2.20 (0.46)
NAP × 1997	−0.19 0.36	−1.78 (1.32)	−0.47 (0.24)	−0.70 (0.94)
Targets (number)		0.13 (0.02)		0.06 (0.01)
Targets × 1997		0.02 (0.02)		0.06 (0.01)
Targets squared × 1000		−0.51 (0.05)		−0.25 (0.03)
Targets squared × 1000 × 1997				−0.17 (0.08)
Targets × NAP		0.15 0.05		0.15 (0.03)
Targets × NAP × 1997		−0.14 0.11		−0.03 (0.08)
Targets squared × NAP × 1000		−8.67 3.70		−7.90 (2.28)
Variance Components, Industry-Level				
τ_{CONS}^{2}	0.21	0.37		0.012
τ_{PS4}^{2}	0.23	0.36	0.002	0.055
τ_{PS500}^{2}	1040	841.7	89.56	50.87
$\tau_{CONS/PS4}$	−0.2	−0.38		−0.037
$\tau_{CONS/PS500}$	11.1	16.4		0.31
$\tau_{PS4/PS500}$	−7.8	−13.3	0.25	−0.97
Variance Components, Firm–Level				
σ_{1997}^{2}	21.2	21.4	14.1	13.6
σ_{1996}^{2}	27.0	26.0	12.2	11.8
$\sigma_{PS4/1997}$	−5.57	−6.30	−4.37	−4.60
$\sigma_{PS4/1996}$	−8.5	−8.26	−4.07	−4.03
$\sigma_{PS9/1997}$	−9.01	−9.21	−5.99	−5.58
$\sigma_{PS9/1996}$	−11	−10.7	−5.42	−5.28
$\sigma_{PS19/1997}$	−7.51	−7.89	−5.53	−5.41
$\sigma_{PS19/1996}$	−8.05	−8.43	−4.4	−4.29
$\sigma_{PS99/1997}$	48.8	40.3	21.8	17.0
$\sigma_{PS99/1996}$	16.4	18.7	10.0	10.3
$\sigma_{PS199/1997}$	57.0	57.1	29.0	25.2
$\sigma_{PS199/1996}$	121.7	124.9	35.0	36.0
$\sigma_{PS499/1997}$	402.6	457.4	136.6	182.7
$\sigma_{PS499/1996}$	430.2	458.2	173.3	177.8
$\sigma_{PS500/1997}$	2045	1966	1362	1396
$\sigma_{PS500/1996}$	2196	2650	303.2	331.8

Note: Reference group: APP companies; ps4 = 1–4 employees.

Source: Labour Inspectorate, *Employment Conditions Survey 1997, 1998*. Authors' calculations.

5. Fighting Unemployment without Worsening Poverty: Basic Income versus Reductions of Social Security Contributions

Bruno Van der Linden[1]

5.1 INTRODUCTION

At least four types of policies have been advocated to fight unemployment without worsening poverty: reductions of social security contributions (RSSC), an unconditional basic income, the negative income tax and the earned income tax credit (EITC). The reader is referred to Van Parijs (1998) for an insightful introduction to these policies. Drèze (1993) and Drèze and Gollier (1993) look for institutions that achieve both production efficiency and risk-sharing between workers and employers. According to their analysis, minimum wage legislation should put a floor on earnings and employers' social insurance contributions (ESIC) should be adjusted in order to bring labour costs down to a level compatible with full employment. The proposal of Drèze and Malinvaud et al. (1994) to exempt minimum wages from ESIC has to some extent been implemented in some Member States, such as France and Belgium.[2] Yet, several authors (for example Nickell and Bell 1997) have questioned this policy. According to them, most of the effect is on take-home pay and not on unemployment. Moreover, the acquisition of skill would be slowed down.

A first aim of this chapter is to clarify the debate about the effects of RSSC in fully unionised economies. Since the critique of Nickell and Bell is based on the so-called 'wage-setting/price-setting' model (henceforth, WS-PS), the present chapter adopts the same approach, first with homogeneous workers and later with two types of workers. For simplicity, ignoring RSSC, taxation is linear. With a single type of labour, a dynamic general equilibrium analysis shows that in the long run RSSC affect unemployment if and only if they introduce some non linearity in the tax schedule[3]. This result holds because, under appropriate conditions, the WS curve is vertical in a steady state. Therefore, proportional taxes are in the long run absorbed entirely by workers and have no influence on unemployment, because the proposal of Drèze and Malinvaud et al. (1994) concerns an exemption, the elasticity of the wage cost with respect to the bargained (gross) wage is higher than one. This non-linearity in the tax schedule has a favourable effect on the steady-state unemployment rate. With two skills and a fixed supply, the chapter shows how a proportional cut in payroll taxes on the low skilled affects the long-run equilibrium unemployment rate if the low skilled wage presents some rigidity (as it does in Continental Europe at least). If skill-specific labour supply is endogenous but not perfectly elastic in the long run, cutting payroll taxes on the low-skilled workers has an effect on their unemployment rate. It is even a major policy response to tackle the well-documented skilled-biased technical progress without worsening poverty.

A basic income is an unconditional allowance handed out to (almost) every adult citizen. It has also been called 'universal income', 'social dividend' (Lange 1936; Meade 1989) or 'participation income' (Atkinson 1995a). With the analytical tools used in this chapter, the negative income tax and the basic income are strictly equivalent. For Drèze (1993) and Drèze and Sneessens (1997), a basic income could be an alternative to RSSC if it was associated with some deregulation of the labour market. A second objective of this chapter is therefore to analyse how a basic income performs in the WS-PS setting and how it compares with RSSC. In contrast to Drèze and Sneessens, it is here assumed that unions keep their bargaining power when the basic income is implemented. Furthermore, if the basic income is lower than pre-existing unemployment benefits, the latter do not disappear. They are simply reduced in such a way that the net income of the unemployed remains unchanged at given wages.

The analysis considers first only one type of labour. With a constant marginal tax rate, the introduction of a basic income generates a non-linear tax schedule. The latter becomes progressive in the sense that the elasticity of the net income of an employed worker with respect to the bargained (gross) wage is negatively related to the basic income level. This has a favourable effect on equilibrium unemployment. So, the basic income and an exemption of payroll taxes influence the unemployment rate in a very similar way. However, the basic income also affects unemployment through a second channel. Unemployment benefits raise the reservation wage of job seekers and this effect is typically amplified by collective bargaining. Allowing workers to keep (part of) their unemployment allowance if they are hired influences wage-setting and eventually unemployment. If at given wages the basic income favours in-work income without increasing the revenue of the unemployed, equilibrium unemployment shrinks. The opposite is true if the basic income favours both in-work and out-of-work incomes of risk-averse agents. In both cases, however, the equilibrium level of net wages decreases. If, in equilibrium, both the unemployment benefits and the basic income are proportional to net earnings, the decrease in net wages can have a negative effect on the instantaneous income of those currently unemployed. Even if an increase in the basic income–net wage ratio can improve the intertemporal utilities of the unemployed and the employed, the instantaneous effect on the income of the unemployed is a matter of concern. The chapter deals with this issue.

Second, with two types of workers, it is shown that a basic income and RSSC on low-skilled workers influence the unemployment rates in different ways. As long as low-skill wages are rigid and skill-specific labour supply is not perfectly elastic in the long run, introducing a basic income has a favourable effect on the unemployment rate of the low-skilled.

Increasing the income of the 'inactive' population through a fully unconditional income could have a direct positive effect on the welfare of the labour force. The model ignores this possibility. Under this assumption, the analysis points to a conflict of interest between the 'active' and the 'inactive' population. The increase in the tax rate needed to keep a balanced budget has a detrimental effect on the wellbeing of the labour force. To avoid this conflict of interest, the chapter puts more emphasis on the limiting case where the inactive population becomes ineligible to the basic income. With this, the institutional setting comes close to an EITC. This holds true if the basic income (what one could call an 'active citizen's income') does not influence the income of the unemployed (at given wages). Still at least one difference remains. Compared to the EITC implemented in the US, the stylised policy considered here is lump sum (no phasing-in, nor phasing-out).

This chapter is linked to various strands in the literature. It is evidently not possible to review all the contributions here. What follows is a selective and very condensed survey of the literature. First, the link between progressive taxation, wage setting and unemployment has now been extensively analysed, often in a static framework. Papers like Lockwood and Manning (1993) or Holmlund and Kolm (1995) found some empirical support for the claim that, loosely speaking, progressive taxes induce wage moderation and boost employment (see also the tax-based income policy of Layard et al. 1991). Yet, the analysis should be extended to deal with tax evasion or with intertemporal issues such as investment in skills (see, for example, Andersen and Rasmussen 1997). Tax evasion is not introduced below but the supply of skills will be endogenous in Section 5.3. Second, there is a growing and closely connected literature about the effects of the structure of labour taxation in unionised economies. This literature identifies reasons why it can matter whether labour taxation is levied on firms or workers (see for example Rasmussen 1994; Koskela and Schöb 1999; Picard and Toulemonde 1999). Tax credits and non-linear RSSC are examples considered in this literature. Third, several papers have used an efficiency wage set-up to analyse the effects of the replacement of unemployment insurance schemes by a basic income (see Bowles 1992; Atkinson 1995a; and also Groot and Peeters 1997). In a bargaining framework, the partial-equilibrium and static analysis of Késenne (1993) should also be mentioned. Fourth, earlier papers have already introduced a lump-sum allowance or tax subsidy in static versions of the WS-PS model (see Holmlund and Kolm 1995; and Pissarides 1998). Both papers present static models and only the first disaggregates the labour force. These papers conclude that these lump-sum policies have favourable effects on unemployment.[4] Given their effects on wages, these papers call for a welfare analysis, which is done in this article. Finally, one should recall that it has been argued that social insurance contributions (SIC) should not be considered as taxes. SIC entitle those who pay them to deferred benefits such as retirement benefits or compensation for workplace injuries (see for example Gruber 1997). However, the present chapter adopts the usual assumption according to which wage-setters take SIC as if they were taxes.

The chapter is organised as follows. Section 5.2 develops a dynamic general equilibrium model of a unionised economy with one type of skill. Section 5.3 distinguishes two types of workers. Section 5.4 concludes the chapter.

5.2   HOMOGENOUS UNIONISED WORKERS AND EQUILIBRIUM UNEMPLOYMENT

This section develops a dynamic general equilibrium model of a small unionised economy facing an exogenous interest rate r.[5] The model draws upon Cahuc and Zylberberg (1999). There are three goods, namely homogeneous labour (L), capital (K) and a produced and consumed good. The market for the produced good is perfectly competitive. Its price is taken as the numeraire. The setting is deterministic with, in each period t, n identical firms,[6] endowed with a decreasing returns-to-scale Cobb–Douglas technology $(A_t L_t)^\alpha K_t^{\theta-\alpha}$, $A_t > 0, 0 < \alpha < 1, \alpha < \theta < 1$,[7] N risk averse workers and M inactive individuals (whose role is here simply to increase the budgetary cost of a basic income if the latter is not restricted to the labour force). n, N and M are given.[8] Wage bargaining over the (gross) wage w_t is decentralised and involves a firm-specific union and the firm owner. Wages are only set for the current period. The firm owner decides on employment L_t

and on the level of investment (the 'right-to-manage' assumption). Firms and workers are infinitely lived agents with perfect foresight. In a given period t, the sequence of decisions is as follows:

Each firm decides upon its current investment level which will increase its capital stock in $t + 1$. Therefore, the capital stock is predetermined in t. If the decentralised bargaining leads to an agreement, the firm determines labour demand for the current period as a function of the real wage cost $(1+\tau_t)w_t - E_t$. τ_t is the constant marginal ESIC rate $(\tau_t \geq 0)$ and E_t is an ESIC exemption $(E_t \geq 0)$.[9] Employment is fixed by labour demand, production occurs and the employees receive each a net real wage $(1-s_t)w_t$ at the end of the period. In this expression, s_t is the constant marginal tax on earnings formally incident on workers.[10] Without an agreement, workers immediately leave the firm and start searching for a job. They are immediately rehired in another firm with an endogenous probability a_t. In such a case, nothing is produced during the current period. Yet, the firm will have the opportunity to bargain and to hire workers (without hiring costs) in $t + 1$. At the end of the period, an exogenous fraction q of the employees leaves the firm and enters unemployment. They will be hired in $t + 1$ with probability $a_{t + 1}$. Moreover, the marginal tax rates are adjusted to keep the budget of the State in equilibrium.

Due to space limitation, the exposition only focuses on the main features of the model. For a more detailed exposition, see Cahuc and Zylberberg (1999) and Van der Linden (1999a, 1999b).[11]

Firms

When it determines its labour demand and the level of investment, each firm takes as given the sequence of real wage costs $[(1+\tau_t)w_t - E_t, t \geq 0]$, the (constant) interest rate r and the (constant) depreciation rate δ. In period t, given the initial capital stock K_t, each firm chooses its investment level I_t, such that $K_{t+1} = (1-\delta)K_t + I_t$. Along an equilibrium path, there is a collective agreement in each period. So, at time $t = 0$, given K_0, the firm maximises the following objective function:

$$\max_{\{L_t, K_{t+1}\}_{t \geq 0}} \sum_{t=0}^{\infty} \left[\frac{1}{1+r}\right]^t \left\{(A_t L_t)^\alpha K_t^{\theta-\alpha} - [(1+\tau_t)w_t - E_t]L_t - [K_{t+1} - (1-\delta)K_t]\right\}$$

(5.1)

The first-order conditions of this problem can be written as:

$$L_t = \frac{K_t^{\theta - \alpha/1 - \alpha}}{A_t}\left(\frac{(1+\tau_t)w_t - E_t}{\alpha A_t}\right)^{1/\alpha - 1}$$

(5.2)

$$K_{t+1}^{1-\theta/1-\alpha} = \frac{\theta - \alpha}{r + \delta}\left(\frac{(1+\tau_{t+1})w_{t+1} - E_{t+1}}{\alpha A_{t+1}}\right)^{\alpha/\alpha - 1}$$

(5.3)

Let $\pi_t(K_t)$ be current optimal profits net of investment. The optimal discounted profits at time t are denoted by $\Pi_t(K_t)$. If $\beta = 1/(1 + r)$ is the discount factor, it is easily seen that:

$$\pi_t(K_t) = (1 - \alpha)K_t^{\theta - \alpha/1 - \alpha}\left(\frac{(1+\tau_t)w_t - E_t}{A_t}\right)^{\alpha/\alpha - 1}$$

(5.4)

$$\Pi_t(K_t) = \pi_t(K_t) - I_t + \beta\Pi_{t+1}(K_{t+1}).$$

(5.5)

Workers

Each of the N workers supply zero or one unit of labour. The instantaneous utility is a function of real net income R_t: $v(R_t)$, $v' > 0$, $v' \leq 0$. It is later assumed that $v(R_t)$ is iso-elastic:

$$v(R_t) = \frac{R_t^\lambda}{\lambda}, \ \lambda \leq 1, \ \lambda \neq 0.$$

(5.6)

Let V_e^t (respectively, V_g^t, V_u^t) denote the intertemporal discounted utility of a worker employed at time t in a given firm (respectively, a redundant worker, an unemployed). If B_t denotes the real level of the basic income, V_e^t verifies the following recursive relationship:

$$V_e^t = v(R_{et}) + \beta\left\{q\left[a_{t+1}\overline{V_e^{t+1}} + (1 - a_{t+1})V_u^t\right] + (1 - q)V_e^{t+1}\right\}$$

(5.7)

where R_{et} denotes the instantaneous real net income of a currently employed worker $[R_{et} = (1 - s_t)w_t + B_t]$ and $\overline{V_e^{t+1}}$ is the intertemporal discounted utility of a job on average in the economy in period $t + 1$. $\overline{V_e^{t+1}}$ is of the same form as (5.7) with only one difference: The average net real wage in the economy, $\overline{w_t}$, replaces w_t. $\overline{V_e^{t+1}}$ and V_u^{t+1} actually are (perfectly) anticipated utilities. The intertemporal discounted utility of being unemployed at time t is such that:

$$V_u^t = v(R_{ut}) + \beta \left[a_{t+1}\overline{V_e^{t+1}} + (1 - a_{t+1})V_u^{t+1} \right] \tag{5.8}$$

where R_{ut} is the instantaneous real income of those currently unemployed. If Z_t is the current level of unemployment benefits, then $R_{ut} = \max[Z_t, B_t]$. Given the above assumptions, the outside option of the workers, V_g^t, is given by:

$$V_g^t = a_t \overline{V_e^t} + (1 - a_t)V_u^t. \tag{5.9}$$

Collective Bargaining at the Firm Level

Following Manning (1993), let us assume the following flexible union's objective $L_t^\psi (V_e^t - V_g^t)$, where ψ is a nonnegative parameter representing the union's preferences for employment relative to an intertemporal rent for currently occupied workers. The firm owner and the firm-specific union bargain over the real gross wage for the current period during which the capital stock is given. When they bargain, they also take the tax parameters (s_t, τ_t), the level of exemption (E_t) and the income in case of unemployment (R_{ut}) as given. Assume that the current real (gross) wage w_t is set to maximise a Nash product. Without an agreement, nothing is produced but future profits and, hence, investment are not affected. Therefore, the firm´s component in the Nash product, that is the difference between intertemporal discounted profits in case of an agreement, Π_t, and in the absence of an agreement, $-I_t + \beta \Pi_{t+1}$, is simply π_t. Ignoring constant and predetermined terms, from (5.2) and (5.4), the Nash program can be conveniently written as:

$$\max_{w_t} \left[(1 + \tau_t)w_t - E_t \right]^{\alpha(1-\gamma) + \psi \gamma / \alpha - 1} (V_e^t - V_g^t)^\gamma \tag{5.10}$$

where γ is the so-called bargaining power of the union $(0 \leq \gamma \leq 1)$. The first-order condition of this problem can be written in the following way:

$$\frac{V_e^t - V_g^t}{\left[B_t + (1-s_t)w_t\right]^v \left[B_t + (1-s_t)w_t\right]} = \mu\zeta_t, \ \mu = \frac{\gamma(1-\alpha)}{\alpha(1-\gamma)+\psi\gamma} \geq 0, \ \zeta_t = \frac{\eta_t^e}{\eta_t^f} > 0. \ (5.11)$$

On the left-hand side of condition (5.11), one finds the difference in inter-temporal utilities between an employed and a redundant worker (the 'rent') scaled by the current net income of an employed worker (if $v = 1$ and a function of it otherwise). This 'scaled rent' is increasing with the time-invariant parameter μ. The latter is positively related to γ and negatively related to ψ and to the absolute value of the elasticity of labour demand, $1/(1 - \alpha)$. To satisfy the second-order condition, it is assumed that $\mu < 1$.[12]

Let us now turn to the second parameter, ζ_t. The latter is the ratio of two elasticities which in general are functions of w_t. The numerator is simply the elasticity of the real net income R_{et} with respect to the real gross wage w_t (also called the 'coefficient of residual income progression'):

$$\eta_t^e = \frac{(1-s_t)w_t}{(1-s_t)w_t + B_t} < 1.$$

Imagine that η_t^e diminishes (say, because the basic income level B_t increases). Then a 1-percentage point of increase in the gross wage has a lower relative effect on the net income of the employed. Yet, it has unchanged negative effects on employment and profits. Therefore, the bargained 'scaled rent' is reduced. The denominator of ζ_t is the elasticity of the real wage cost with respect to the real gross wage:

$$\eta_t^f = \frac{(1+\tau_t)w_t}{(1+\tau_t)w_t - E_t} > 1.$$

Imagine that η_t^f increases (say, because the exemption E_t is higher). Then a 1 percentage point of increase in the gross wage raises the wage cost relatively more. This is detrimental to employment and profits but does not change the relationship between the real gross wage and real net income. Therefore, the bargained 'scaled rent' is reduced. So, ζ_t summarises the degree of non linearity of the tax schedule. As in Lockwood and Manning

(1993) and chapter 8 of Cahuc and Zylberberg (1996), ζ_t captures the role of progressive taxation on wage bargaining. Finally, since ζ_t is positive, it should be noticed that the 'rent' is definitely positive if $\gamma > 0$.

Symmetric Equilibrium

In a symmetric equilibrium, since firms, workers and unions are identical, $V_e^t = \overline{V_e^t}$ and $w_t = \overline{w_t}$. Then (5.9) implies that:

$$V_e^t - V_g^t = (1 - a_t)(V_e^t - V_u^t). \qquad (5.12)$$

The exit rate from unemployment, a_t, can be rewritten as a function of the current and previous unemployment rate (hence, a_t is endogenous). The current unemployment level is made of those who where unemployed at the beginning of this period and who are not currently hired. After division by the size of the labour force, N, this definition can be written as:

$$u_t = (1 - a_t)[u_{t-1} + q(1 - u_{t-1})], \qquad (5.13)$$

where u_t is the unemployment rate in period t. Combining (5.7), (5.8), (5.11), (5.12) and (5.13) yields an equation that implicitly defines the current real gross wage as a function of: (i) the current and anticipated levels of the marginal rate of taxes formally incident on the employees (s); (ii) the current and anticipated progressivity of the tax system (ζ); (iii) the current and anticipated levels of allowances (B and R_u); (iv) the previous and current unemployment rate u; (v) the characteristics of the union and the technology (captured by μ); (vi) the exogenous separation rate q. This equation can be written in the following way:

$$\frac{v(R_{et}) - v(R_{ut})}{\mu \zeta_t R_{et} v'(R_{et})} + \beta(1 - q) \frac{\zeta_{t+1} R_{e,t+1} v'(R_{e,t+1})}{\zeta_t R_{et} v'(R_{et})} = \frac{q + (1 - q)u_{t-1}}{u_t}. \qquad (5.14)$$

The dynamic properties of a similar model have been analysed by Van der Linden (1999b). Let us henceforth focus on a steady state. The second term on the left-hand side of (5.14) is then simply equal to $\beta(1 - q)$. Furthermore, the right-hand side of (5.14) becomes equal to $q/u_t + 1 - q$. So, in a steady state, equation (5.14) can be written in the following way:

$$\frac{v[(1 - s_t)w_t + B_t] - v(R_{ut})}{\mu \zeta_t[(1 - s_t)w_t + B_t]v'((1 - s_t)w_t + B_t)} - (1 - \beta)(1 - q) = \frac{q}{u_t}. \qquad (5.15)$$

For sufficiently risk averse workers, this wage-setting curve ('WS') is an implicit decreasing relationship between the real (gross) wage w_t and the unemployment rate u_t. The price-setting curve ('PS') is here simply an aggregate labour demand curve (immediately derived from (5.2) and (5.3)). This 'PS' curve is upward sloping in a (w_t, u_t) space:

$$N(1-u_t) = \frac{n}{A_t}\left(\frac{\theta-\alpha}{r+\delta}\right)^{\theta-\alpha/_{1-\alpha}}\left[\frac{(1+\tau_t)w_t - E_t}{\alpha A_t}\right]^{-1+\alpha-\theta/_{1-\theta}}. \qquad (5.16)$$

If B_t and Z_t are fixed (in real terms), the model (5.15–5.16) is such that balanced growth (A_t increases at a constant rate) reduces the unemployment rate. Such a tendency is historically not observed and, hence, sounds implausible. Therefore, it is standard in this literature to assume that unemployment benefits are indexed to wages. This assumption then leads to a vertical 'WS' curve: the equilibrium unemployment rate is fixed by the wage-setting behaviour and shifts in labour demand only affects the real (gross) wage rate. To see this and to simplify the following analysis, let us from now on make use of assumption (5.6). In addition, let the real level of (untaxed) unemployment benefits and basic income be proportional to the real net earnings:[13]

$$\frac{Z_t}{(1-s_t)w_t} = z, 0 < z < 1 \text{ and } \frac{B_t}{(1-s_t)w_t} = b, 0 \le b < 1. \qquad (5.17)$$

From (5.17), the real net instantaneous income of the unemployed is now $R_{ut} = \max(z,b)(1-s_t)w_t$. When $0 < b < z$, the basic income is said to be 'partial'. The income of the unemployed is here the sum of the basic income and an unemployment benefit reduced by the amount of the basic income. So, there is a switch in the type of benefit received but the cash amount is unchanged at given wages. The opposite case ($b \ge z$) is the so-called 'full basic income'. Now, the unemployment benefits disappear and are replaced by a basic income which is at least equivalent at given wages. To keep the analysis as simple as possible, let the ESIC exemption, E_t, be proportional to the wage cost:

$$\frac{E_t}{(1+\tau_t)w_t} = e, 0 \le e < 1. \qquad (5.18)$$

Henceforth, z, b and e will be considered as 'policy parameters'. From (5.17) and (5.18), it is easily checked that the two elasticities η_t^e and η_t^f become time-invariant:

$$\eta^e = \frac{1}{1+b}, \eta^f = \frac{1}{1-e} \Rightarrow \zeta = \frac{1-e}{1+b}. \tag{5.19}$$

Then, the steady-state unemployment rate, u, is determined by the 'WS' curve (5.15). The latter becomes:

$$u = \frac{q}{\frac{1}{\mu\lambda\zeta}\left\{1-\left[\frac{\max(z,b)}{1+b}\right]^\lambda\right\} - (1-\beta)(1-q)} \tag{5.20}$$

The higher q and μ, the higher the equilibrium unemployment rate. The equilibrium unemployment rate decreases with the degree of relative risk-aversion. These are rather intuitive results. As far as the policy parameters are concerned, the message delivered by equation (5.20) can be decomposed in two parts. First, introducing a basic income or an ESIC exemption has an influence on the equilibrium unemployment rate because taxation is now progressive (namely, ζ becomes lower than one). Let us call this the 'progressivity effect'.

As far as this mechanism is concerned, the two policies are strictly equivalent provided that they generate the same level of ζ. By the way, as is well-known in this literature, linear taxes have no effect on the unemployment rate in steady state (namely, neither s nor τ play a role in (5.20)). Their value only affects net income (through equation (5.16)). So, as z, b or e changes, at least one of the marginal tax rates s or τ will have to adjust to keep the public budget balanced. This adjustment is borne by employees with no effect on the allocation of labour. Taking (5.17) and (5.18) into account, the steady-state 'PS' curve (5.16) can be written as:

$$w = \frac{C}{(1-e)(1+\tau)(1-u)^\kappa}, \kappa = \frac{1-\theta}{1+\alpha-\theta} > 0, \tag{5.21}$$

where C is a positive constant easily derived from (5.16). From (5.21), the real net income of an employed worker, $R_e = (1+b)(1-s)w$, is immediately computed.

Second, the basic income influences the unemployment rate through the ratio between income in case of unemployment and income in-work (the 'replacement ratio'). From (5.11), it is intuitively clear that the unions try to generate a 'rent' for the occupied workers. This rent is measured in comparison with the outside option (the intertemporal utility of a redundant worker). Equation (5.12) establishes a clear link between this rent $(V_e^t - V_g^t)$ and the difference in utility between an employed and an unemployed worker $(V_e^t - V_u^t)$. Due to the simplifying assumptions (5.6) and (5.17), what matters in steady state is simply the replacement ratio $\max(z, b)/1 + b$. By assumption (5.17), real unemployment benefits are indexed to net earnings, not to the net income of an employed worker. Therefore, the partial basic income favours in-work net income (for a given z, as b increases, the replacement ratio $z/(1 + b)$ decreases). This has a favourable effect on wage formation and eventually on unemployment. The opposite holds in the case of the full basic income. For then, the replacement ratio is $b/(1 + b)$ which increases with b. This second mechanism, which could be called the 'replacement ratio effect', is specific to the basic income.

<h3 style="text-align:center">Figure 5.1
Steady-state properties of an increase in:</h3>

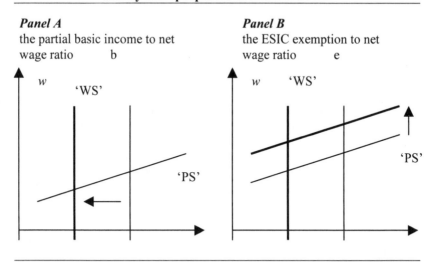

Panel A
the partial basic income to net wage ratio   b

Panel B
the ESIC exemption to net wage ratio   e

To sum up, an exemption of ESIC, captured by the policy parameter e, has a favourable effect on unemployment through the 'progressivity effect' (see Panel B of Figure 5.1). A partial basic income has a favourable effect, too, but now through both mechanisms (see Panel A of Figure 5.1). A full basic income has a favourable effect on unemployment through the 'progressivity effect'. On the other hand, it has a detrimental effect on unemployment through the 'replacement ratio effect'. It is easily seen that the two effects cancel out if workers are risk neutral. If they are risk averse, it can be checked that a marginal increase in the full basic income-net earnings ratio b raises the equilibrium unemployment rate.[15] These conclusions rely upon the way bargaining is modeled. If a collective agreement is not reached, the workers have been assumed to immediately leave the firm and start searching a job. This implies that the fall-back position of a union member is his outside option. In a setting where the lack of an agreement leads to a strike, the income during this period would be positively influenced by an unconditional basic income. Without an offsetting effect on the level of strike payments or other changes in the bargaining set-up, this would introduce a wage-push effect detrimental to employment.

Welfare and Profits

From (5.7) and (5.8), the inter-temporal levels of utility can be written as follows in a steady state:

$$V_e = \frac{[1 - \beta(1-a)]v(R_e) + \beta q(1-a)v(R_u)}{(1-\beta)[1 - \beta(1-a)(1-q)]},$$ (5.22)

$$V_u = \frac{\beta a v(R_e) + \{1 - \beta[1 - q(1-a)]\}v(R_u)}{(1-\beta)[1 - \beta(1-a)(1-q)]} < V_e,$$ (5.23)

$$V_0 = \frac{v(B)}{1-\beta},$$

where V_0 stands for the intertemporal utility of the inactive population. In (5.22) and (5.23), a is derived from (5.13) expressed in a steady state and from (5.20). From (5.6) and (5.17), it is easily checked that (5.22) and (5.23) are proportional to w^λ / λ, with w defined by (5.21). It can be verified that a lower unemployment rate (that is an improvement in the exit rate from unemployment, a) increases V_e and V_u at given wages (see Van der Linden 1999a). In that way, an increase in the partial basic income–net wage ratio, b, has a favourable effect on V_e and V_u. So does an increase in e. However, the effect on wages should also be taken into account. From (5.21) and Panel A of Figure 5.1, an increase in the partial basic income–net wage ratio also lowers w. This has a detrimental effect on V_e and V_u. On the contrary, Panel B of the same figure illustrates that an increase in e has an ambiguous effect on w.

Given (5.2) to (5.4) and (5.21), steady-state optimal inter-temporal profits Π can be written as:

$$\Pi = \left(\frac{\theta-\alpha}{r+\delta}\right)^{1-\alpha/1-\theta} \frac{1}{1-\beta}\left[\frac{C}{\alpha A(1-u)^k}\right]^{-\alpha/1-\theta}\left[\left(\frac{1-\alpha}{\theta-\alpha}\right)r + \left(\frac{1-\theta}{\theta-\alpha}\right)\delta\right], \quad (5.24)$$

which is negatively related to the unemployment rate.

The Budget Constraint of the State

Up to now, the budget of the State (including the unemployment insurance system) has been ignored and it has been implicitly assumed that profits are untaxed. Under a balanced budget constraint, the marginal tax rates, s and τ, have to vary with the level of parameters e and b. Put another way, if, as it turns out, a reduction of social security contributions or a basic income increases net public expenses, this can only be financed through additional taxes on income from salaried employment.[16] This obviously has negative effects on the inter-temporal level of utility within the labour force.

To write the budget constraint of the State, an additional parameter has to be introduced. The inactive population and the n firm-owners are eligible to the basic income if the latter is truely unconditional. More generally, there could exist more restrictive criteria (see, for example, the 'participation income' of Atkinson 1995b). So, let v be the ratio between the eligible inactive population (extended to firm-owners) and the workforce $(v \leq [(M + n)/N])$. Given the focus of this chapter on the unemployment insurance mechanism, let us ignore the other components of the welfare state. Under assumptions (5.17) and (5.18) and after division by the size of the labour force and by the real gross wage rate, the balanced budget can then be written as:

$$(s+\tau)(1-u) = (1-s)\max(z,b)u + b(1-s)(1-u+v) + (1+\tau)e(1-u). \quad (5.25)$$

A Numerical Illustration

The analytical properties of the model are clear-cut as far as the steady-state unemployment rate is concerned. On the contrary, due to their effects on the real gross wage and on tax rates, it is unclear whether the introduction of an

ESIC exemption or a basic income will raise the utility level of the various types of agents. For this very reason and to provide orders of magnitude of the various effects, this subsection develops a numerical analysis based on plausible values of the parameters.[17] This simulation exercise showed that the introduction of an active citizen's income or an exemption in ESIC can be a Pareto improvement in a unionised economy. This is true when inter-temporal utility and profit levels are used. However, if the unemployment benefit is proportional to net earnings, the income position of the unemployed deteriorates in the short run when a partial active citizen's income is introduced. Yet, the level of the active citizen's income can be defined in a different way to avoid this effect without loosing the Paretian property. Then, an exemption and an active citizen's income have rather similar properties. The analysis also highlighted a plausible conflict of interest between the active and the inactive people if the latter are eligible to a basic income.

5.3   HETEROGENEOUS UNIONISED WORKERS AND EQUILIBRIUM UNEMPLOYMENT

This section also uses the WS-PS model but now two types of workers are distinguished (low-skilled, with subscript l, and high-skilled, with subscript h). Nickell and Bell (1997, 321) summarise the rather pessimistic view on the effect of cutting payroll taxes on the less-skilled in two claims:

- If there are no barriers to acquisition of training, shifts in the demand for unskilled relative to skilled workers may have little long-run impact on relative unemployment rates because changes in unemployment rates and wages will tend to be offset by 'migration' from the unskilled to the skilled.
- In the long run, if wages are flexible, payroll taxes are borne by labour. So labour costs and employment are unaffected although take-home pay will change.

As Gregg and Manning (1997) explain, these results heavily rely on a set of additional assumptions introduced in the WS-PS model by Layard et al. (1991). First, it is assumed that the two skill groups are separable on the supply side, which means that the wage rate of a given skill group is only influenced by its own unemployment rate. Second, the supply of skills is perfectly elastic in the long run. Gregg and Manning (1997) give reasons why these hypotheses are fragile. So, in this section, I follow the viewpoint of Gregg and Manning (1997) and relax these assumptions. The model of this section also draws upon Chapter 9 of Cahuc and Zylberberg (1996). The effect of (nonlinear) taxation in a unionised economy with two types of workers has been analysed by Holmlund and Kolm (1995). Their approach is, however, embedded in the one of Layard et al. (1991). Moreover, their purpose is not to compare exemption of ESIC and basic income schemes. Recently, Lehmann (1999) has looked at the effect of a basic income in an equilibrium matching model that distinguishes two types of skill.

At the outset, it should be recognised that developing a rigorous and fully-fledged general equilibrium model of a unionised two-skills economy turns out to be quite a challenge in its own right. Due to space limitation, the model is only sketched. As in the abovementioned papers, the focus is on the long-run effects. In a first stage, labour supply is fixed. This will allow to discuss the second claim. In order to adress the first claim, the hypothesis of exogenous labour supply is relaxed in a second stage. Due to space limitation, as far as the basic income is concerned, this section only considers the partial scheme.

A Model with Exogenous Labour Supply

Consider a decreasing returns-to-scale Cobb–Douglas technology $L_t^\alpha K_t^{\theta-\alpha}, 0 < \alpha < \theta < 1$. And let L_t be a C.E.S. function of the two types of workers:

$$L_t = G_t \left[\left(A_{ht} L_{ht} \right)^{\sigma-1/\sigma} + \left(A_{lt} L_{lt} \right)^{\sigma-1/\sigma} \right]^{\sigma/\sigma-1}, G_t, A_{lt}, A_{ht}, \sigma > 0. \tag{5.27}$$

The firm produces a homogeneous good and sells it on a competitive market at a price normalised to 1. When it determines labour demand and the investment level, each firm takes as given the sequence of real wage costs, the (constant) interest rate r and the (constant) depreciation rate δ. In any period t, given the initial capital stock K_t, each firm chooses its investment level I_t such that $K_{t+1} = (1-\delta)K_t + I_t$. Along an equilibrium path, there is a collective agreement in each period. So, at time $t = 0$, given K_0, the firm maximises the following objective function:

$$\max_{\{L_t, K_{t+1}\}_{t \geq 0}} \sum_{t=0}^{\infty} \left\{ L_t^\alpha K_t^{\theta-\alpha} - w_t^f L_t - \left[K_{t+1} - (1-\delta)K_t \right] \right\} \tag{5.28}$$

with $w_t^f L_t = w_{ht}(1 + \tau_{ht})L_{ht} + w_{lt}(1 + \tau_{lt})L_{lt}$ \hfill (5.29)

In the latter expression, w_{jt} denotes the real (gross) wage of skill j and $\tau_{jt} \geq 0$ the skill-specific ESIC rate, $(j = h,l)$. The first-order conditions of this problem are:

$$L_t = K_t^{\theta - \alpha/1 - \alpha} \left(\frac{w_t^f}{\alpha} \right)^{1/\alpha - 1} \tag{5.30}$$

$$K_{t+1}^{1-\theta/1-\alpha} = \frac{\theta - \alpha}{r + \delta} \left(\frac{w_{t+1}^f}{\alpha} \right)^{\alpha/\alpha - 1}. \tag{5.31}$$

Combining these two conditions yields the 'PS' curve:

$$L_t = \left[\frac{\theta - \alpha}{r + \delta} \right]^{\theta - \alpha/1 - \theta} \left[\frac{w_t^f}{\alpha} \right]^{-1 + \alpha - \theta/1 - \theta}. \tag{5.32}$$

Conditional on this optimal level of L_t, the minimisation of the wage bill solves the following problem:

$$\min_{\{L_{ht}, L_{lt}\}} w_{ht}(1 + \tau_{ht})L_{ht} + w_{lt}(1 + \tau_{lt})L_{lt} \tag{5.33}$$

subject to $G_t \left[(A_{ht}L_{ht})^{\sigma - 1/\sigma} + (A_{lt}L_{lt})^{\sigma - 1/\sigma} \right]^{\sigma/\sigma - 1} \geq L_t \tag{5.34}$

The first-order conditions of this problem can be summarised as follows:

$$\frac{L_{ht}}{L_{lt}} = \left[\frac{(1 + \tau_{ht})w_{ht}}{(1 + \tau_{lt})w_{lt}} \right]^{-\sigma} \left(\frac{A_{ht}}{A_{lt}} \right)^{\sigma - 1}. \tag{5.35}$$

From (5.27), (5.29) and (5.35), it can be checked that w_t^f is a C.E.S. function of the two wage costs:

$$w_t^f = \frac{1}{G_t} \left\{ \left[\frac{(1+\tau_{ht})w_{ht}}{A_{ht}} \right]^{1-\sigma} + \left[\frac{(1+\tau_{lt})w_{lt}}{A_{lt}} \right]^{1-\sigma} \right\}^{\frac{1}{1-\sigma}}. \tag{5.36}$$

Assume that the current income of an employed worker is $B_t + (1 - s_{jt}) w_{jt}$, $j = h,l$, where $s_{jt} \geq 0$ and $B_t \geq 0$ are respectively the constant tax rate on earnings (SIC paid by employees and the income tax) and the real level of the basic income. There is assumed to be a union negotiating on behalf of the high-skilled workers. Leaving aside the bumping down or ladder effect,[18] in a steady state, there should be a relationship such as (5.20) defining the high-skilled unemployment rate.[19] Let us write this relationship in a compact way as:

$$B_t + (1-s_{ht})w_{ht} = Z_{ht} I_h(u_{ht}), I_h'(.) < 0, \tag{5.37}$$

where Z_{ht} is the unemployment benefit paid to a high-skilled worker and u_{ht} is the corresponding unemployment rate. As in the previous section, let us assume that in a steady state the level of unemployment benefits is indexed on net earnings. Assume also that the real level of the basic income is proportional to the net wage of high-skill workers. It will turn out later that the basic income is actually indexed on the wages of both types of workers. So,

$$Z_{ht} = z_h(1-s_{ht})w_{ht}, 0 < z_h < 1 \text{ and } B_t = b(1 - s_{ht})w_{ht}, 0 \leq b < 1 \tag{5.38}$$

This implies that the unemployment rate of the high-skilled is fixed by wage setting. Because, combining (5.37) and (5.38) yields:

$$u_{ht} = \Omega_h \left(\frac{z_h}{1+b} \right), \Omega_h'(.) > 0. \tag{5.39}$$

So, as far as high-skilled workers are concerned, we are in the setting of Layard et al. (1991).[20] A first departure from their perspective will be to assume that, even in the long run, the real (gross) wage of the low-skilled presents a form of rigidity. The assumption that the reservation wage of the low-skilled depends on the wage of the high-skilled could do the trick. As a shortcut, let there simply be a strict proportionality between gross wages:

$$w_{lt} = w_{ht}, 0 < \omega < 1. \tag{5.40}$$

In Continental Europe, this assumption is not broadly in accordance with historical trends (see Table 3.1 in OECD 1996, Table 8.3 in Drèze and Sneessens 1997; Gottschalk and Smeeding 1997). Given (5.40), expression

(5.35) can be rewritten as an equation defining the unemployment rate of the low-skill workers:

$$1 - u_{lt} = (1 - u_{ht}) \frac{N_{ht}}{N_{lt}} \left(\frac{A_{ht}}{A_{lt}} \right)^{1-\sigma} \left[\frac{1 + \tau_{ht}}{\omega(1 + \tau_{lt})} \right]^{\sigma}. \qquad (5.41)$$

In this expression, L_{jt} has been replaced by $N_{jt}(1-u_{jt})$, $j = l, h$, where N_{jt} designates the (exogenous) level of skill-j labour supply. Skilled-biased technical progress is defined as an exogenous change in the production function that increases the ratio L_{ht}/L_{lt} at the current wage cost level. Given (5.35), if $\sigma > 1$ (respectively, $\sigma < 1$), this occurs if A_{ht}/A_{lt} has an upward (respectively, downward) trend. According to Nickell and Bell (1997) and Gregg and Manning (1997), $\sigma > 1$ is a very plausible assumption. On the other hand, Manacorda and Petrongolo (1999) cannot reject the hypothesis that $\sigma = 1$. Henceforth, the maintained assumption is nevertheless $\sigma > 1$.

Equation (5.41) allows a comparison of the effects of a partial basic income and a cut in payroll taxes on the low-skill workers when labour supply is exogenous. Because wages are rigid at the low end of the labour market, cutting payroll taxes on the low-skilled has in the long run a favourable effect on their unemployment rate and no effect on the unemployment rate of the high-skilled workers.[21] The effectiveness of this policy depends on the magnitude of the elasticity of substitution σ. The partial basic income acts through a different channel. In the long run, it lowers the unemployment rate of the high-skilled workers and since the optimal mix of workers is governed by (5.35), the employment ratio is adjusted in such a way that the unemployment rate of the low-skilled improves as well.

Finally, the aggregate WS-PS equations determine the high-skill real wage rate w_{ht}. Equality (5.36) and assumption (5.40) imply that w_t^f is now simply:

$$w_t^f = \frac{w_{ht}}{G_t} \left\{ \left[\frac{(1 + \tau_{ht})}{A_{ht}} \right]^{1-\sigma} + \left[\frac{(1 + \tau_{lt})\omega}{A_{lt}} \right]^{1-\sigma} \right\}^{\frac{1}{1-\sigma}} \qquad (5.42)$$

Let us rewrite the aggregate employment level L_t as $N_t(1-u_t)$ with $N_t = N_{ht} + N_{lt}$ and $u_t = s_{ht}u_{ht} + s_{lt}u_{lt}$ ($s_{jt} = N_{jt}/N_t$). Given (5.42), the 'PS' curve (5.32) is now an upward-sloping relationship between w_{ht} and the aggregate unemployment rate u_t. By assumptions (5.38) and (5.40), the aggregate 'WS' curve is vertical. Combining (5.39) and (5.41) yields the following vertical 'WS' curve:

$$u_t = s_{ht}\Omega_h\left(\frac{z_h}{1+b}\right) + s_{lt}\left\{1 - \left[1 - \Omega_h\left(\frac{z_h}{1+b}\right)\right]\frac{N_{ht}}{N_{lt}}\left(\frac{A_{ht}}{A_{lt}}\right)^{1-\sigma}\left[\frac{1+\tau_{ht}}{\omega(1+\tau_{lt})}\right]^{\sigma}\right\} \quad (5.43)$$

As expected, neutral technical progress (G_t) does note influence the level of aggregate unemployment but it affects the real wage level. Yet, skill-biased technical progress affects the aggregate unemployment rate and the PS curve and, hence, wages. To sum up, if the supply of skills is exogenous, the plausible assumption of rigid relative (gross) wages implies that a reduction of social security contributions on the low skilled and a basic income have a long-run favourable effect on the low-skilled unemployment rate. This conclusion is not in contradiction with the second reported claim of Nickell and Bell (1997) that relies upon the (at least in Continental Europe) counterfactual assumption of relative wage flexibility.

A Model Where Labour Supply is Endogenous

The rate at which low-skill workers become trained and enter the high-skill group will not be treated in a structural way. As in Layard et al. (1991) and Gregg and Manning (1997), the rate at which low-skilled workers 'migrate' will be a reduced form of plausible (endogenous) current indicators.[22] In Layard et al. (1991), skill-specific labour supply is perfectly elastic in the long run. This happens because the second partial derivative of the following 'migration' function, H, is by assumption zero:

$$\frac{d}{dt}\left(\frac{N_{ht}}{N_{lt}}\right) = H\left(\Re, \frac{N_{ht}}{N_{lt}}\right), H_1 \geq 0, H_2 \leq 0, \quad (5.44)$$

where $\Re$ is a measure of net returns in case of migration, to be defined below. For Layard et al. (1991, ch. 6), since the partial derivative $H_2 = 0$, there is one and only one level of $\Re$ such that N_{ht}/N_{lt} is constant in the long run and any level of N_{ht}/N_{lt} can be observed for this equilibrium value of $\Re$. This is a restrictive assumption (see Gregg and Manning 1997). Therefore, a second departure from the Layard et al. (1991) approach will be to consider expression (5.44) with $H_2 < 0$. Therefore, in the long run, when N_{ht}/N_{lt}

reaches a steady state, there is an upward sloping relationship between N_{ht}/N_{lt} and $\Re$. Following Gregg and Manning (1997), this assumption is more plausible than the one of Layard et al. (1991). One interpretation could be that the group of low-skilled workers is actually heterogeneous as far as the cost of acquiring skill is concerned. Then, to increase the steady state N_{ht} /N_{lt} ratio, a higher net return $\Re$ is needed in order to compensate the cost of 'migration'. An ad hoc, yet plausible, specification of $\Re$ could be:

$$\Re = \Re\left[\frac{1-u_{ht}}{1-u_{lt}}, \frac{(1-s_{ht})w_{ht}}{(1-s_{lt})w_{lt}}\right], \Re_1 \geq 0, \Re_2 \geq 0. \tag{5.45}$$

Because it makes sense to assume that the incentive to acquire a high-skill level increases with the relative employment rate and the high- to low-skilled net earnings ratio. In the long run, when 'migration' vanishes, (5.44) and (5.45) lead to:

$$H\left\{\Re\left[\frac{1-u_{ht}}{1-u_{lt}}, \frac{(1-s_{ht})w_{ht}}{(1-s_{lt})w_{lt}}\right], \frac{N_{ht}}{N_{lt}}\right\} = 0. \tag{5.46}$$

It is convenient to assume an explicit form for (5.46) and more specifically a homogeneous function of degree one. So, in the long run, let

$$\frac{N_{ht}}{N_{lt}} = D\left(\frac{1-u_{ht}}{1-u_{lt}}\right)^{\rho}\left[\frac{(1-s_{ht})w_{ht}}{(1-s_{lt})w_{lt}}\right]^{1-\rho}, 0 \leq \rho \leq 1, \tag{5.47}$$

where D is a positive parameter. Still adopting a long-run perspective, we can now substitute (5.47) into (5.41). Remembering (5.40), this leads to the following long-run expression for u_{lt} when skill-specific labour supply is endogenous:

$$(1-u_{lt})^{1+\rho} = D(1-u_{ht})^{1+\rho}\left(\frac{1-s_{ht}}{1-s_{lt}}\right)^{1-\rho}\left(\frac{A_{ht}}{A_{lt}}\right)^{1-\sigma}\left(\frac{1+\tau_{ht}}{1+\tau_{lt}}\right)^{\sigma}\omega^{\rho-1-\sigma}, \tag{5.48}$$

with u_{ht} still defined by (5.39).[23] Expression (5.48) deserves the following comments. First, in the long run, skilled-biased technical progress requires an adjustment of ω (the indicator of real wage rigidity) and/or of the tax/allowance rates in order to stabilise the unemployment rate of the less-skilled. Put differently, the acquisition of skills is not a sufficient answer. Acting on wage-push factors (z_h, ω) is one available strategy that reduces the income of the low-skilled and/or the unemployed. Restructuring taxation on labour is an alternative that does no have these direct effects (yet, as we saw in Section 2, one should care about indirect effects through wage formation and adjustments in taxes). Clearly, without one type of adjustment or another, the unemployment rate among the less-skilled workers would in the long run tend to 1. This result is at odds with the first claim of Nickell and Bell (1997). It heavily relies on assumption (5.44) with $H_2 < 0$. Second, as far as this restructuring is concerned, it does matter which side of the market is taxed. Cutting payroll taxes on the low-skilled workers (that is lowering τ_{lt}) still has the effect emphasised when labour supply was exogenous. Changing taxes formally incident on workers influences the labour supply mix (through an impact on the acquisition of skills). As equation (5.48) shows, there is no reason to expect that these two approaches have the same effect on the unemployment rate of the low-skilled. By the way, it is worth noticing that reducing the tax rate formally incident on low-skilled workers, s_{lt}, has an unfavourable effect on their unemployment rate since this lowers the net return of acquiring skills. The opposite is true if s_{ht} is reduced. Loosely speaking, this illustrates that 'more progressive taxes' can have negative effects when the acquisition of skills is taken into account (on this issue, see also Andersen and Rasmussen 1997). Finally, the mechanism through which the partial basic income affects the unemployment rates is in essence the same whether labour supply is endogenous or not. From (5.41), it should be clear that the ratio $(1-u_{lt})/(1-u_{ht})$ is the same whatever the value of b. Therefore, the long-run labour supply mix given by (5.47) is not modified by b. This conclusion should obviously be reconsidered if the basic income is financed by a restructuring of the tax rates s_{jt} that modifies the ratio $(1-s_{ht})/(1-s_{lt})$.

5.4   CONCLUSION

Long periods of high unemployment and of large inequalities in the risk of unemployment are very detrimental as they are synonymous to wasted resources, they enhance poverty and they raise distributional problems. Therefore, reforms such as those studied in this chapter should be analysed from different viewpoints. Do they improve the allocation of resources? Do they contribute to income maintenance (that is do they contribute to keep each individual's income above a certain minimum)? Do they improve the distribution of wellbeing? Instead of raising the latter ex post question, it is sensible to raise a different ex ante question: do these reforms improve the way risks are borne by the socio-economic groups?

To such broad questions, this chapter has only given a partial answer. It has dealt with two possible reforms (cutting payroll taxes on the less-skilled and introducing a basic income) financed by taxes levied on salaried employment. It has focussed on general equilibrium steady-state effects in a sufficiently simple deterministic setting. The analysis was conducted for unionised and (strongly) regulated economies. Distributional problems could only be lightly touched on because the degree of agents' heterogeneity was very limited. Furthermore, the very diverse effects of the reforms on the informal economy have been ignored. This clearly points to the need for further research.

However, facing the sharp contrast between the recommendations of Drèze and Malinvaud (1994) and those of Nickell and Bell (1997), it was worth trying to clarify how reductions in social security contributions (RSSC) work in the 'wage setting-price setting' (WS-PS) model made popular by Layard et al. (1991). Since this model is one of the major references to deal with imperfect labour markets and is at the root of Nickell and Bell's pessimistic view on RSSC, this chapter has tried to develop a rigorous WS-PS model in order to scrutinise the reasons of this view. This examination has taken place with homogeneous labour and with two types of workers. It turns out that the pessimistic view of Nickell and Bell relies upon questionable assumptions at least if RSSC are not implemented accross-the-board but are instead appropriately non linear. More precisely, targetting RSSC on low-skilled workers or introducing a lump-sum cut in employers social security contributions has a long-run favourable effect on (less-skilled) unemployment. With two types of skills, this is true if relative real gross wages are rigid and if the supply of skills is not perfectly elastic in the long run. These are plausible assumptions, at least in Continental Europe. These non-linear RSSC cannot claim to solve the unemployment problem. However, if one agrees that biased-technical progress is a major trend, this chapter has argued that cutting payroll taxes on the less-skilled or in a lump-sum way is one, at least partial, response to this problem that does not worsen the position of low-wage groups.

The chapter had a second objective. It intended to discuss the performances of an alternative to RSSC, namely basic income schemes. In the WS-PS framework, without questioning unions' bargaining power, it turns out that appropriately designed partial basic income schemes have interesting long-run effects on (less-skilled) unemployment. This conclusion hinges upon the assumption that unions do not care about their members' net earnings but do about their net incomes. Put differently, they accept that real wages decrease as the level of the basic income rises.

This chapter has also shown that an analysis that focuses on the unemployment rate is very incomplete, because the reforms considered here induce adjustments in wages. Furthermore, the reduction in unemployment is insufficient to cover the additional costs generated by the reforms. Hence, an increase in marginal tax rates seems unavoidable. This chapter has therefore developed an analysis of the impact of these reforms on the utility levels and on profits. In this respect, the distinction between instantaneous and inter-temporal effects turns out to be important in some cases. For instance, if unemployment benefits are proportional to net earnings, a basic income can both raise the intertemporal utility of the unemployed and have very gloomy effects on their income in the very short run. Therefore, the precise design of these reforms crucially matters. This is also true as far as the degree of unconditionality is concerned. To avoid a trade-off between the utility of the inactive population and the active one, this chapter recommends to restrict the basic income to the labour force. This viewpoint has been developed under a set of assumptions. First, the distinction between the active and the inactive population is costlessly made. Second, before the introduction of the basic income, the inactive population is not eligible for a (means-tested) minimum income guarantee. Third, the informal productive activities that a fully unconditional basic income could promote have not been taken into account. Since it leaves the income of the unemployed unchanged at given wages, such an 'active citizen's income' can then be reinterpreted as a lump-sum allowance handed out to the employed. This policy clearly presents some similarity with the EITC. In an unreported numerical simulation, it has been shown that well-defined RSSC and active citizen's income schemes can have very similar properties. To broadly the same extent, they reduce the unemployment rate and raise both profits and the inter-temporal utility levels of each group without worsening the position of the unemployed in the very short run. Yet, the rise in marginal tax rates is always substantial. Although the models developed in this chapter have paid attention to the general equilibrium effects of these increases in taxes, more research is needed to deal with this issue in non competitive labour markets.

A final question needs to be raised. Do we really have good reasons to believe that the WS-PS model is the most appropriate framework to use? To generate persistent unemployment, it relies on efficiency wage stories or bargaining. Now, the former has been under attack (the so-called bonding critique) and authors like Frank and Malcomson (1994) and Booth (1997) have challenged the view that wage bargaining is really a sufficient condition for equilibrium unemployment to emerge. In the latter case, one clearly needs additional (often implicit) assumptions (such as the absence of two-tier contracts or the hypothesis that redundancy payments are not bargained over). This final question is a very large one. Even if it lies out of the scope of this chapter, there is no doubt that it is a priority at the research agenda of the economists.

NOTES

1. This research is part of two programmes supported by the Belgian government (Interuniversity Poles of Attraction Programmes PAI P4/01 and P4/32 financed by the Prime Minister's Office – Federal Office for Scientific, Technical and Cultural Affairs). Comments of Henri Sneessens, Etienne Wasmer and an anonymous referee are gratefully acknowledged.
2. Hiring or marginal employment subsidies are even more frequently observed. As they are only issued for newcomers, these subsidies improve the efficiency of a given expenditure. However, they introduce new and often neglected distortions. They generate substitution effects at the margin of the targeted groups. Moreover, they raise moral hazard problems such as internal displacement (that is simultaneous hiring and firing by the same firm to benefit from the subsidy) or fictitious recruitment (by transferring workers across firms). In addition, they do not tackle the problem of (skill-specific) job destruction. This and space limitation explain why this chapter does not consider these subsidies.
3. Similar results are found in the matching literature (see Chapter 8 of Pissarides 1990). However, in an overlapping-generations model, linear taxes can affect unemployment (see Daveri and Tabellini 1997).
4. For an analysis of the same type of policies in a general equilibrium search model see Pissarides (1990, Chapter 8) and Mortensen and Pissarides (1998).
5. Implicitly, there is an international financial market with perfect mobility. An alternative would be to consider savings and the interest rate as endogenous. However, the level of saving of a given individual would then be a function of his employment/unemployment status in the past. To avoid such a difficulty, Danthine and Donaldson (1990) have assumed that actuarially fair unemployment insurance contracts are available without transaction costs. At the optimum, risk-averse workers are then fully insured. So, their savings behaviour is independent of their past trajectory on the labour market. However, some ad hoc assumption is then needed to generate a genuine loss of utility when a worker loses his job. In this chapter that focuses on steady-state properties, the assumption of an exogenous interest rate seems preferable.
6. To simplify the notations, no subscript is added to designate a particular firm.
7. The case with constant returns-to-scale is developed in Van der Linden (1999a and b).
8. Van der Linden (1999a) introduces an extension where M and N become endogenous.
9. In a model with homogeneous workers, E_t captures the Drèze, Malinvaud et al. (1994) proposal.
10. Hence, s_t captures both the SIC paid by the employees and the income tax.
11. The latter paper deals with the dynamic properties of the model, that are not considered here.
12. This condition is always fulfilled if $\psi = 1$. Otherwise, this inequality imposes an upper-bound on γ.
13. Although Figure 2.2 in OECD (1996) uses the pre-tax level of benefits divided by gross wages, this figure offers some support to this assumption.

14. In actual economies where marginal income taxes are increasing, combining a basic income and a flat tax (Atkinson 1995a) would therefore not be the best thing to do. See however the discussion in Andersen and Rasmussen (1997).
15. A formal proof is provided in Van der Linden (1999b).
16. Hence, this chapter does not raise the interesting question whether some broadening of the tax base can be implemented.
17. Available from the author on request and reproduced in Van der Linden (1999c)
18. This phenomenon is essentially a cyclical one. Ignoring it is not a major shortcoming since this chapter focuses on long-run effects.
19. A more rigorous treatment should take into account the fact that the elasticity of labour demand depends on the wage cost of the two types of workers.
20. The function Ω_h varies with the progressivity parameter ζ, which is here equal to $(1 + b)^{-1}$. In the compact notation used in (5.39) this relationship is implicit.
21. The last assertion should be revised in an extended setting where the outcome of the bargaining process is influenced by the fact that the elasticity of labour demand depends on the wage cost of the two types of workers.
22. This specification is linked to the cobweb model of labour supply.
23. Notice that (5.48) does not guarantee that $0 \leq u_{lt} < 1$. To satisfy these conditions, appropriate constraints need to be imposed on D.

REFERENCES

Andersen, T. and B. Rasmussen (1997), *Effort, Taxation and Unemployment*, Working Paper 11, Department of Economics, University of Aarhus, Denmark.

Atkinson, A. (1995a), *Public Economics in Action: The basic income/flat tax proposal*, Oxford University Press, Oxford.

Atkinson, A. (1995b), 'Beveridge, the National Minimum and its Future in a European Context', in A. Atkinson (ed.), *Incomes and the Welfare State*, Cambridge University Press, Cambridge.

Booth, A. (1997), 'An Analysis of Firing Costs and their Implications for Unemployment Policy', in D. Snower and G. de la Dehesa (eds), *Unemployment Policy: Government options for the labour market*, Cambridge University Press, Cambridge.

Bowles, S. (1992), 'Is Income Security Possible in a Capitalist Economy? An Agency-Theoretic Analysis of an Unconditional Income Grant', *European Journal of Political Economy*, **8**, 557–78.

Cahuc, P. and A. Zylberberg (1996), *Economie du travail: la formation des salaires et les déterminants du chômage*, De Boeck-Université, Paris et Bruxelles.

Cahuc, P. and A. Zylberberg (1999), 'Le modèle WS-PS', Annales d'Economie et de Statistique, 53, 1–30.

Daveri, F. and G. Tabellini (1997), *Unemployment, Growth and Taxation in Industrial Countries*, CEPR Discussion Paper No. 1681, Centre for Economic Policy Research, London.

Danthine, J. and J. Donaldson (1990), 'Efficiency Wages and the Business Cycle Puzzle', *European Economic Review*, **34**, 1275–301.

Drèze, J. (1993), 'Can Varying Social Insurance Contributions Improve Labour Market Efficiency?', in A. Atkinson (ed.), *Alternative to Capitalism: The Economics of Partnership*, Macmillan, London.

Drèze, J. and C. Gollier (1993), 'Risk Sharing on the Labour Market and Second-Best Wage Rigidities', *European Economic Review*, **37**, 1457–82.

Drèze, J., E. Malinvaud et al. (1994), 'Growth and Employment, the Scope for a European Initiative', *European Economy*, **1**, 75–106.

Drèze, J. and H. Sneessens (1997), 'Technological Development, Competition from Low-Wage Economies and Low-Skilled Unemployment', in D. Snower and G. de la Dehesa (eds), *Unemployment Policy: Government Options for the Labour Market*, Cambridge University Press, Cambridge.

Frank, J. and J. Malcomson (1994), 'Trade Unions and Seniority Employment Rule', *European Economic Review*, **38**, 1595–611.

Gregg, P. and A. Manning (1997), 'Skill-Biased Change, Unemployment and Wage Inequality', *European Economic Review*, **41**, 1173–200.

Gottschalk, P. and T. Smeeding (1997), 'Cross-National Comparisons of Earnings and Income Inequality', *Journal of Economic Literature*, **35** (2), 633–87.

Groot, L. and H. Peeters (1997), 'A Model of Conditional and Unconditional Social Security in an Efficiency Wage Economy: The Economic Sustainability of a Basic Income', *Journal of Post-Keynesian Economics*, **19**, 573–97.

Gruber, J. (1997), 'The Incidence of Payroll Taxation: Evidence from Chile', *Journal of Labor Economics*, **15**, S72–101.

Holmlund, B. and A.-S. Kolm (1995), Progressive Taxation, Wage Setting, and Unemployment: Theory and Swedish Evidence, Tax Reform Evaluation Report No. 15, August, National Institute of Economic Research, Economic Council, Stockholm and *Swedish Economic Policy Review*, **2** (2), Autumn, 423–60.

Késenne, S. (1993), *The Unemployment Impact of a Basic Income*, Report 93/286, Studiecentrum voor Economisch en Sociaal Onderzoek, Universitaire Faculteiten Sint-Ignatius, Antwerp, Belgium.

Koskela, E. and R. Schöb (1999), 'Does the Composition of Wage and Payroll Taxes Matter under Nash Bargaining?', *Economics Letters*, **64**, 343–9.

Lange, O. (1936), 'On the Economic Theory of Socialism: Part 1', *Review of Economic Studies*, **4**, 53–71.

Layard, R., S. Nickell and R. Jackman (1991), *Unemployment: Macroeconomic Performance and the Labour Market*, Oxford University Press, Oxford.

Lockwood, B. and A. Manning (1993), 'Wage Setting and the Tax System: Theory and Evidence for the United Kingdom', *Journal of Public Economics*, **52**, 1–29.

Lehmann, E. (1999), *Replacing Unemployment Benefits by Basic Income: A numerical evaluation in a matching wage bargaining model with heterogeneous skills*, Paper presented at the 11th Annual Conference of the European Association of Labour Economists, Regensburg, Germany, 23–26 September.

Manacorda, M. and B. Petrongolo (1999), 'Skill Mismatch and Unemployment in OECD Countries', *Economica*, **66**, 181–208.

Manning, A. (1993), 'Wage Bargaining and the Uppercase Phillips Curve: The Identification and Specification of Aggregate Wage Equations', *The Economic Journal*, **103**, 98–118.

Meade, J. (1989), *Agathotopia: The economics of Partnership*, Aberdeen University Press, Aberdeen.

Mortensen, D.T. and C.A. Pissarides (1998), Taxes, Subsidies and Equilibrium Labor Market Outcomes, mimeo, North-western University and London School of Economics.

Nickell, S. and B. Bell (1997), 'Would Cutting Payroll Taxes on the Unskilled have a Significant Impact on Unemployment?' in D. Snower and G. de la Dehesa (eds),

Unemployment Policy: Government Options for the Labour Market, Cambridge
University Press, Cambridge.

OECD (1996), *Employment Outlook*, OECD, Paris.

Picard, P. and E. Toulemonde (1999), *On the Equivalence of Taxes Paid by
Employers and Employees*, Cahiers de la Faculté des Sciences Economiques,
sociales et de gestion, Série recherche, N°215-1999/5, Facultés Universitaires de
Namur, Belgium.

Pissarides, C.A. (1990), *Equilibrium Unemployment Theory*, Basil Blackwell, Oxford.

Pissarides, C.A. (1998), 'The Impact of Employment Tax Cuts on Unemployment and
Wages: The role of unemployment benefits and tax structure', *European
Economic Review*, **42**, 155–83.

Rasmussen, B. (1994), *Wage Formation, the Structure of Labour Taxation and
Welfare*, Centre for Labour Market and Social Research, Institute of Economics,
University of Aarhus, Denmark.

Van der Linden, B. (1999a), *Active Citizen's Income, Unconditional Income and
Participation under Imperfect Competition: A Normative Analysis*, Discussion
Paper No. 9923, Institut de Recherches Economiques et Sociales, Université
Catholique de Louvain, Belgium.

Van der Linden, B. (1999b), *Is Basic Income a Cure for Unemployment in Unionised
Economies? A General Equilibrium Analysis*, Document de Travail No. 49,
Chaire Hoover d'Ethique Economique et Sociale, Université Catholique de
Louvain, Belgium.

Van der Linden, B. (1999c), *Fighting Unemployment without Worsening Poverty:
Basic Income versus Reductions of Social Security Contributions*, Discussion
paper No. 9928, Institut de Recherches Economiques et Sociales, Université
Catholique de Louvain, Belgium.

Van Parijs, Ph. (with Laurence Jacquet and Claudio Salinas) (1998), 'Basic Income
and its Cognates', Document de travail 46, Chaire d'Ethique Economique et
Sociale de l'Université Catholique de Louvain, forthcoming, in L. Groot and R.J.
van der Veen (eds), *Basic Income on the Agenda. Policies and Politics*,
Amsterdam University Press, 2000.

PART TWO

Long-Run Policy Issues of Low Pay

6. Competitive and Segmented Labour Markets and Exclusion from Retirement Income

Gerard Hughes and Brian Nolan[1]

6.1   INTRODUCTION

Interest in the causes and consequences of low pay is, understandably, primarily focused on the mechanisms which bring about social exclusion and their immediate effects on inequality and poverty. There are, however, lifetime consequences of employment in low-paying jobs which result in exclusion of certain categories of employees from employer-provided occupational pension schemes. The effects of this exclusion will not be felt by individuals in these groups until it is impossible, or too late, for them to make their own pension arrangements. In these circumstances a significant minority of employees who work in low-paid jobs may be almost totally dependent on the State for an income during old age. If the social exclusion which many of them suffer during their working lifetime is not to continue into old age it is critical that the State should put in place arrangements, either in its own pension schemes or through private schemes, which will provide an adequate income for the elderly.

A strong commitment to social solidarity, high fertility rates and long-term economic growth over the last half century or so have ensured that most states in Europe developed pension systems which resulted in dramatic reductions in poverty among the elderly in the two decades after World War II. Despite some economic and social difficulties in the 1970s and 1980s most governments in Europe have continued to emphasise the importance of social solidarity and the need for the elderly to share in the benefits of continuing economic growth. Now circumstances are beginning to change. Fertility rates are falling, Europe's population is projected to age significantly in the next twenty years or so and the commitment to social solidarity is threatened by conservative ideologies which prescribe a very limited role for the State. If action is not taken soon to address the ageing problem there is a distinct possibility that population ageing and reductions in social security benefits could lead to the re-emergence of poverty rates in Europe and the United States among the elderly which have not been seen for a generation or more (see Delhausse et al. 1996). Even in countries like Ireland where the demographic profile of the population is more favourable than in other countries, there is a possibility of an increase in poverty among the elderly. The Economic and Social Research Institute (ESRI) survey of poverty in the 1990s by Callan et al. (1996) shows that an increasing proportion of households headed by a pensioner are living in poverty. The main reason for this is that State pension benefits have not been indexed in line with increases in earnings in recent years.

Economists often treat pensions as a form of deferred pay. However, it is clear from surveys of pension coverage that there are certain groups of employees who are far less likely than other groups to benefit from deferred pay arrangements. It is also clear that there is a very strong interaction between pay during the working lifetime and membership of an occupational pension scheme. Since belonging or not belonging to such a scheme will ultimately decide eligibility for an occupational pension it is necessary to investigate what factors determine pension entitlement.

There are two main theories of pay determination which claim to explain the interaction between present and deferred pay. The theory of compensating pay differentials suggests that employees with a preference for future over present consumption can trade off lower wages now in return for deferred pay in the form of a pension in the future. By contrast, the theory of segmented labour markets suggests that differences in rates of time preference have limited influence on membership of occupational pension schemes because employees are constrained in the exercise of their preferences by the structural characteristics of the industry in which they work and its employment practices. Segmentation theory predicts that it is the kind of jobs which employers offer that will determine membership of occupational pension schemes.

Competitive labour market theory suggests that in the first case work force characteristics (supply-side variables) will be important determinants of whether employees belong to occupational pension schemes. Segmented labour market theory suggests that in the second case demand side variables such as industry, duration of employment, type of employment (full-time/part-time), degree of unionisation, sex composition of the work force and size of employer are likely to be the important determinants of pension entitlement (see Ghilarducci 1992, 59–60). Elliott (1991, 313) points out that the competitive theory of pension provision implies that 'the employer's only concern is with the level, not the composition, of compensation'. Employees who wish to join an occupational pension scheme will finance it by contributing part of their current pay towards the cost of a future pension. The competitive theory, therefore, suggests that wages and pensions are substitutes and that the coefficient of a pension entitlement variable in a wage equation ought to be negative.

Ghilarducci (1992, 59–60) notes that under segmented labour market theory firms in sectors with the worst jobs (typified by high turnover, low pay and atypical employment) do not compensate for poor terms and conditions of employment by providing generous pension plans while firms in sectors with the best jobs (typified by low turnover, high pay and permanent employment) attract workers by providing good terms and conditions of employment which include generous pension plans. Pension coverage will therefore be strongly influenced by industry of employment. Where labour markets are segmented pension entitlement will be poorest in sectors offering the worst jobs. Segmented labour market theory, therefore, suggests that pensions and wages are complements and that the coefficient of a pension entitlement variable will depend on the sector in which someone is employed.

Our objective in this chapter is to investigate which of the main theories of pay determination best explain membership of occupational pension schemes. We will begin by describing our data and will present a series of cross tabulations of pension coverage (which we also refer to as pension entitlement) on age, sex, occupation, industry and earnings. Next, we will outline our tests of competitive and dual labour market models and of a four-sector segmentation model which we have adapted for work with Irish data. Finally, we will consider some of the implications of our results for the development of the Irish pension system in the light of the recent report by the Pensions Board (1998) on *Securing Retirement Income*. This report proposes a framework for the future development of pension provision in Ireland. If its proposals are implemented in full it will represent a fundamental reform of the existing approach to pension provision.

6.2   PENSION COVERAGE

The *Living in Ireland Survey*, the Irish element of the European Community Household Panel survey, provides data for Ireland for 1994 which enables us to explore the extent to which competitive and segmented labour market hypotheses can account for individual pension entitlement. The survey provides data for 4048 households. The response rate for the survey was 62.5 per cent. The responding households were reweighted for analysis to correct for non-response bias. The reweighting ensures that the sample for analysis broadly agrees with the Labour Force Survey in terms of the number of adults in the household, urban/rural location, socio-economic group and age of household head. The sample households contained 3300 employees for whom information is available on pension entitlements and personal and employment characteristics.

Table 6.1 shows the age distribution of employees with a pension entitlement in 1995 classified by age and sex. Just over half of all employees have a pension entitlement and this is positively related to age. Less than

Table 6.1
Employees with pension entitlement by age and sex, 1994

Age	With pension entitlement (%)		
	All	Men	Women
Under 25	16.8	13.6	20.4
25–34	52.1	53.9	50.0
35–44	64.6	74.4	47.3
45–54	64.2	79.2	37.1
55–64	63.7	75.6	42.1
65+	13.5	30.6	0.0
All	51.0	58.7	39.8

Source: Living in Ireland Survey 1994.

one-fifth of those aged under 25 were covered by a pension scheme. The proportion covered increases to over half for the age cohort 25–34 and to two-thirds for those aged 35–44. It stabilises at this level for the remaining cohorts in the working ages 45–54 and 55–64 and falls to about one-seventh for those aged 65 and over who continue to work after normal retirement age. There are significant differences in the pattern of coverage for men and women. Almost three-fifths of men have a pension entitlement while less than two-fifths of women have. Entitlement for both men and women increases from a low level for the youngest age cohort to around 50 per cent for the cohort aged 25–34. It increases to around 75 per cent for men but falls back to around 40 per cent for women for the remaining working age cohorts.

The percentage of employees with a pension entitlement classified by major occupational group is shown in Table 6.2. There are significant differences in entitlement by occupational group. Agricultural and sales workers have very low pension coverage with only 20 and 27 per cent respectively belonging to a pension scheme. Producers and transport and communication workers have moderate coverage ranging from 44 to 50 per cent. Professional workers have good coverage with almost 70 per cent having a pension entitlement.

Table 6.2
Employees with pension entitlement by occupation, 1994

Occupational group	With pension entitlement (%)
Agricultural workers	20.1
Producers etc.	44.2
Labourers	43.4
Transport and communication workers	50.2
Clerical workers	57.1
Sales workers	27.5
Service workers	33.3
Professional workers etc.	69.6
Others	85.7
All	51.0

Source: Living in Ireland Survey 1994.

Table 6.3
Employees with pension entitlement by sector, 1994

Sector	With pension entitlement (%)
Agriculture	16.3
Building	46.6
Other production	47.3
Wholesale	37.2
Retail	17.0
Insurance, finance and business services	70.1
Transport, communication and storage	71.1
Professional services	39.8
Teaching etc.	76.0
Health	60.9
Public administration	94.2
Personal services	9.2
Others	31.1
All	51.0

Source: Living in Ireland Survey 1994.

Coverage classified by the major industrial sector in which the employee is working is shown in Table 6.3. There is considerable variation in coverage by industry. The lowest coverage rates are in personal services, agriculture and retail services where only 9, 16 and 17 per cent of employees respectively have a pension entitlement. Moderate coverage is provided in the building and other production sectors where approaching half of the employees have a pension entitlement. The highest coverage occurs in the public administration sector with almost 95 per cent of employees belonging to a pension plan.

The percentage of employees in each decile of the earnings distribution who are covered by a pension scheme is shown in Table 6.4. There is a very strong positive relationship between the percentage covered in each decile and the level of earnings. Employees in the bottom two deciles of the earnings distribution have virtually no pension entitlement while virtually all of those in the top two deciles have such an entitlement. In the remaining six deciles the percentage of employees with a pension entitlement increases steadily with earnings from 20 per cent for those in the third decile to almost 78 per cent for those in the eighth decile.

Table 6.4

Employees ranked by hourly gross earnings showing the percentage with pension entitlements by deciles, 1994

Decile	With pension entitlement (%)
First	3.2
Second	6.7
Third	20.3
Fourth	41.4
Fifth	51.6
Sixth	57.7
Seventh	72.4
Eight	77.8
Ninth	88.9
Tenth	88.7

Source: Living in Ireland Survey 1994.

The variations in employees' pension entitlements classified by age, sex, occupation, industry and level of earnings are striking. Are these variations the product of differences in the age composition of the labour force across occupations and sectors or are the variations produced by differences in industrial sector with pension entitlement determined by industry of employment? A multivariate approach in which the effects of these and other factors on pension entitlement are allowed for is needed to identify the influence of employee preferences associated with the competitive model and job characteristics associated with the segmented labour market model (see Piore 1970; and Doeringer and Piore 1971).

6.3 TESTS OF COMPETITIVE AND DUAL SEGMENTATION MODELS

In testing competitive and segmented labour market models of pension entitlement we will follow the approach used in our earlier work on earnings (Hughes and Nolan 1997) and pensions (Hughes and Nolan 1996). We begin by testing the relationship between earnings and pension entitlement. We estimate regression models for our sample of employees which include variables that are key determinants of earnings according to competitive and segmentation theories. In these regressions the dependent variable is the log of average gross hourly earnings of employees. The independent variables are those suggested by competitive and segmented models to be important determinants of earnings: age, sex, marital status, education, occupation, industry, type of employment (part-time/full-time) and trade union membership. We also include a pension entitlement variable to test whether earnings and pension entitlement are postively related, as the segmentation theory suggests, or negatively related, as the competitive theory predicts.

We recognise that the test of the competitive theory is an imperfect one. Ideally we would like to test whether the total compensation packages which employers offer to workers of equal productivity are equalised over the working lifetime. The most straightforward way to test this would be to use Schiller and Weiss's (1980) approach in which the wage rate in the standard earnings function:

$$\log W = a + bX$$

is replaced by total compensation $(W + P)$, where W is the wage rate, X is a vector of productive characteristics and P is the value of the occupational pension. Making the substitution and rearranging gives:

$$\log W = a + bX - c \log (1 + p)$$

where $p = P/W$ is the ratio of the value of the occupational pension contribution to the wage. If wages and pensions are perfect substitutes, as predicted by the competitive theory, the elasticity of the wage with respect to the pension wage ratio should be equal to -1. Unfortunately, our data set does not provide any information on the value of each employee's occupational entitlement. In the absence of such data our strategy is to use a set of control variables which are believed to affect the lifetime values of both pay and pension entitlement and to insert a dichotomous variable for pension coverage. The competitive theory predicts that the coefficient on the pension coverage variable should be negative because members of pension schemes who receive the same total compensation and who have the same personal characteristics as employees who are not members should have lower earnings. Segmentation theory predicts that the coefficient of the pension coverage variable will be positive because employees in good, well-paid, jobs will be more likely to be members of occupational pension schemes than employees in poor, badly paid, jobs.

Table 6.5
Allocation of occupational and industrial groups to primary and secondary labour market segments

Primary sector	Secondary sector
Occupational group	
Producers, Makers and Repairers	Agricultural
Transport, Communications and Storage	Labourers
Clerical	Sales
Professional and Technical	Service
Other occupations	
Industrial group	
Other production	Agriculture
Insurance	Building and Construction
Transport	Wholesale
Professional service	Retail
Teaching	Personal service
Health	Other industries
Public administration	

Following our earlier work we first test a basic dual version of the segmentation model rather crudely, by dividing major industry groups into those which would generally be thought of as in the primary sector versus the secondary sector. The relevant allocation is shown in Table 6.5 and in the 1994 survey this would categorise 34 per cent of employees as in the secondary sector. According to the dual version of segmented labour market theory the primary and secondary sectors should differ in terms of the sex composition of the work force, unionisation, the proportion working part-time, the provision of fringe benefits such as pensions, the existence of earnings ladders and the duration of employment. Table 6.6 shows that the secondary sector does have significantly higher proportions of part-time employees and lower proportions of trade union members than the primary sector (though not many more female employees). It also has fewer with a pension entitlement. Evidence from a similar survey carried out by the ESRI in 1987 reported in Hughes and Nolan (1996) also showed the secondary sector (defined in this way) to have fewer employees on incremental scales than the primary sector, as well as considerably less stability of employment (with an average length of job of only five years compared with more than eight years in the primary sector).

Hence, our rough division of occupations and industries into primary and secondary sectors looks to be consistent with segmentation arguments that the primary sector offers employees more stable. jobs with good conditions and terms of employment while the secondary sector offers employees more precarious employment with few fringe benefits and limited opportunities for advancement up the earnings ladder.

Table 6.6
Characteristics of primary and secondary labour markets, 1987

Sector	Female	Union members	Part-time	With pension entitlement	On incre-mental scale	Average length of job
	%	%	%	%	%	years
Primary	35.2	62.1	2.6	58.9	42.8	8.5
Secondary	40.9	19.3	7.9	18.5	18.5	5.3

Source: ESRI Survey 1987.

Table 6.7 presents three earnings equations for all employees in the 1994 *Living in Ireland Survey*. Equation (1) explains almost two-thirds of the variation in employees′ average gross hourly earnings. The number of years an employee has been employed has the expected positive effect on earnings although it decreases as the number of years employed increases. Time spent out of employment has the expected negative effect on earnings with the effect declining as the number of years out of employment increases. Being female reduces earnings relative to being male while for both sexes being married increases earnings relative to being single.

The omitted occupation and industry variables are 'labourer' and 'other production'. It will be seen from Table 6.5 that labouring occupations are allocated to the secondary sector and that other production industries are allocated to the primary sector. Hence, earnings in primary sector occupations should be higher relative to the omitted occupation variable while earnings in secondary sector industries should be lower relative to those in the other production sector. These hypotheses are generally borne out by our regression results. Earnings in the primary sector occupation groups – producer, clerical, professional and other occupations – are higher relative to labouring occupations. In addition, the higher coefficients of the professional and other occupation groups conform with prior expectations about the relationships between earnings for these occupations and such occupations as clerical and sales which generally require lower level educational qualifications. The coefficients of the industry variables in equation (1) also generally accord with expectations generated by the

Table 6.7
OLS regression earnings level on pension entitlement and other variables

Variable	Equation					
	(1)		(2)		(3)	
Constant	1.14	(32.66)	0.94	(22.90)	−0.81	(0.98)
Age					0.05	(11.93)
Age^2					−0.01	(9.56)
Years employed	0.03	(12.20)	0.03	(15.03)		
Years employed^2	−0.05	(9.62)	−0.05	(10.44)		
Years out of employment	−0.02	(4.61)	−0.01	(2.29)		
Years out of employment^2	0.04	(9.62)	0.02	(2.06)		
Female	−0.07	(3.42)	−0.08	(3.64)	−0.06	(2.94)
Married man	0.17	(7.41)	0.14	(6.68)	0.17	(7.06)
Married woman	0.09	(3.71)	0.07	(3.10)	0.06	(2.28)
Group certificate			0.06	(2.07)	0.14	(4.60)
Intermediate certificate			0.13	(4.57)	0.23	(7.71)
Leaving certificate			0.22	(7.70)	0.37	(12.99)
Diploma/third level			0.26	(7.97)	0.45	(13.74
University degree			0.57	(15.70)	0.92	(29.77)
Occupational Group:						
Agricultural worker	0.08	(1.92)	−0.21	(3.23)		
Producer etc.	0.11	(3.35)	0.10	(3.06)		
Transport etc.	0.02	(0.51)	0.01	(0.21)		
Clerical	0.27	(7.23)	0.18	(4.91)		
Sales	0.13	(3.00)	0.04	(1.06)		
Service	0.08	(1.92)	0.02	(0.46)		
Professional workers etc.	0.56	(14.67)	0.32	(8.21)		
Other	0.49	(11.73)	0.34	(8.24)		
Industrial Sector:						
Agriculture	−0.38	(6.12)	−0.37	(6.19)		
Building	−0.11	(3.74)	−0.09	(2.96)		
Wholesale	−0.07	(2.13)	−0.04	(1.20)		
Retail	−0.24	(7.01)	−0.20	(5.90)		
Insurance	0.09	(2.77)	0.09	(2.63)		
Transport	−0.03	(0.89)	−0.03	(0.97)		
Professional	−0.14	(2.18)	−0.20	(3.26)		
Teaching	0.31	(9.37)	0.18	(5.45)		
Health	−0.10	(3.30)	−0.06	(1.94)		
Public administration	−0.13	(4.41)	−0.11	(3.80)		
Personal service	−0.29	(8.59)	−0.24	(7.33)		
Other	−0.11	(3.38)	−0.10	(3.11)		
Trade union member	0.12	(7.67)	0.14	(9.17)	0.18	(11.05)
Part-time	0.13	(4.32)	0.13	(4.62)	0.01	(0.36)
Pension entitlement	0.27	(15.12)	0.24	(14.02)	0.34	(19.01)

Variable	Equation		
	(1)	(2)	(3)
Number of observations	3,288	3,270	3,270
Adjusted R^2	0.65	0.68	0.59
F	200.89	197.81	367.60
Std. Error of regression	0.37	0.35	0.39

Note: control group is: male, no formal education qualifications, labourer and other production.

Source: See text.

segmented model. Earnings in agriculture, building, wholesale, retail, personal service and other industries, which are in the secondary sector, are lower than in the omitted other production sector. Being a trade union member increases earnings and being part-time also does so. The latter result is somewhat surprising as we expected the association between earnings and part-time employment to be negative. Finally, having a pension entitlement is positively related to the level of earnings – the higher an employee's earnings the more likely that he or she will have a pension entitlement. This suggests that earnings and pensions are complements, as the segmented model predicts, rather than substitutes, as the competitive model suggests.

Equation (2) in Table 6.7 examines the effect on our results of including education variables which human capital theory predicts will have a strong effect in explaining variation in earnings. The omitted variable in this case is 'no formal educational qualifications'. As human capital theory predicts, an increase in the level of education has a strong positive influence on earnings. Thus, employees with low level educational qualifications have higher earnings than those who have no qualifications while those with high level qualifications have the highest level of earnings relative to those without qualifications. The inclusion of the education variables improves the performance of the regression. It increases the variation in earnings explained from 65 to 68 per cent. Their impact on the coefficients of the other variables is noticeable but relatively minor in most cases. In the case of the pension entitlement variable, for example, the coefficient is reduced from 0.27 to 0.24 but it remains highly significant, as indicated by its t-value.

Equation (3) shows what happens if the occupation and industry variables are omitted from the regression. The percentage of the variance explained falls from 68 to 59 per cent so that the overall performance of the regression deteriorates. In addition the coefficient of the part-time variable becomes insignificant while the coefficents and significance of the trade union and pension entitlement variables increase. Thus, these variables 'pick up' some of the explanatory power associated with the excluded segmentation variables.

6.4   PENSION ENTITLEMENT AND LABOUR MARKET SEGMENTATION

Our regression results suggest that further consideration should be given to the segmentation model's arguments about pension entitlement. In this section we will consider the explanatory power of these arguments by directly testing the relationship between pension entitlement and dual and multi-segment versions of the segmentation model. The crucial issue in testing the segmentation model is how to allocate individuals to primary versus secondary sector, as Hughes and Nolan (1997) note. There is a danger that the allocation procedure can bias the results in favour of the segmentation hypothesis. Heckman and Hotz (1986) deal with the problem by doing the allocation on the basis of the observed wage and correcting for sample selection bias, Dickens and Lang (1985) deal with it by using a switching regression model and Gordon (1986) deals with it by doing the allocation on the basis of job characteristics. Since the first two approaches allocate workers on the basis of the wage or individual characteristics whereas the core idea is that it is job rather than individual characteristics that matter, we favour the third approach since it has the potential to link hypothesis testing to an underlying theoretical perspective. We begin by testing the two-sector version of the model in this section. Table 6.8 presents the results of three logit regressions of the probability of having a pension entitlement. The dependent variable in these regressions is the dichotomy 'has/has not a pension entitlement'. It takes a value of 1 for those who have an entitlement and 0 for those who do not. The independent variables are generally the same as those included in the earnings equations in Table 6.7.

In equation (1) in Table 6.8 pension entitlement is strongly associated with increasing age. The probability of having a pension entitlement rises with age but at a decreasing rate as the stock of employees who need to make such arrangements falls. While the coefficient on the female variable is negative it is not significantly different from zero. This contrasts with our earlier finding that being female did result in a lower probability of having a pension entitlement, as suggested by the segmentation model (see Hughes and Nolan 1996). Being married and female results in a lower pension entitlement whereas being married and male leads to a higher entitlement. These results accord with our expectation that marital status should have a different effect for men and women. The primary sector occupation variables have the expected signs relative to the omitted group 'labourers'. Relatively, earnings are higher in clerical, professional and other occupations or are not significantly different from the control group in the case of producer and transport occupations. Similarly, the coefficients of the industry groups agriculture, retailing, personal service and other industries in the secondary

Table 6.8
Estimates of logit model for probability of having pension entitlement

Variable	Equation					
	(1)		(2)		(3)	
Constant	−6.14	(10.01)		(10.83)	−5.89	(16.12)
Age	0.21	(6.83)	0.10	(2.75)		
Age^2	−0.01	(5.75)	−0.01	(2.25)		
Years employed					0.08	(4.25)
Years employed^2					−0.10	(2.55)
Years out of employment					−0.12	(4.04)
Years out of employment^2					0.37	(2.98)
Female	−0.14	(0.84)	0.15	(0.84)	0.19	(1.07)
Married man	0.88	(5.48)	0.44	(2.55)	0.31	(1.79)
Married woman	−0.61	(3.64)	−0.57	(0.19)	−0.35	(1.83)
Occupational Group:						
Agricultural worker	0.60	(1.07)	0.49	(0.81)	0.44	(0.71)
Producer etc.	−0.09	(0.36)	−0.46	(1.93)	−0.55	(2.26)
Transport workers etc.	−0.44	(1.50)	−0.54	(2.45)	−0.65	(2.15)
Clerical worker	1.09	(3.97)	0.33	(1.13)	−0.24	(0.83)
Sales worker	0.57	(1.87)	0.19	(0.59)	0.10	(0.33)
Service worker	0.08	(0.26)	0.02	(0.08)	0.02	(0.06)
Professional workers etc.	1.54	(5.61)	0.02	(0.08)	0.01	(0.04)
Other	1.74	(5.38)	0.27	(0.77)	0.19	(0.53)
Industrial Sector:						
Agriculture	−1.87	(3.60)	−1.19	(2.13)	−1.28	(2.26)
Building	0.29	(1.41)	0.46	(2.14)	0.43	(1.96)
Wholesale	−0.20	(0.87)	−0.11	(0.45)	−0.15	(0.62)
Retail	−0.90	(3.45)	−0.38	(1.37)	−0.51	(1.81)
Insurance	0.79	(3.45)	0.62	(2.44)	0.62	(2.40)
Transport	0.71	(3.21)	0.73	(3.08)	0.72	(3.00)
Professional	−0.37	(0.87)	−0.11	(0.23)	−0.16	(0.31)
Teaching	0.38	(1.60)	−0.19	(0.73)	−0.14	(0.52)
Health	0.58	(2.76)	0.93	(3.91)	0.95	(3.90)
Public administration	2.28	(7.50)	2.95	(8.19)	2.92	(8.02)
Personal service	−1.36	(4.52)	−0.82	(2.48)	−0.85	(2.57)
Other	−0.75	(3.27)	−0.48	(1.94)	−0.54	(2.19)
Trade union member	1.99	(18.84)	1.53	(13.39)	1.50	(12.92)
Part-time			−4.53	(9.56)	−4.54	(9.43)
Hourly earnings			2.57	(15.15)	2.44	(14.29)
Number of observations	3289		3289		3289	
% of cases correctly predicted	80.7		84.9		84.8	
−2 Log-likelihood	2713.9		2288.8		2251.1	

sector are lower than in the primary sector control group. Finally, trade union membership has a strong positive influence on pension entitlement. Overall, the influence of the segmentation variables in equation (1) appears to be exercised in the direction predicted by the segmented labour market model. Industries which have relatively stable product demand have a higher probability of offering their employees a pension entitlement than industries in the secondary sector where product demand is more uncertain. The explanatory power of the first regression equation in Table 6.8 is quite high with almost 81 per cent of the individual cases of pension entitlement being predicted correctly.

As noted earlier in connection with the dual version of the segmented model part-time workers are more likely to be found in the secondary sector while high pay is associated with the primary sector. In equation (2) in Table 6.8, therefore, we include two variables, part-time employment and hourly earnings, which help to differentiate between employment in the two sectors. The inclusion of these variables increases the explanatory power of the regression from 81 to 85 per cent. The coefficient of the hourly earnings variable suggests that the higher the employee's earnings the greater the chance that he or she will have a pension entitlement. The coefficient of the part-time variable suggests that working less than the standard number of hours is likely to result in a significant reduction in the probability of having a pension entitlement. The inclusion of the part-time and earnings variables reduces the coefficients of the married woman variable and all but two of the occupation variables to insignificance. However, almost all of the industry variables which were significant in equation 1 remain significant in equation (2). This suggests that industry is a more important determinant of pension entitlement than occupation. This accords with an implication of the segmented model that since firms in the primary sector generally have higher recruitment and training costs they are more likely to offer fringe benefits such as pensions as an incentive for employees to remain with them.

Equations (1) and (2) in Table 6.8 show that pension entitlement is positively related to age. In order to test whether age or labour market experience, with which of course age is closely related, is the more useful predictor of pension entitlement, we substitute employment experience variables in equation (3) for the age variables. The effect of employment experience on the probability of having a pension entitlement is little different from age. However, it is preferable to use the employment experience variables in the regression instead of age to allow them to have a direct impact on the dependent variable rather than an indirect effect through the age variable.

6.5   A FOUR-SECTOR SEGMENTATION MODEL

The two-sector segmented labour market model is a simple dualist version mainly used for expository purposes. More advanced treatments of the model posit multiple segments (see Gordon et al. 1982, and McNabb and Whitfield 1998) rather than two segments consisting of primary and secondary labour markets. In earlier work on earnings and labour market segmentation in Ireland (Hughes and Nolan 1997) we tried to take account of this diversity by applying Gordon's (1986) procedure for the allocation of industry and occupation groups to four labour market segments: independent primary professional and technical, independent primary craft, subordinate primary and secondary. Details of how the employees in our sample are allocated to these segments are given in Hughes and Nolan (1997).

Table 6.9
Distribution of employment in four labour market segments in Ireland in 1994 and in the United States in 1987

Labour market segment	Ireland (%)	United States (%)
Independent primary professional	29.4	29.3
Independent primary craft	11.4	10.8
Subordinate primary	30.9	33.9
Secondary	28.3	26.0

Source: Living in Ireland Survey 1994 and Hughes and Nolan (1996).

Table 6.10
Percentage female, unionised, part-time, with pension entitlement and average length of job in four labour market segments in Ireland in 1994

	Female	Union members (1987)	Part-time (18 hours)	With pension entitlement	Average job length (1987)
	%	%	%	%	years
Independent primary professional and technical	40.2	54.0	4.3	70.0	9.95
Independent primary craft	13.3	51.4	0.8	47.4	7.43
Subordinate primary	38.2	61.4	3.5	63.6	7.05
Secondary	55.9	29.1	16.2	18.9	6.16

Source: Living in Ireland Survey 1994 and Fichtenbaum et al. (1994).

Table 6.9 compares the distribution of the workforce across the four segments in Ireland and the United States. The distribution is remarkably similar in the two countries. About a quarter of employees in both countries work in the secondary sector, around a third work in the subordinate primary sector and a quarter and a tenth respectively work in the independent primary professional and technical and independent primary craft sectors.

The characteristics of the four sectors in Ireland in terms of gender, unionisaton, type of employment, pension entitlement and duration of employment are shown in Table 6.10. As described in the literature on labour market segmentation the secondary sector has a higher percentage of women in its labour force than sectors in the primary labour market and a higher percentage of part-time employment. In addition it has lower levels than the primary sectors of unionisation and pension entitlement and lower percentages of its employees on incremental scales and in jobs with a long duration of employment.

Table 6.11
Logit regression of pension entitlement on marital status, years in and out of the employment, trade union membership, hourly earnings and labour market segment

Variable	Whole sample	
Constant	−6.49	(22.49)
Female	0.41	(2.59)
Married man	0.22	(1.33)
Married woman	−0.30	(1.68)
Years employed	0.09	(4.95)
Years employed^2	−0.12	(3.11)
Years out of employment	−0.12	(4.13)
Years out of employment^2	0.37	(3.20)
Part-time	−4.12	(8.59)
Trade union member	1.41	(13.45)
Hourly earnings	2.45	(16.02)
Independent primary professional and technical		
Independent primary craft	0.39	(2.25)
Subordinate primary	0.99	(7.18)
Number of observations		3289
% of cases predicted correctly		82.9
−2 Log likelihood		2457.9

Note: The control groups are males and secondary sector.

The results of testing the four-segment version of the model are given in Table 6.11. Being female increases an employee's chance of having a pension entitlement relative to being male. This result is unexpected as segmentation theory suggests the opposite. Being a married man or a married woman does not effect the probability of pension entitlement relative to being a single man. Employment experience, as measured by years in and out of employment, has the expected positive impact on pension entitlement. The more years an employee has been employed the greater the likelihood that he or she will have a pension entitlement. However, the squared employment experience variable shows that the rate of increase diminishes over time. Conversely, the more years an employee has been without a job the greater is the probability of not having a pension entitlement. Being a part-time worker has a strong negative impact on pension entitlement while being a trade union member and having high hourly earnings have strong positive effects on entitlement. In the case of the segmentation variables the reference group is the secondary sector and we expect the coefficients of the primary sector variables to be higher relative to this control group. The results in Table 6.11 show that this expectation is borne out with all three coefficients of the primary sector variables being higher relative to the secondary sector.

The four-sector regression results presented in Table 6.11 contain less than half the explanatory variables used in the two-sector results in Table 6.9 but the explanatory power is greater than that for equation (1) in Table 6.9 with 83 per cent of the cases being predicted correctly versus 81 per cent.

Table 6.12
Predicted probability of having a pension entitlement based on results for four-sector segmented labour market model

Characteristics	Predicted probability
Benchmark: employed 15 years, earns £5 per hour, full-time, As benchmark except:	
Works in independent primary professional sector	0.64
Works in independent primary craft sector	0.57
Works in secondary sector	0.47

Source: See text.

The implications of the results in Table 6.11 for the average employee's probability of having a pension entitlement if employed in jobs with characteristics typical of primary or secondary sectors can be considered by using the four-sector regression equation to predict the probability of having such an entitlement. This is done in Table 6.12. As a benchmark we use an employee who has worked for 15 years, earns £5 per hour in a full-time job, is a trade union member and works in the subordinate primary sector. This employee has 71 chances out of 100 of having a pension entitlement. If the employee works in the independent primary professional and technical sector the chances are reduced to 64 and to 57 if working in the independent primary craft sector. However, if the employee works in the secondary sector the chances of having a pension entitlement fall from 71 to 47 in a 100. Hence, an employee working in the subordinate primary sector has a 50 per cent greater chance of having a pension entitlement as someone with exactly the same characteristics working in the secondary sector.

6.6   CONCLUSIONS AND IMPLICATIONS FOR PENSIONS POLICY

The *Living in Ireland Survey* data for 1994 for Ireland has allowed us to test the power of the two main labour market theories to explain pension entitlement. The competitive and segmented labour market theories lead to conflicting hypotheses about the relationship between earnings and pension entitlement. The competitive theory suggests that individual preferences for current over future consumption will determine whether an employee is likely to have a pension entitlement. In this case the coefficient on a pension entitlement variable in an earnings equation should be negative, reflecting the fact that all other things being equal earnings will be reduced to pay for the pension.

The segmentation theory emphasises the employer's role in making provision for a pension scheme for the employees. The labour market divides into a number of different segments according to the characteristics of product demand curves. In the dual version of the model there is a primary sector in which good jobs are generally provided and a secondary sector in which the jobs offered are mainly of poor quality. Employers in the primary sector have stable product demand curves so continuity of supply of labour of the quantity and quality they desire is important to them. Having an occupational pension scheme gives them an instrument with which they can reward employees who give long service to the firm or punish employees who quit the firm's employment. Such an instrument is, generally, not required by employers in the secondary sector because the demand for their products is less stable. and they need to be able to hire and fire staff in response to fluctuations in demand. The segmentation theory predicts that having a pension entitlement will be positively related to the level of earnings. Hence, in an earnings equation the coefficient of a pension entitlement variable should be positive.

Our tests of these two theories favour the segmentation model over the competitive model. The coefficient of the pension entitlement variable in our earnings equation is positive and significant, contrary to the competitive hypothesis. Logit regressions testing both dual and multi-sector versions of the segmentation model show that pension coverage conforms to the patterns predicted by the segmentation model. In the four-sector version of the model, those employed in primary sectors of the labour market are far more likely to have a pension entitlement than those working in the secondary sector. An analysis of the factors which are likely to result in differences in pension entitlement shows that an employee in the subordinate primary sector has a 50 per cent greater chance of having a pension entitlement than an employee working in the secondary sector.

These results strongly suggest that most employees in the secondary sector and a significant minority of employees in primary sectors are excluded from occupational pension schemes because it is not in the interest of their employers to provide such schemes. Previous research, in which we were able to test only a dual version of the segmented labour market model, provided similar results and we concluded that 'employers throughout the economy are unlikely to extend employer-provided pension cover on a voluntary basis to all employees' (Hughes and Nolan 1996, 182). A recent survey of trends in occupational pension coverage provides evidence which supports these arguments (see Hughes and Whelan 1996). The survey shows that coverage of occupational pension schemes fell from over 54 per cent of public and private sector employees in 1985 to 52 per cent in 1995 despite strenuous efforts by the pensions industry to increase coverage during those years.

The trend in coverage in Ireland is in line with experience in other countries which have relied on occupational schemes to provide an earnings-related pension during retirement. Private-sector coverage in Canada, the United Kingdom and the United States has peaked at around 50 per cent or less of the labour force. Efforts to push private sector coverage above 50 per cent in these countries have not been successful. In our view this is largely due to the existence of segmentation in the labour market. Labour market segmentation means that the great majority of workers in the secondary sector and a significant minority of workers in primary sectors will have to rely on the State to provide an income in retirement. The nature of their jobs, their low pay and their broken employment histories make it extremely difficult for them to accumulate enough savings during their working lives to provide even a modest earnings-related supplement to the State pension. This has significant implications for the proposals which the Pensions Board (1998) has made for the future development of pensions policy in Ireland.

The Pensions Board has produced a strategy for the development of the national pension system which has 'a particular objective of bringing into supplementary pension coverage groups hitherto not covered such as younger people, lower paid and atypical workers' (Pensions Board 1998, v). The Board argues that the best way of providing coverage for these and other groups is by introducing Personal Retirement Savings Accounts (PRSAs).

These accounts would be similar to 401(k) plans in the United States or Private Personal Pension plans in the United Kingdom.[2] They would be available to everyone regardless of employment status, so an employee who quits work or becomes self-employed could continue to make contributions to an individual retirement savings account. It will be mandatory for employers to provide facilities for their employees to contribute to PRSAs through payroll deductions if the employees wish it, but the employer will not be obliged to make contributions. Significant age-related tax relief would be given on contributions to encourage individuals to take out PRSAs and it is envisaged that they would be marketed by a wide range of providers such as banks, insurance companies, credit unions and the Post Office.

Having argued that the way to increase coverage for younger people, the lower paid and atypical workers is by providing PRSAs, the Board seems to expect that not many of them will avail of the opportunity to save for their retirement through an individual savings account. It notes that such accounts have high administrative costs and states that:

> Since those on lower pay are, at best, only likely to be in a position to fund a small pension this additional expense is likely to fall most heavily on those on lower incomes and those working in small employments. Based on the results of the ESRI Survey 1995, this sector experiences very low coverage at present and, in addition, it must be accepted that it is least likely to be in a position to contribute towards a supplementary pension. (Pensions Board 1998, 87)

Experience in the United States and the United Kingdom shows that take-up of individual retirement savings accounts is greatest for middle and higher income groups and least for low-income groups (see Sabelhaus 1996). It also shows that such accounts are mainly used by middle and higher income groups as a tax-favoured shelter for their savings. This means that they redistribute income from lower to higher income groups and result in little, if any, increase in national savings (see Engen et al. 1996) for evidence that individual retirement accounts do not increase national savings and Poterba et al. (1996) for the contrary view). A striking demonstration of the validity of this point was provided in the United States when the tax reform act of 1986 excluded high income tax-payers with employer-provided pensions from contributing to Individual Retirement Accounts and 'contributions immediately fell by 62 per cent' as Banks (1998, 3) points out.

Since the lower paid are unlikely to benefit much from the introduction of Personal Retirement Saving Accounts it will be necessary to ensure that the State's contributory and non-contributory pension benefits are set at levels which are high enough to prevent poverty. It is also necessary that the benefits should be indexed in line with increases in average earnings to ensure that the living standards of the elderly are maintained and that they share in any increase in living standards which occurs. It is encouraging that the Pensions Board recommends this should be done by raising the current contributory old-age pension level of 28.5 per cent of average industrial earnings for a single person to 34 per cent over a five to ten year period, that a minimally acceptable income level should be maintained by indexing the pension in line with prices and, if circumstances permit, that the pension should be increased in line with average industrial earnings to reflect the broadly based commitment in Irish society to social inclusion.

If these proposals to improve Social Welfare pensions are acted upon, lower-paid workers in segmented labour markets in Ireland could look forward to having a flat-rate pension which would provide a reasonable replacement rate and an adequate income during retirement.

NOTES

1. We are grateful to an anonymous referee and to the participants in the LoWER conference in Groningen in November 1998 for helpful comments on an earlier draft.
2. The acronym 401 (k) refers to the section of the United States Internal Revenue Act of 1978 which enabled the establishment of defined contribution pension plans to which employees can make voluntary contributions on a tax-deferred basis.

REFERENCES

Banks, J. (1998), 'Tax Incentives for Saving: The UK Experience', Paper on Institute for Fiscal Studies web site.

Callan, T., B. Nolan, B.J. Whelan, C.T. Whelan and J. Williams (1996), *Poverty in the 1990s: Evidence from the 1994 Living in Ireland Survey*, Dublin: Oaktree Press, General Research Series No. 146.

Delhausse, B., S. Perlman and P. Pestieau (1996), 'Retirement and Growing Old: Which Model of Protection?', in E. Reynaud, L. apRoberts, B. Davies and G. Hughes (eds), *International Perspectives on Supplementary Pensions*, Quorum Books, Westport, Connecticut.

Dickens, W.T. and K. Lang (1985), 'A Test of Dual Labor Market Theory', *American Economic Review*, **75** (4).

Doeringer, P. and M. Piore (1971), *Internal Labor Markets and Manpower Analysis*, Heath Lexington Books, Lexington, Mass..

Elliott, R. (1991), *Labor Economics: A Comparative Text*, McGraw-Hill, London.

Engen, E.M., W.G. Gale and J.K Scholz (1996), 'The Illusory Effects of Saving Incentives on Saving', *Journal of Economic Perspectives*, **10** (4).

Fichtenbaum, R., K. Gyimah-Brempong and P. Olson (1994), 'New Evidence on the Labour Market Segmentation Hypothesis', *Review of Social Economy*, **LII** (1).

Ghilarducci, T. (1992), *Labor's Capital: The Economics and Politics of Private Pensions*, MIT Press, Cambridge, Mass.

Gordon, D.M. (1986), *Procedure for Allocating Jobs Into Labor Segments*, New School for Social Research (mimeo).

Gordon, D.M., R. Edwards and M. Reich (1982), *Segmented Work, Divided Workers: The Historical Transformation of Labor in the United States*, Cambridge University Press, Cambridge.

Heckman, J.J. and J.V. Hotz (1986), 'An Investigation of the Labor Market Earnings of Panamanian Males: Evaluating the Sources of Inequality', *Journal of Human Resources,* **21**.

Hughes, G. and B. Nolan (1996), 'Pension Plans and Labor Market Structure: Evidence from Ireland', in E. Reynaud, L. apRoberts, B. Davies and G. Hughes with the collaboration of T. Ghilarducci and J. Turner (eds), *International Perspectives on Supplementary Pensions: Actors and Issues*, Quorum Books, Westport Ct.

Hughes, G. and B. Nolan (1997), 'Segmented Labour Markets and Earnings in Ireland', *Economic and Social Review*, **28** (1).

Hughes, G. and B. Whelan (1996), *Occupational and Personal Pension Coverage 1995*, Economic and Social Research Institute, Dublin.

McNabb, R. and K. Whitfield (1998), 'Testing for Segmentation: an establishment-level analysis', *Cambridge Journal of Economics*, **22** (3).

Pensions Board (1998), *Securing Retirement Income: National Pensions Policy Inititative Report of the Pensions Board*, The Pensions Board, Dublin.

Piore, M. (1970), 'The Dual Labour Market: Theory and Applications' in R. Barringer and S.H. Beer (eds), *The State and the Poor*, Winthrop, Cambridge, Mass.

Poterba, J.M., S.F. Venti and D.A. Wise (1996), 'How Retirement Saving Programs Increase Saving', *Journal of Economic Perspectives*, **10** (4).

Sabelhaus, J. (1996), 'How Does Pension Coverage Affect Household Saving?', in P.A. Fernandez, J.A. Turner and R.P. Hinz (eds), *Pensions, Savings and Capital Markets*, U.S. Department of Labor, Pension and Welfare Benefits Administration, Washington, DC.

Schiller, B. and R. Weiss (1980), 'Pensions and Wages: A Test for Equalising Differences', *Review of Economics and Statistics*, **62**.

7.   From Childhood Poverty to Labour Market Disadvantage: Changes in the Intergenerational Transmission of Social Exclusion

Abigail McKnight[1]

7.1   INTRODUCTION

It is intuitive to believe that parental income can influence a young person's 'success' in the labour market. Higher levels of parental income can provide access to extra education and other benefits during childhood in addition to financial support during the first few years of labour market entry. This means that young people growing up in low-income households can be disadvantaged in the labour market. In recognition of the potential inequality of opportunity governments have sought to improve the life chances of young people growing up in low-income households. Policies have included the provision of a comprehensive education for all, widening access and financial support through further and higher education. However, employment and earnings inequalities have increased over the last two decades. In 1977 employees in the top 10 per cent of the earnings distribution were earning 2.75 times as much as employees in the bottom 10 per cent, by 1997 they were earning four times as much; an increase of 45 per cent (McKnight 2000). The proportion of children in Britain growing up in poverty has also increased. A recent study has shown that the number of children living in poverty has increased from 1.4 to 4.3 million between 1968 and 1995/96 (Gregg et al. 1999). In terms of percentages this represents an increase from 10 per cent of all children living in poverty to 30 per cent.

If parental income is a determinant of early labour market success, then over the longer term, the increase in inequality and the growth in the number of children living in poverty is greater cause for concern than if labour market success is independent of parental income. Parents on high incomes will continue to improve the chances of their children through whatever means are available and if earnings inequality continues to increase inequality will not only perpetuate across generations but the gap between the advantaged and disadvantaged will widen; thus producing rich and poor dynasties.

Over the last two decades the transition from school to work has elongated with a much greater proportion of young people staying on at school after the age of 16 and a higher share of school leavers going on to further and higher education. In addition, it is not uncommon for young people to take a 'gap year' or 'year out' between school and higher education, some even take additional time off after completing their education and before entering a chosen career. Consequently, young people now tend to enter the labour market much later than they did in the past and this extends the time to when they become economically independent adults. These longer transitions between school and work undoubtedly create an additional financial burden on parents. If the cost of helping young people enter high-level jobs has increased over time the link between parental income and labour market success may have strengthened.

Intergenerational transmission of labour market disadvantage can only be explored using surveys which track individuals over time within a family context. The National Child Development Study (NCDS) and the British Cohort Study (1970) (BCS70) provide a unique opportunity to both estimate the effect of parental income on young people's labour market success and to test whether this relationship has changed over time. Members of NCDS were born in 1958 and finished compulsory education around 1974. Individuals in BCS70 were born in 1970 and finished compulsory education in 1986. The timing of the interviews for the two cohorts vary slightly. Labour market status in early adulthood is available for the NCDS members at age 23 (1981) and BCS70 members at age 26 (1996). As a result the BCS70 cohort at age 26 will be more established in the labour market than the NCDS cohort at age 23, but the differences should not be too great.

This study seeks to establish whether or not there exists a link between low-income background and later labour market disadvantage and to test whether this relationship has changed over time. This is achieved by estimating the correlation between household income at age 16 and labour market 'success' at age 23/26. Labour market 'success' is estimated in terms of labour market status, whether employed, unemployed, or economically inactive, and the earnings of those in employment.

7.2   INTERGENERATIONAL TRANSMISSION

The literature on intergenerational transmission of economic or social status looks at the transmission of a particular variable between parents and their children: for example, earnings, education, unemployment, social class, welfare dependency, extra-marital births, teenage pregnancy.

The transmission of social status across generations has interested sociologists for some time. Economists' interest in the process and consequences of intergenerational transmission of economic status has been more recent. Atkinson produced one of the first studies for Britain (Atkinson 1981) which focused on intergenerational transmission of earnings. His study used a sample of 307 father/son pairs. Fathers' earnings were measured in 1950 and sons' earnings in the period 1975–78. He finds a significant degree of earnings immobility with an earnings advantage for the children of the top quartile relative to the bottom of some 50 per cent. Evidence from transition matrices suggests that the probability of a son whose father's earnings were in the bottom quartile entering the top quartile is only 28 per cent of that of a son from the top quartile, and his relative chance of being in the bottom quartile is nearly 2.5 times that of someone from the second quartile. Dearden et al. (1997) adopted and refined the methodology used in the Atkinson study and applied it to a much larger, more representative, sample of fathers and sons.[2] They also extended the analysis to fathers and daughters. They found that the extent of mobility is limited in terms of both earnings and education. Their results support an earlier finding of Atkinson's that an asymmetry exists with upward mobility from the bottom of the earnings distribution more likely than downward mobility from the top.

The US literature in the area of intergenerational mobility has largely concentrated on estimating the correlation in lifetime earnings between parents and children (usually between fathers and sons). The early empirical models (surveyed in Becker and Tomes 1986) suggested a high degree of intergenerational earnings mobility with an elasticity of children's earnings with respect to their parent's earnings at around 0.2 (for example, Sewell and Hauser 1975; Behrman and Taubman 1985). More recent studies have argued that these results are biased downwards due to measurement error in lifetime earnings and/or the use of unrepresentative samples (Solon 1989). Corrections for measurement error along with empirical estimates using more representative samples have led to lower estimates of intergenerational earnings mobility with an elasticity in the region of 0.4 (Solon 1992; Zimmerman 1992). These US studies have concentrated on the search for an equilibrium rate of intergenerational transmission rather than exploring the possibility that intergenerational mobility may have changed over time.

There are a number of additional studies that have exploited the richness of the British National Child Development Study (NCDS) to explore intergenerational transmission. Hobcraft (1998) looks at how experiences during childhood are linked to a wide variety of outcomes in adulthood. He focuses on the issue of social exclusion and looks particularly at the effect of poverty, family disruption and contact with the police during childhood on adult outcomes. Adult outcomes at age 33 are divided into demographic, psychological, welfare dependency, educational qualifications and economic. He concludes that 'There is little doubt that social exclusion, as captured by the adult outcomes and childhood factors, is transmitted across the generations and through the lifecourse.' Hobcraft's measure of childhood poverty is derived from responses to a question on whether or not the child's family experienced financial difficulties at age 7, 11 and 16 and whether or not any child in the family received free school meals[3] when the cohort member was aged 11 and 16. He finds that low income in adulthood is related to childhood poverty along with poor performance at school and lack of parental interest in schooling.

Machin (1998) 'unpacks' some of the linkages between the transmission of earnings and education across generations. Once again using the NCDS he shows that the cognitive achievement of children in their early years is significantly related to labour market earnings of their parents and consequently affects the child's earnings in adulthood.

Elias and Blanchflower (1987) used the NCDS to identify factors affecting the likelihood of a 23-year-old being in an above average paying job. They found that an important predictive factor was the result of a standard test in English and mathematics taken at around 11 years of age. A maths test score below average was associated with a 10 per cent decrease in the probability of employment in an above average paying job at age 23. However, they did not look directly at the financial circumstance of the individual during childhood. Together these earlier studies suggest that the linkage runs from parental earnings to childhood educational achievement to adulthood earnings and so on across generations.

All of these previous studies have sought to establish a link between the economic and social status of parents and that of their children. Although they are informative in terms of identifying a link across generations in terms of economic and social factors it is not possible to generalise from these findings and state that the same link exists between other age cohorts. The strength of the present study is the ability to identify the extent of intergenerational transmission within a cohort and then to compare the experience between cohorts to see whether the degree of transmission has changed over time.

Some recent analysis comparing the experience of the two birth cohorts has started to explore some of these issues looking at a number of childhood factors and their relationship with adult outcomes. Bynner et al. (1999) found that childhood poverty was an intermediate factor in poor educational achievements, and comparison between the two cohorts identified a lower pay-off in terms of occupational attainment for the later cohort. The probability of unemployment among males who received free school meals as children was higher in the more recent cohort. However, they chose to compare the cohorts at age 26 and age 33 and this seven year difference may distort the results. Breen and Goldthorpe (2000) have also compared the experience of the two cohorts. They were interested in testing whether or not British society could now more accurately be described as a meritocracy than in the past. In terms of social class mobility they found even after controlling for merit – using measures of ability, motivation and educational attainment – class inequalities in mobility rates for both cohorts and no evidence to support the theory that Britain has moved further towards a meritocracy.

7.3　THE BIRTH-COHORT STUDIES

This study draws on information from two British birth-cohort studies. The first contains all individuals living in Britain who were born between 3 and 9 March 1958, the National Child Development Study (NCDS). The more recent cohort, the 1970 British Cohort Study (BCS70), is a study of all those living in Britain who were born between 5 and 11 April 1970. Table 7.1 shows the age at which each birth cohort was revisited and the sample size achieved.

Table 7.1
NCDS and BCS70 interview dates and sample size

National Child Development Study (NCDS)						
Year	1958	1965	1969	1974	1981	1991
Age	Birth	7	11	16	23	33
Sample	17414	16883	16835	16915	16457	15600
British Cohort Study 1970 (BCS70)						
Year	1970	1975	1980	1986	1996	
Age	Birth	5	10	16	26	
Sample	16135	13135	14875	11628	9003	

It is inevitable that the longer the time period over which individuals are tracked, the greater the number of the original sample fail to be contacted or fail to respond to the study questionnaires and requests for interviews (attrition). During the earlier stages of their lives it was easier to trace cohort members (for example, through the school system) but as they age and move house they increasingly become difficult to trace. In addition, particular events are known to have influenced the response rate. For example, the teachers strike in 1986 affected the BCS70 16 year follow up and the BCS70 26 year follow up was only a 4-in-5 sample from the address file, consequently the response rate appears low.

Attrition and question non-response are unlikely to be random. The consequence of which is that ignoring attrition and non-response can lead to biased estimates. The problem of attrition and question non-response is confounded further when it is necessary to draw on information from more than one survey and from different sections of a survey. As soon as a number of restrictions are applied the valid sample quickly diminishes. These issues will be explored further in future work.

Potential Problems Associated with Comparing the Two Cohorts

Comparison of two birth cohorts, one born in 1958 and the other in 1970, has a lot of potential. However, such a comparison in the context of the present analysis gives rise to a few problems. The present study is concerned with comparing an origin variable, household income, with a selection of outcome variables, economic activity and earnings. The origin variable, household income, is measured for both cohorts at age 16 but the NCDS variable is *net* monthly income while BCS70 only contains a measure for *gross* monthly income. The computation of a measure of equivalent household income[4] using McClement's scale is based on an approximation for NCDS because only grouped information is available for age of household members. Three levels of household income are defined: households with above average income; households with below average income and households with below 50 per cent of average income.

The outcome variables, economic activity and earnings, are available for both birth cohorts in their early twenties but unfortunately not at the same age. The NCDS cohort was interviewed in 1981 at the age of 23. The BCS70 cohort was interviewed in 1996 at the age of 26. Ideally, comparisons should be made at the same age and future work will involve exploiting the event history file for the NCDS cohort to compare both cohorts at age 23. However, this may not be too much of a problem as the transition between school and work has elongated. The consequence of this is that the two cohorts might well be at the same 'career age' even if they are not at the same chronological age.

When young people reach the age of 16 in the UK they, along with their parents, face their first major labour market decision: whether or not to stay on in post-compulsory education. At this age their alternative choices are either employment or a place on a training scheme. If they fail to secure a job or a place on a training scheme they will be unemployed. Unless a young person is still in full-time education of at least 12 hours a week at a recognised educational establishment studying for a qualification up to and including A level/(G) NVQ level 3 or equivalent, their parents can no longer claim Child Benefit. This means that young people who leave education at the age of 16 and fail to take up a training place or find a job will largely be financially dependent on their parents. The financial circumstance of the household when the cohort members were age 16 seems to be a reasonable point at which to assess the impact of low household income on future labour market outcomes. Low household income at age 16 is assumed to proxy for lack of resources available during childhood as well as the lack of future available resources to finance continuing educational investments and ease the transition from school to work. It is envisaged that future work will attempt to identify individuals who grew up in households which were consistently poor during their childhood from those who experienced poverty for only a limited period of time.

The appendix contains some descriptive statistics for the two cohorts. Two important changes recorded are the increases in qualification levels from NCDS to BCS70 (only 5 per cent of BCS70 members have no qualification by age 26 compared with 17 per cent of NCDS members by age 23) and the share of 16-year-olds who where living in households with incomes 50 per cent below the average from 11 per cent in NCDS to 20 per cent in BCS70.

7.4 THE RELATIONSHIP BETWEEN CHILDHOOD POVERTY AND ADULT EMPLOYMENT

To assess the relationship between childhood poverty and the economic circumstance of cohort members in their early to mid twenties we begin with a simple comparison between the economic status of individuals from households with above-average income with those from households with below-average income and 50 per cent below-average income.

Figure 7.1 shows the distribution of economic activity at age 23 (1981) by household income at age 16 (1974) for the 1958 birth cohort (NCDS). It is clear from this chart that individuals from low-income households are less likely to be in employment and more likely to be unemployed or at home full-time than 23-year-olds from higher-income households. Higher levels of household income are associated with increased likelihood of being in employment. Over 70 per cent of 23-year-olds who were in households with above-average income (HAAI) at age 16, compared with 61 per cent of those from households with below-average income (HBAI), and 56 per cent of

Long-Run Policy Issues of Low Pay

those from households below 50 per cent of average income (HB50AI) were in employment at age 23.

Figure 7.1
Economic activity at age 23 by household income at age 16, NCDS

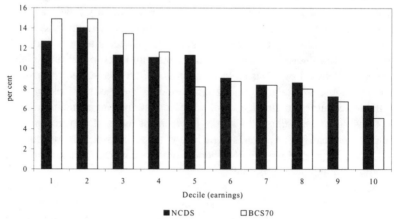

Source: NCDS.

Figure 7.2
Economic activity at age 26 by household income at age 16, BCS70

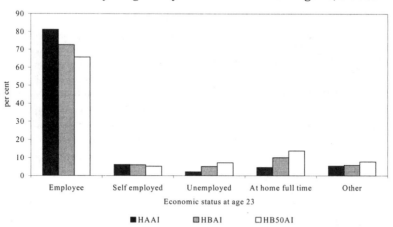

Source: BCS70.

The positive association between unemployment at 23 years and a low-income background was also found between the experience of long-term unemployment and a low-income background. Only 7 per cent of individuals from HAAI at age 16 had experienced a spell of unemployment lasting one year or more by the age of 23 compared with 16 per cent of individuals from HBAI and nearly one-quarter (24 per cent) of all individuals from HB50AI.

For the younger cohort, BCS70, Figure 7.2 shows the distribution of economic activity at age 26 by household income at age 16. It is clear from this chart that individuals from low-income households are less likely to be in employment at age 26 than individuals from higher-income households. Individuals from low-income households are more likely to be unemployed or at home full-time. The relationship between low income at age 16 and non-employment at age 26 is even stronger for individuals who were in households with incomes 50 per cent below average at age 16. Less than two-thirds of individuals from households below 50 per cent of average income were employees at age 26 compared with over 80 per cent of individuals from households with income above the average at age 16.

These charts have combined the outcomes for men and women, but economic activity patterns are very different for men and women. Women are more likely than men to be at home full-time caring for children or working part-time and in Britain men are more likely than women to register as unemployed. Table 7.2 shows the distribution of economic activity by household income for men and women separately in the 1970 birth cohort. The table shows economic activity in terms of full-time and part-time work rather than employment and self-employment and the share who were in full-time education at age 26.

Table 7.2
Economic activity at age 26 by household income at age 16 by gender, BCS70

| | Age 16 | | | | | |
| | | Men | | | Women | |
Age 26	HAAI	HBAI	HB50AI	HAAI	HBAI	HB50AI
Full-time work	88.5	82.8	76.1	74.2	59.1	45.7
Part-time work	2.4	2.9	3.4	10.3	14.2	19.0
Unemployed	3.5	8.2	12.3	1.2	2.9	3.4
Full-time education	3.0	2.8	3.1	2.5	1.8	1.0
At home full-time	0.3	0.4	0.8	8.4	17.6	23.8
Other	2.2	2.8	4.2	3.4	4.4	7.2
Total (100%)	907	1092	381	1070	1423	501

Source: BCS70.

In the 1970 cohort 26-year-old men from low-income households are less likely to be in full-time work and more likely not to be in any type of work than 26-year-old men from households with above-average income at the age of 16 years. Over one-fifth of 26-year-old men from households with incomes 50 per cent below the average are not in work. The majority of these young men are unemployed (60 per cent) but a significant share were in full-time education (15 per cent) or long-term sick (14 per cent) (included in the 'other' category).

Women from households with incomes 50 per cent below the average are 62 per cent less likely to be in full-time work at age 26 than women from households with above-average income. Women from low-income households are more likely to be in part-time work and much more likely to be at home full-time.[5] Overall these results suggest that childhood poverty is associated with adult unemployment for men and an increased likelihood of being at home full-time for women.

Figure 7.3
Economic activity at age 23/26 for individuals from households 50 per cent below average income

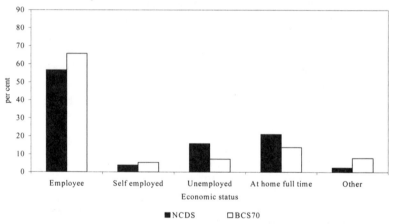

Sources: NCDS and BCS70.

These findings may partly be an artefact of the different age of the young adults in the two cohorts but the results in Figure 7.3 suggest that this is unlikely to be the most important factor. If age was the main influence then we might expect to find a smaller percentage of the older BCS70 cohort members still in full-time education and a larger share at home full-time caring for children. In fact the reverse is true, with a higher percentage in the 'other' category which includes full-time education and a smaller percentage at home full-time.

One major change which occurred between these two time periods (1981 and 1996) was the overall rise in labour force participation rates of women irrespective of household income background. Table 7.3 shows the distribution of economic activity for all women in the two cohorts in 1981 and 1996. This table highlights the reduction in the proportion of young women at home full-time and the corresponding increase in the proportion of women in work between the 1958 cohort and the 1970 cohort irrespective of household income background.

Table 7.3
Economic activity of young women in 1981 and 1996

	NCDS Age 23	BCS70 Age 26
In work	58.2	78.1
Not in work	8.5	6.0
At home full-time	30.2	13.7
Other	3.0	2.2
Total (100%)	2738	2493

Source: NCDS and BCS70.

We know that women from low-income households are less likely to be in employment and more likely to be at home full-time than women from higher income households. However, although increases in female labour force participation rates are reflected in the higher share of women from low-income households in employment in their early to mid twenties in 1996 than in 1981, it is interesting to note that the share of women at home full-time does not fall by as much for women from low-income households as for women from high-income households. While the share of women at home full-time for all women falls by 55 per cent, it falls by 50 per cent for women from households below average income and 38 per cent for women from households 50 per cent below average income.

An important factor is the economic climate in which these young people find themselves. The unemployment rate in 1996 (8.3 per cent) was over one percentage point lower (the time at which we observe the BCS70 cohort) than in 1981 (9.6 per cent) (the time at which we observe the NCDS cohort), and, more importantly, unemployment was falling in 1996 but rising in 1981 (Nickell 1999). Overall the improved economic climate in 1996 compared with 1981 meant that the experience of unemployment was much lower among the BCS70 cohort members than among members of NCDS.

While the unemployment prospects of the whole group are of interest the main focus here is on the relative prospects of the low-income group compared with the high-income group. We might expect that due to the observed correlation between low-income backgrounds and low levels of qualification that during economic downturns the employment prospects of individuals from low-income backgrounds would suffer by most. If this is the case then the relative prospects of the low-income group are likely to follow a cyclical pattern. We are interested in identifying the trend – has the penalty of growing up in a low-income household changed over time? To answer this question we should separate out the trend from any cyclical influence. This is beyond the scope of the present study, but if the hypothesis that the relative employment prospects of individuals from low-income backgrounds are lower during economic downturns is true, then we would expect to observe an increase in the relative prospects of the low-income group between 1981 and 1996.

A more rigorous analysis of the trends can be conducted in an econometric framework modelling the probability of being in employment at age 23/26 years and its association with household income at age 16. The results from a very simple logistic regression for the two cohorts, males and females separately and for the two levels of household income, can be found in Table 7.4. Concentrating first on males, the top portion of the table shows the negative correlation between low household-income background and the probability of employment. Comparison of the NCDS and BCS70 shows that the odds of being employed for males from HBAI has decreased over time. The same is true for males from HB50AI suggesting that, in terms of employment, the penalty of growing up in low-income households has increased over time. The lower portion of the table shows the results for females. A similar increase in the penalty of growing up in a low-income household is observed.

Table 7.4
The effect of childhood poverty on adult employment

	NCDS	BCS70		NCDS	BCS70
Males					
HBAI	0.461*	–0.517*	HB50AI	–0.445*	–0.853*
	(0.111)	(0.145)		(0.155)	(0.152)
Model χ^2	17.76*	13.25*	Model χ^2	7.77*	29.18*
Observations	2495	1999	Observations	2495	1999
Females					
HBAI	–0.484*	–0.685*	HB50AI	–0.482*	–0.877*
	(0.080)	(0.104)		(0.118)	(0.110)
Model χ^2	37.14*	45.95*	Model χ^2	16.78*	60.84*
Observations	2738	2493	Observations	2738	2493

Notes:
* denotes statistical significance at the 5% level. Standard errors are shown in parentheses. Models include a constant term.

Education has a strong influence on the employment prospects of individuals and the relationship between low household income and low levels of qualification is fairly well established. To understand how much of the difference in employment prospects is due to education a separate model has been estimated including the highest level of qualification obtained by 23/26 years as an explanatory variable.

It is clear from the results contained in Table 7.5 that higher levels of qualification are associated with higher relative odds of employment at age 23/26. The influence of education on the likelihood of being employed appears to be stronger for women than for men. The results show that even after controlling for education, household-income background continues to have a separate and significant influence on the relative probability of being employed at age 23/26, individuals from low-income households having a lower probability of being employed.

Table 7.5
The effect of childhood poverty and education on adult employment

	NCDS	NCDS		BCS70	BCS70
Males					
HBAI	−0.431*		HBAI	−0.419*	
HB50AI		−0.346*	HB50AI		−0.741*
CSE/other	0.561*	0.564*	CSE/other	0.530	0.464
O levels	0.835*	0.876*	O levels	0.949*	0.891*
A levels	1.202*	1.275*	A levels	0.991*	0.929*
Higher quals	1.426*	1.506*	Higher quals	0.947*	0.894*
Degree	−0.325	−0.196	Degree	0.578*	0.535
Model χ^2	97.10*	87.81*	Model χ^2	35.78*	48.69*
Observations	2495	2495	Observations	1999	1999
Females					
HBAI	−0.185*		HBAI	−0.385*	
HB50AI		−0.177	HB50AI		−0.564*
CSE/other	0.561*	0.560*	CSE/other	1.312*	1.238*
O levels	1.159*	1.175*	O levels	1.800*	1.717*
A levels	2.167*	2.206*	A levels	2.220*	2.159*
Higher quals	2.137*	2.163*	Higher quals	2.255*	2.200*
Degree	1.755*	1.790*	Degree	2.260*	2.207*
Model χ^2	294.86*	292.22*	Model χ^2	169.81*	179.81*
Observations	2738	2738	Observations	2493	2493

Notes:
* denotes statistical significance at the 5% level. Models include a constant term; 'no qualifications' is reference category.

Comparisons between the two cohorts suggest that the decrease over time in the relative odds of being employed for males from below-average income households can be explained by differences in the level of education. This maybe because the increases in educational attainment have not been evenly distributed across individuals. However, for males from HB50AI there remains a decrease in the odds of employment for males between the two cohorts even after controlling for the level of education. For females the decrease in the odds of employment remains for both thresholds of low household income even after controlling for the level of education.

7.5   THE RELATIONSHIP BETWEEN CHILDHOOD POVERTY AND ADULT EARNINGS

There are a number of ways of examining the relationship between low parental income and low pay. Firstly, we could pick a definition of low pay, such as 2/3 of median, 68 per cent of the mean, half of male median earnings, and compare the likelihood of being low paid for individuals from low-income households with individuals from higher-income households. The weakness of this approach is that it provides very limited information. A more informative approach is to examine the decile earnings distribution of individuals from low-income households and contrast the distribution with that of individuals from higher income households.

Figure 7.4 shows the decile earnings distribution of 26-year-old workers in BCS70 by household-income background. This figure shows the percentage of workers in each earnings decile using the three thresholds: above-average income (HAAI); below-average income (HBAI) and below half average income (HB50AI). If no relationship exists between household income at age 16 and earnings at age 26 then 10 per cent of these individuals would be found in each decile. For the 1970 cohort the figure shows that 26-year-olds from low-income households are more likely to be in the lowest four earnings deciles – and individuals from households with below 50 per cent of average income even more – than individuals from higher-income households. Conversely individuals from households with above-average income are much more likely to be in the top earnings deciles.

Figure 7.5 compares the decile earnings distribution of individuals from households below average income (HBAI) at 16 years for the 1958 cohort at age 23 and for the 1970 cohort at 26 years. The results from NCDS support the finding from BCS70 that young adults are more likely to be at the lower end of the earnings distribution if they were in a low-income household at the age of 16 than if they were in a higher income household.

Comparison between the two cohorts suggests that the likelihood of young adults from low-income households being at the lower end of the earnings distribution has increased between the two cohorts; shown by the higher percentage in deciles one, two and three for the 1970 cohort.

Figure 7.4
Decile earnings distribution at age 26 by household income at age 16

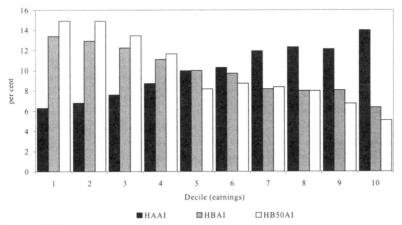

Source: BCS70.

Figure 7.5
Decile earnings distribution at age 23 (NCDS) and age 26 (BCS70) for individuals from below-average income households

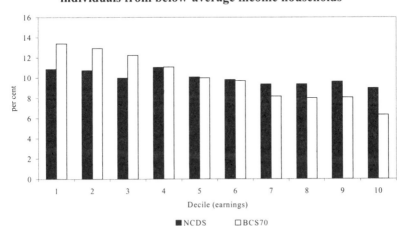

Sources: NCDS and BCS70.

The greater concentration of individuals from low-income households in low earnings deciles is even more accentuated for individuals from households with below 50 per cent of average income (Figure 7.6).

Figure 7.6
Decile earnings distribution at age 23 (NCDS) and age 26 (BCS70) for
individuals from households below 50 per cent of average income

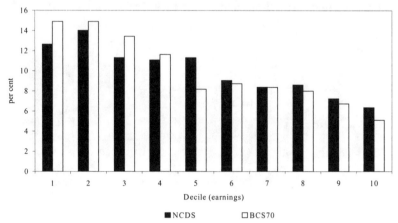

Sources: NCDS and BCS70.

Table 7.6
The effect of childhood poverty on adult earnings

	NCDS	BCS70		NCDS	BCS70
Males					
HBAI	–0.034*	*–0.147	HB50AI	–0.082*	–0.121*
	(0.016)	(0.019)		(0.027)	(0.026)
Adjusted R^2	0.002	0.037	Adjusted R^2	0.005	0.014
Observations	1795	1539	Observations	1795	1539
Females					
HBAI	–0.077*	–0.155*	HB50AI	–0.105*	–0.154*
	(0.018)	(0.017)		(0.031)	(0.023)
Adjusted R^2	0.011	0.047	Adjusted R^2	0.007	0.025
Observations	1447	1749	Observations	1447	1749

Note: * denotes statistical significance at the 5% level. Models include a constant term.

A simple model of earnings using relative household income as an explanatory variable (Table 7.6) shows the negative effect of low household-income background on adult earnings. Naturally the explanatory power of such a model is very low but the results do suggest that there is a greater negative influence on earnings associated with lower household-income backgrounds and that the penalty of such a background in terms of earnings has increased for males and females over time.

A more realistic model of earnings including educational qualifications (Table 7.7) shows the positive influence of higher levels of qualifications on earnings. It is interesting to see that even after education has been controlled for, low household-income background continues to have a significant and negative influence on adult earnings. The results suggest that the lower the household income the greater is the negative effect on earnings and for men and women the penalty of a low-income background in terms of earnings has increased over time.

Table 7.7
The effect of childhood poverty and education on adult earnings

	NCDS	NCDS		BCS70	BCS70
Males					
HBAI	−0.010		HBAI	−0.092*	
HB50AI		−0.061*	HB50AI		−0.067*
CSE/other	0.072*	0.068*	CSE/other	0.101	0.094
O levels	0.146*	0.142*	O levels	0.187*	0.188*
A levels	0.138*	0.132*	A levels	0.239*	0.252*
Higher quals	0.179*	0.175*	Higher quals	0.217*	0.224*
Degree	0.149*	0.144*	Degree	0.337*	0.356*
Adjusted R^2	0.023	0.026	Adjusted R^2	0.089	0.080
Observations	1795	1795	Observations	1539	1539
Females					
HBAI	−0.031		HBAI	−0.077*	
HB50AI		−0.049	HB50AI		−0.077*
CSE/other	0.095*	0.093*	CSE/other	0.056	0.050
O levels	0.177*	0.178*	O levels	0.210*	0.207*
A levels	0.308*	0.311*	A levels	0.364*	0.366*
Higher quals	0.392*	0.392*	Higher quals	0.310*	0.317*
Degree	0.440*	0.442*	Degree	0.459*	0.468*
Adjusted R^2	0.132	0.132	Adjusted R^2	0.175	0.171
Observations	1447	1447	Observations	1749	1749

Notes:
* denotes statistical significance at the 5% level. Models include a constant term; 'no qualifications' is reference category.

7.6   SUMMARY

It is not surprising that parental income is linked to labour market success of children when they leave education. It is only natural that parents use whatever means are at their disposal to help their children succeed in the labour market during their adult life. Increases in earnings inequality suggest that those at the bottom end of the earnings distribution now have relatively less means at their disposal than previously and this may well be behind the dramatic increases in child poverty in Britain since the end of the 1960s. Using two rich data sources this study has shown that above-average household income at age 16 increases the likelihood of young adults being in employment and receiving higher levels of pay in their twenties.

The findings presented here suggest that there is a substantial labour market 'penalty' associated with childhood poverty. Young people in low-income households at age 16 are much more likely to be unemployed, or out of the labour force in their early twenties than young people from households with higher incomes. In addition, if young people from poor backgrounds are in employment in their early twenties they are disproportionately observed in the lower end of the earnings distribution. Children who grow up in poverty are more likely to be employed in low-paid jobs than individuals from higher-income backgrounds.

The influence of parents' income on the level of qualifications gained by their children is clearly evident. Individuals from households with above average income are more than three times as likely to have gained a degree than individuals from households with incomes less than 50 per cent below average. Although it was fairly unusual for any of the 1970 cohort to have no formal qualifications by the age of 26, this was the case for 13 per cent of individuals from households with incomes below 50 per cent of the average compared with 2 per cent of individuals from households with above-average income. Clearly differences in education affect employment prospects. However, although the level of education 'explains' some of the observed labour market disadvantage associated with low income in childhood, even after controlling for differences in education there remains a clear negative influence associated with growing up in poverty.

As well as the high penalty associated with growing up in poverty a comparison of the experience of these two cohorts has revealed an increase over time. The young adults from low-income backgrounds in the more recent cohort (individuals born in 1970) face a greater relative disadvantage in the labour market than the cohort born in 1958. This disadvantage is observed in terms of the relative chances of being in employment and the relative earnings for those who are in employment even though the labour market was more favourable for the younger cohort. These findings imply that the 'penalty' associated with growing up in a low-income household has increased over time.

The policy implications are clear. The rise in the proportion of children growing up in poverty is alarming, not just because of the disadvantages these children inevitably suffer in their childhood but because they carry this disadvantage into their adult working lives. One way that policy can be directed at this problem is to ensure that all children receive good quality education and that any barriers to academic success faced by children in poverty are identified and eroded. However, the analysis conducted here suggests that education is not enough. The second message is that the poverty of the parents must be directly addressed by ensuring that periods of low income do not lead to long-term poverty traps. New initiatives such as earned income tax credits must be accompanied by additional services which help recipients move from 'poverty in work' to full economic independence.

Previous studies have highlighted the extent that poverty is associated with lone parenthood. The findings in this chapter suggest that welfare-to-work programmes targeted at lone parents, such as the New Deal for Lone Parents in the United Kingdom, aimed at helping lone parents move from means-tested benefits to employment can have significant effects, not only in terms of improving their current circumstance but also on the long-term prospects of their children. If these issues are not addressed then the cycle of deprivation will continue.

NOTES

1. This research was partly funded by the Joseph Rowntree Foundation. I would like to thank seminar participants at the LoWER conference in Groningen and the Schooling, Training and Transitions conference in Orléans for comments on an earlier draft.
2. Atkinson's study was based on a sample of low-income families living in York in 1950. Dearden et al. (1997) used the NCDS which provided 1565 father/son pairs and 747 father/daughter pairs.
3. In Britain children from low-income households qualify for free school meals.
4. Equivalent household income is computed by adjusting gross household income for household size and composition.
5. This finding is consistent with earlier research which has shown that women from low-income households are more likely to have children at a young age.

REFERENCES

Atkinson, A.B. (1981), 'On Intergenerational Income Mobility in Britain', *Journal of Post Keynesian Economics,* Winter 1980–81, **3** (2).

Becker, G.S. and N. Tomes (1986), 'Human Capital and the Rise and Fall of Families', *Journal of Labor Economics,* **43** (July), S1–S39.

Behrman, J. and P. Taubman (1985), 'Intergenerational Earnings Mobility in the United States: Some Estimates and a Test of Becker's Intergenerational Endowments Model', *Review of Economics and Statistics,* **67** (February), 144–51.

Breen, R. and J.H. Goldthorpe (2000), 'Class, Mobility and Merit: the Experience of two British Birth Cohorts', *European Sociological Review* (forthcoming).

Bynner, J., H. Joshi and M. Tsatsas (1999), 'Obstacles and Opportunities on the Route to Adulthood: evidence from Rural and Urban Britain', Centre for Longitudinal Studies, Institute for Education, mimeo.

Dearden, L., S. Machin and H. Reed (1997), 'Intergenerational Mobility in Britain', *Economic Journal,* **107** (January), 47–66.

Elias, P. and D. Blanchflower (1987), *The Occupations, Earnings and Work Histories of Young Adults – Who Gets the Good Jobs?,* Department of Employment Research Paper No. 68.

Gregg, P., S. Harkness and S. Machin (1999), *Child Development and Family Income,* Joseph Rowntree Foundation, YPS, York.

Hobcraft, J. (1998), *Intergenerational and Life-Course Transmission of Social Exclusion: Influences of Childhood Poverty, Family Disruption, Contact with the Police,* CASE Paper No. 15, November 1998.

Machin, S. (1998), 'Childhood Disadvantage and Intergenerational Transmissions of Economic Status', in A. Atkinson and J. Hills (eds), *Exclusion, Employment and Opportunity,* CASE Paper No. 4, January 1998.

McKnight, A. (2000), *Trends in Earnings Inequality and Earnings Mobility 1977–1997: The Impact of Mobility on Long-Term Inequality,* Department of Trade and Industry, Employment Relations Research Series.

Nickell, S. (1999), 'Unemployment in Britain', in P. Gregg and J. Wadsworth (eds), *The State of Working Britain,* Manchester University Press, Manchester.

Sewell, W.H. and R.M. Hauser (1975), *Education, Occupation and Earnings,* Academic Press, New York.

Solon, G. (1989), 'Biases in the Estimation of Intergenerational Earnings Correlations', *Review of Economics and Statistics,* **71**, 172–4.

Solon, G. (1992), 'Intergenerational Income Mobility in the United States', *American Economic Review,* **82** (June), 393–408.

Zimmerman, D.J. (1992), 'Regression Toward Mediocrity in Economic Stature', *American Economic Review,* **82** (June), 409–29.

APPENDIX

Table 7.A1

Descriptive statistics

	NCDS	BCS70
	%	%
Male	47.7	44.5
Female	52.3	55.5
Economic activity		
Employee	65.1	76.4
Self-employed	4.8	6.1
Unemployed	11.8	3.9
At home full-time	15.8	7.7
Other	2.5	5.9
Highest qualification		
Degree	6.3	22.3
Higher qualification	7.8	4.9
A level	7.8	11.3
O level	44.2	40.7
CSE/Other	17.4	15.9
No qualification	16.5	4.8
Household income at age 16		
Above average	41.9	44.0
Below average	58.1	56.0
50% below average	11.4	19.6
Total valid cases*	5233	4492

Note: *To be included in the dataset individuals must have a valid measure of household income at age 16 and their economic activity must be known at age 23/26.

PART THREE

Demand for Low-Paid Labour

8. Industrial Change, Stability of Relative Earnings and Substitution of Unskilled Labour in West Germany

Viktor Steiner and Robert Mohr

8.1 INTRODUCTION

The differential labour market developments in Germany[1] and the United States are often cited to support the hypothesis of a trade-off between more jobs for unskilled workers on the one hand, and a less equal earnings distribution on the other. In contrast to the United States, unemployment of unskilled German workers has increased substantially since the early 1980s while the distribution of earnings changed little (Gottschalk and Smeeding 1997; Steiner and Wagner 1998a and b). Given that the German economy is affected by technological change and international competition to a similar extent as the American economy, these differential labour market developments are usually explained by the much greater importance of institutional factors in Germany which are hypothesised to lead to a rigid wage structure. These factors include effective wage floors set by collective bargaining agreements, the 'solidaristic wage policy' of the unions aiming at uniform relative wage increases, and income support schemes characterised by high earnings replacement ratios (Abraham and Houseman 1995; Siebert 1997). However, not all observers seem convinced that these factors have contributed significantly to the high unemployment rates of unskilled workers in Europe, and in Germany in particular (Nickell 1997, for a pessimistic view).

Although the relationship between (changes in) the employment of unskilled workers and relative wages has been analysed in a number of empirical studies, no consensus view seems to have emerged so far. For a small cross-section of developed market economies, OECD (1996) reports a significant positive relationship between unemployment rates and a measure of earnings inequality; this correlation disappears, however, when first differences of unemployment rates rather than their levels are considered. In a study covering a larger number of countries, Blau and Kahn (1996) find that employment ratios of low-skilled workers are lower in countries with a more compressed earnings distribution than the US, but this correlation, too, seems far from conclusive, to say the least. After comparing the development of relative unemployment rates and wages for various skill groups in a number of OECD countries, Nickell and Bell (1995, 46) conclude that 'there seems to be no evidence for a relationship between the unemployment rate effects [of the fall of the relative demand for unskilled workers] are any more severe in countries where the wage effects are small'. On the basis of a comparative study including the US, Canada and France, Card et al. (1996) find little evidence for the hypothesis that the more compressed earnings distribution in France, which hardly changed during the observation period, generated significantly different employment trends than in the other two countries characterised by a higher degree of wage flexibility.

For Germany, Krueger and Pischke (1998) on the basis of a similar methodology as employed by Card et al. (1996) find that there is no significant correlation between the change in the employment-to-population ratio disaggregated by a small number of age-education cells and the respective wage in the base period. Other studies for Germany, which rely on the estimation of standard partial-equilibrium labour demand models, tend to find a significant negative relationship between the relative employment of unskilled labour and relative wages.[2] However, estimated substitution elasticities between unskilled and skilled labour vary a great deal between the various studies, depending on the economic sector analysed, the time period, the way skills are measured and the specification of the production technology. The same is also true regarding the estimated effects of skill-biased technological change on the relative demand for labour.

This paper builds on previous work for Germany by Steiner and Wagner (1998a) who found a rather low substitution elasticity between unskilled and skilled male labour for the whole manufacturing sector of about – 0.3 and a trend decline in the skills ratio of about 3 per cent per year. Given these estimates, the authors conclude that even reductions in the relative earnings of unskilled workers on a scale observed for the US labour market would not have been sufficient to bring employment of unskilled workers in West German manufacturing back to previous levels. In this paper, we extend their analysis for the manufacturing sector to the whole German economy and analyse the economic factors which have contributed to the dramatic decline of the employment share of unskilled labour in German manufacturing, in particular the role played by the relatively rigid earnings structure.

In the next section, we present some stylised facts on relative earnings and employment trends in the German economy since the mid-1970s. The econometric model of substitution between unskilled and skilled labour and its relation to the development of relative earnings are set out in Section 8.3. Estimation results are presented and discussed in Section 8.4, and Section 8.5 concludes.

8.2 SOME STYLISED FACTS

To set the scene for the empirical analysis, we first present some stylised facts on employment and earnings trends in West Germany. We first describe general trends referring to the whole economy before sectoral evidence is presented for the period 1975 to 1990, for which individual-level earnings information differentiated by skills is available. Then we look at the development of relative employment and earnings at a more disaggregated level.

Between the recession year 1975 and the pre-unification year 1990, overall employment in West Germany increased by almost 14 per cent from 22.4 to 25.5 millions. The strongest increase occurred in the second half of the 1980s when about 2 million jobs net were created. Since labour supply increased strongly throughout the period, even the relatively large employment increase in the second half of the eighties was insufficient to bring down overall unemployment to its level before the recession of the early eighties. In 1990, the unemployment rate as measured by the OECD stood at 6 per cent, compared with a level of 4 per cent in the recession year 1975. The increase of unemployment in the 1980s mainly occurred among the unskilled and older male workers. The strong increase in female labour supply did not result in higher unemployment of women, but an increasing share of female employment throughout the period. In the high-growth period in the second half of the 1980s alone, the female share in employment increased by five percentage points.[3] This increase was both related to changes in the educational attainment of females, the expansion of the service sector and the extension of female part-time work. Between 1985 and 1990 the service sector expanded by more than 2 million employees, while the share of women in this sector increased from about 55 to 60 per cent. The share of the part-time employed among all female employees increased by about 5 percentage points to 36 per cent in this period. Part-time employment is concentrated in services and the public sector.

In the period from the mid 1970s to the end of the 1980s, employment of unskilled workers in the West German economy as a whole dropped by almost 36 per cent, while the number of skilled employees increased by 30 per cent. Employment losses for the unskilled in manufacturing were markedly higher than in the service sector, but even there employment of this group dropped by more than 20 per cent. Within the manufacturing sector, these employment losses ranged from 35 per cent in industries producing investment goods to almost 50 per cent in mining and energy production (Sachverständigenrat 1994, Table 51).

In the following, we present some sectoral evidence on the development of skill-specific trends in employment and earnings in the period 1975 to 1990. The data set used here and also for the subsequent regression analyses derives from merging data from the disaggregated national accounts for two-digit manufacturing industries and individual-level employment and earnings information from social security records for the period 1975 to 1990 (see data appendix). The main advantage of the social security data for the present purpose is that it allows us to calculate employment shares and earnings ratios for meaningfully defined skill groups and also by labour market experience.[4] We use median rather than average earnings here because the latter are affected by the change in the coding of fringe benefits in the social security data in 1983/84 (see Steiner and Wagner 1998b).

As in Steiner and Wagner (1998a), we define workers as unskilled if they neither have obtained a vocational qualification (apprenticeship) nor a degree in higher education. Workers with a vocational degree and/or university entry level degree are classified as skilled and distinguished from those employees with a degree from an university or polytechnical school (*Fachhochschule*) who are called graduates. While the number of skilled male workers in manufacturing slightly increased after the recession in the mid 1970s and then remained fairly constant, employment of unskilled labour decreased and of graduates increased throughout the whole period. The employment decline of the unskilled also seems to have accelerated in the 1980s, while the growth in employment of graduates was particularly strong in the second half of the decade. In principle, this could have contributed to the substitution of unskilled by higher skilled workers. Whereas it seems unlikely that unskilled workers have been directly substituted for by graduates, there may well be some indirect substitution through a 'bumping down' process by which graduates displace skilled workers from skilled jobs and the latter displace unskilled workers from jobs requiring relatively little skills (Borghans et al. 1998). Given that earnings of a very high share of all graduates are censored at the social security threshold (Steiner and Wagner 1998b) and therefore (uncensored) median earnings cannot be calculated, we cannot test this hypothesis here and have to assume that this indirect substitution effect can be neglected.

The plots in Figure 8.1 track the development of employment and earnings growth for unskilled and skilled men (panel A) and women (panel B), respectively. Employment and earnings of unskilled and skilled workers are indexed by the year 1975.[5] In addition, we also plot the real daily wage of the unskilled (full-time workers only) deflated by the 1975 price level. In each case, the analysis is presented for all manufacturing, all services, and the two largest non-manufacturing sectors for each gender.

As for the trends in relative employment, the figures show that, for both men and women, the strongest decline in the employment of unskilled workers occurred in the manufacturing sector, and for men also in construction and in transport. Employment of skilled workers in manufacturing increased, where the increase was substantial for women in the second half of the 1980s. However, most of the increase in employment of skilled workers occurred in services, where the increase was especially strong for women. In contrast, employment of unskilled workers exhibits a negative trend in all sectors shown. Relative to the divergence of employment levels, there was little change in relative earnings, although the figures show some noteworthy sector and gender differences. For males, only the service sector shows some increase in earnings inequality between skilled and unskilled workers. For females, earnings inequality seems to have actually decreased in the whole manufacturing sector and in personal services. Given the strong increase in the employment of skilled relative to unskilled women in personal services, the divergence in earnings implies that the increase in the supply of skilled labour has outpaced its demand. The development of real wages of unskilled workers over time shows both substantial persistent differences in wage levels between men and women within sectors as well as, for a given gender, between sectors. For example, whereas men (women) in the manufacturing sector earn about DM 180 (140) a day, they earn less than DM 160 (120) in wholesale and retail trade.

To provide a more quantitative assessment of the developments of relative employment and earnings trends we ran regressions of, respectively, the log skills ratio and the log earnings ratio on a linear time trend. Estimation results are summarised in Table 8.1. The regressions involving the skills ratio reveal the following stylised facts. The skills ratio has decreased in all sectors, for both men and women. In other words, the growth of skilled employment exceeded the growth of unskilled employment in all sectors of the economy within the observation period. This effect was stronger for women than for men in all sectors. In manufacturing the skills ratio decreased on average by an annual rate of about 3 per cent for males and about 5 per cent for females. Except for business services, this decline is quite uniform across sectors for both men and women. In absolute terms, the strongest decline of the skills ratio occurred for women in business services with an average yearly rate of more than 6 per cent, compared to about 5 per cent for men working in this sector.

Figure 8.1
Employment and earnings trends of unskilled and skilled workers
in West Germany, 1975–1990
real wage deflated by consumer prices of 1975
A. Men

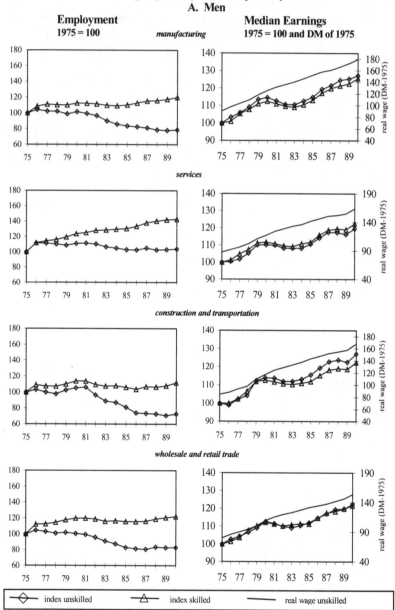

B. Women

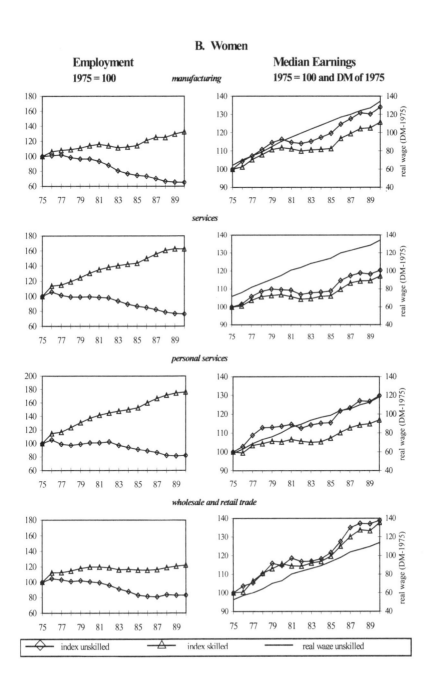

Table 8.1
Regressions of skills and earnings ratios against trend*

	Men		Women	
	log skills ratio	log earnings ratio	log skills ratio	log earnings ratio
Manufacturing	−0.029 (0.001)	0.001 (0.000)	−0.050 (0.002)	0.004 (0.000)
Construction & transportation	−0.030 (0.002)	0.004 (0.001)	−0.056 (0.003)	−0.003 (0.001)
Wholesale & retail trade	−0.026 (0.001)	0.000 (0.000)	−0.047 (0.002)	0.001 (0.001)
All services	−0.024 (0.001)	−0.007 (0.000)	−0.051 (0.001)	0.001 (0.000)
Personal service	−0.023 (0.002)	−0.005 (0.001)	−0.050 (0.002)	0.005 (0.001)
Business services	−0.048 (0.002)	−0.007 (0.001)	−0.062 (0.002)	0.006 (0.001)
Public services	−0.020 (0.001)	−0.004 (0.000)	−0.047 (0.001)	0.001 (0.001)

Note: * Standard errors are given in parentheses.

Sources: IABS data, own calculations.

The regression results relating to the log of the earnings ratio reveal that it changed very little in the observation period. This holds for all sectors of the economy and for both men and women. The main gender differences seem to have occurred in the service sector. Whereas unskilled male workers have experienced a small deterioration in their relative earnings position, relative earnings of unskilled females working in the personal and service sectors have even slightly improved. This confirms what was already apparent from Figure 8.1. For the 1980s, the overall stability of the earnings distribution was also confirmed by Steiner and Wagner (1998b), who showed that the average earnings differential between skilled and unskilled workers has become even slightly smaller in the observation period.

8.3   SUBSTITUTION BETWEEN UNSKILLED AND SKILLED LABOUR

The effects of demand and supply shocks on the relative employment and earnings position of unskilled workers in the domestic economy can be analysed on the basis of a straightforward extension of the standard partial-equilibrium labour market model (Bound and Johnson 1992; Katz and Murphy 1992; Nickell and Bell 1995, 1997). These effects depend on the slope of the relative demand curve for unskilled and skilled labour, that is the substitution elasticity between these two groups, the position and slope of their respective supply curves, and the extent to which trade and technological shocks shift the relative demand curve for labour. A relatively high absolute value of the substitution elasticity between unskilled and skilled labour would indicate that a small change in relative wages has a relatively large impact on relative employment. Under such conditions, a relative supply or demand shock affecting especially unskilled labour could lead to a marked increase in this factor's relative employment in the presence of rigid wages. On the other hand, if the elasticity of substitution is low, then even a large adverse shock would be unlikely to significantly affect relative employment levels. Hence, the size of the substitution elasticity between unskilled and skilled labour is crucial for the evaluation of the hypothesis that, in the presence of non-neutral negative demand shocks, the rigidity of relative wages has caused the decline in the relative employment of unskilled labour.

In their influential studies on the causes of the observed changes in relative wages in the US, Bound and Johnson (1992) and Katz and Murphy (1992) derived substitution elasticities between skilled (college) and unskilled (high school) labour of about –0.7 and –1.4, respectively. For Germany, estimates of this substitution elasticity vary a great deal between the various studies, depending on the economic sector analysed, the time period, the way skills are measured and the specification of the production technology. For example, on the basis of a linear approximation of a two-level CES production function, Fitzroy and Funke (1994) obtained an average substitution elasticity between blue-collar workers and the capital-white-collar subaggregate of –0.5 for a sample of two-digit manufacturing industries. Using a standard CES specification of the production technology, Entorf (1996) estimated a substitution elasticity between unskilled and skilled blue-collar workers in manufacturing of about –1 and, depending on the specification, between –1.5 and –0.5 for white-collar workers. Also relying on a CES production function, Möller (1996) obtained an average substitution elasticity between unskilled and skilled workers of –1.7 for a subsample of male workers in the manufacturing sector, while Beissinger and Möller (1998) reported estimated substitution elasticities of –1.7 for males and –3.3 for females. On the basis of a different functional form specification of the production technology Falk and Koebel (1997a) also found a relatively large substitution elasticity between unskilled and skilled labour for the manufacturing sector producing tradables and somewhat smaller substitution elasticities for several other non-traded sectors. However, in recent work based on a more general specification of the production technology and using disaggregated industry data, Falk and Koebel (1997b) found much lower substitution elasticities between unskilled and skilled labour. However, using the same database with a more disaggregated industry classification, Fitzenberger and Franz (1997) arrived at substitution elasticities between unskilled and skilled labour which vary between −0.4 in mechanical engineering and about −2.5 in trade.

Here, we extend previous work by Steiner and Wagner (1998a) for the manufacturing sector, who found a relatively small substitution elasticity of −0.3, and analyse the relative employment decline in the whole West German economy, where we also differentiate between men and women. As in most of the studies mentioned above, our working hypothesis will be that the decline in the supply of unskilled labour has affected all analysed sectors to a similar extent, and that employment is mainly determined by the demand side of the labour market. Given these assumptions, the substitution elasticity between unskilled and skilled labour can be estimated on the basis of the following simple econometric model (Hamermesh 1993, chapter 2; Shadman-Mehta and Sneesens 1995; Goux and Maurin 1997).

Assuming that technology can be characterised by a constant-returns-to-scale (CES) cost function and strong separability between these two types of labour and all other inputs,[6] and assuming that one can aggregate across firms, the total cost functions

$$C_t = \sum_{i,g} c_{i,g,t} \tag{8.1}$$

can be specified as sum of lower-level CES cost functions of the form

$$c_{i,g,t} = Y_{it} \left[\lambda_{u,t} \alpha_{ig}^{\sigma} w_{u,i,g,t}^{1-\sigma} + \lambda_{s,t} (1 - \alpha_{ig})^{\sigma} w_{s,i,g,t}^{1-\sigma} \right]^{1/(1-\sigma)}. \tag{8.2}$$

Y stands for output, λ is a relative efficiency parameter for each skill group assumed equal across all industries and groups, w is the wage rate (earnings), and σ is the substitution elasticity between the two types of labour; u, s, i, g refer to unskilled workers, skilled workers, industry, and experience group, respectively, and t is a time index measured in years. To take differences in human capital within unskilled and skilled labour into account, following Steiner and Wagner (1998a) we have disaggregated these two groups by the level of labour market experience, which is an important factor for the determination of both employment and earnings. In particular, economic change due to increased import competition or technological change should mainly have affected older workers who find it more difficult to adjust than workers with little labour market experience. Furthermore, individual earnings in Germany increase substantially with labour market experience as implied by human-capital theory (Steiner and Wagner 1998b). The disaggregation of the two skill groups by their level of labour market experience is based on the social security data described in the appendix. Given that too fine a disaggregation would leave us with an insufficient number of observations in certain industry × formal skill × experience cells, we use five experience groups, that is less than 6 years, 6 to 15, 16 to 25, 26 to 35, and more than 36 years of labour market experience.

We use two levels of aggregation of industries. For the analyses covering the whole economy we aggregated manufacturing industries into five subsectors, the other industries were aggregated into eighteen service industries and one sector covering agriculture and mining (see data appendix). Combined with manufacturing, this produces a disaggregation of the whole economy into 24 industries that, when multiplied by the five experience groups and sixteen years of observations, produces a total of 1920 possible observations (cells). In the estimation, observations referring to cells which contained no skilled or unskilled workers are removed from the sample. In addition we will present results for the manufacturing sector only, which rely on a finer disaggregation into 30 manufacturing industries as used in Steiner and Wagner (1998a).

Given the specification of the cost functions form above, the demand functions for the two types of labour can be derived by applying Shephard's lemma, that is:

$$\frac{\partial c_{i,g,t}}{\partial w_{u,i,g,t}} = L_{u,i,g,t} = Y_{i,t}^{1-\sigma} c_{i,g,t}^{\sigma} \lambda_{u,t} \alpha_{i,g}^{\sigma} w_{u,i,g,t}^{-\sigma} \tag{8.3}$$

$$\frac{\partial c_{i,g,t}}{\partial w_{s,i,g,t}} = L_{s,i,g,t} = Y_{i,t}^{1-\sigma} c_{i,g,t}^{\sigma} \lambda_{s,t} (1-\alpha_{i,g})^{\sigma} w_{s,i,g,t}^{-\sigma} . \tag{8.4}$$

Finally, we make the simplifying assumption that the relative efficiency of the two types of labour changes at a constant rate over time, that is:

$$\ln\left(\frac{\lambda_{u,t}}{\lambda_{s,t}}\right) = \gamma \cdot trend . \tag{8.5}$$

Now, it is straightforward to derive a log-linear relative labour demand model by dividing equation (8.3) by equation (8.4) and taking logs on both sides. Adding an error term, $\varepsilon_{i,g,t}$, which accounts for other unobserved time-varying factors affecting relative employment, we get the following estimable relative labour demand equation:

$$\ln\left(\frac{L_{u,i,g,t}}{L_{s,i,g,t}}\right) = k_{i,g} + \gamma \cdot trend - \sigma \ln\left(\frac{w_{u,i,g,t}}{w_{s,i,g,t}}\right) + \varepsilon_{i,g,t} , \tag{8.6}$$

where the dependent variable is the log of the ratio of the number of unskilled (u) to skilled (s) workers in a particular industry (i) and age group (g) in a given year (t). $k_{ig} = \left[\alpha_{ig}/(1-\alpha_{ig})\right]^{\sigma}$ is an industry-experience group fixed effect, which refers to a particular experience group in a given industry and which does not vary over time. , $\varepsilon_{i,g,t}$, is a time-varying error term which is assumed uncorrelated both with the earnings ratio and over time as well as across industry-experience groups.

Clearly, this specification implies a number of strong assumptions, including the restrictions that the elasticity of substitution is constant across industries or sectors, that production is strictly separable between the two types of labour and all other inputs and that, within the two skill groups, there is no substitution across experience groups. The restrictive assumption of a constant substitution elasticity is mitigated in the estimation in that we estimate equation (8.6) for various sectors of the economy separately and thus allow it to vary across these sectors. As for the separability assumption, the two most obvious additional inputs are highly skilled labour (graduates) and capital. For the reason mentioned above, reliable data on earnings of graduates, especially when disaggregated by labour market experience, is not available in our database. However, we do not consider the separability assumption with respect to highly skilled labour a serious restriction, since graduates possess a distinct set of skills which are unlikely to be close complements or substitutes to other types of labour. The maintained assumption that substitution elasticities do not differ between experience groups admittedly is a rather restrictive one, but the data unfortunately do not allow for a more flexible specification.[7] As for capital, Steiner and Wagner (1998a) have shown that the inclusion of the stock or the cost of capital had only minimal effects on either the coefficient for the trend or the estimate for the elasticity of substitution between unskilled and skilled labour in manufacturing. Negligible effects of capital on the relative demand for unskilled and skilled labour were also found for Germany by Fitzenberger and Franz (1997) and Falk and Koebel (1997a, 1997b).

The estimation of equation (8.6) poses two obvious econometric problems. The first is the potential for simultaneity bias. Since relative wages and relative skills are determined simultaneously in the labour market, there exists the possibility that the earnings ratio is correlated with the error term in the relative labour demand equation. We therefore instrument this potentially endogenous variable by its lagged value. Steiner and Wagner (1998a) present results indicating that this type of bias does indeed exist and that it is abased by using this methodology. The second problem relates to the efficiency of our estimates. Applying OLS to grouped data does not account for the relative size of the cells. Though unbiased, the estimates produced by this methodology are inefficient. As an alternative, we estimated the relative labour demand equation by weighted least squares (GLS) thereby incorporating information on cell size in the estimation.

8.4   RESULTS

We first present results for the whole economy and for various broadly defined sectors, where in each case estimation is based on the same specification of the relative labour demand model as given by equation (8.6). For the manufacturing sector, we also present estimation results where industries are differentiated at the two-digit level according to their import intensity and their rate of total factor productivity growth, respectively. Following Steiner and Wagner (1998a), we thus try to shed some light on the issue of the relative importance of international trade and technological change as explanatory factors for the decline of the skills ratio.

Sectoral Analysis

Table 8.2 contains the results of sixteen different regressions (eight for each gender), where the relative labour demand equation was estimated over all industries, the whole manufacturing sector, construction and transportation, retail and wholesale trade, and the service sector. For the latter we also ran separate regressions on three different subsectors, that is personal services, business services and public services (defense and public safety is not included).

In all regressions, group-specific fixed effects were highly significant and, according to standard Hausman tests (Greene 1993, 479) correlated with the regressors in the model. Hence, we estimated the models conditional on the group-specific fixed effects. The results can be summarised as follows.

For the pooled sample of all industries, the estimated coefficient of the time trend implies that the skills ratio has declined by about 3 per cent per year for men (6 per cent for women). These estimates simply reflect the dramatic trend decline in the employment of unskilled labour referred to in Section 8.2, though after taking into account changes in relative earnings and other factors accounted for by the included group-specific fixed effects. The time trend thus accounts for factors that have changed for all industries and experience groups in a similar fashion within the observation period. A negative trend coefficient would therefore not only capture common demand shift factors, but also reflects labour supply factors due to the general upgrading in the level of vocational qualification of the German workforce.

This labour supply explanation of the trend decline of the skills ratio seems consistent with the much faster decline of the skills ratio for women, whose level of qualification has improved markedly more than for men. Furthermore, this explanation is also supported by the quite uniform estimated value of the trend coefficient across broad economic sectors.[8] As the estimation results in Table 8.2 show, the trend coefficient in the regressions for women is always about double the size of that for men. On the other hand, if the trend decline in the skills ratio were mainly related to skill-biased technological change and/or intensified international trade with low-wage countries – the most prominent hypotheses in the economic literature – there would be little reason to expect these rather uniform differences between men and women and across economic sectors.

Table 8.2
Relative labour demand functions by sector, 1975–90

Industry		Men				Women		
	N	trend	$\ln w^r_{t-1}$	R^2 adj.	N	trend	$\ln w^r_{t-1}$	R^2 adj.
all	1584	−0.031**	−0.128	0.951	1641	−0.059**	−0.080	0.974
industries		(0.001)	(0.085)			(0.001)	(0.086)	
Manufac-	375	−0.029**	−0.330*	0.953	375	−0.054**	−0.098	0.962
turing		(0.001)	(0.165)			(0.002)	(0.220)	
Construction	150	−0.030**	−0.372**	0.893	150	−0.064**	−0.165	0.883
& transport		(0.003)	(0.419)			(0.005)	(0.212)	
Wholesale,	75	−0.027**	0.573	0.851	75	−0.055**	0.202	0.954
retail trade		(0.003)	(0.389)			(0.005)	(0.635)	
All services	909	−0.034**	0.026	0.925	966	−0.066**	−0.097	0.951
		(0.002)	(0.118)			(0.002)	(0.112)	
Personal	255	−0.027**	0.058	0.722	300	−0.061**	−0.839**	0.969
services		(0.003)	(0.206)			(0.003)	(0.220)	
Business	360	−0.060**	0.004	0.881	366	−0.086**	0.370*	0.930
services		(0.004)	(0.157)			(0.003)	(0.180)	
Public	294	−0.016**	−0.420*	0.869	300	−0.051**	0.083	0.927
services		(0.003)	(0.250)			(0.003)	(0.165)	

Notes: w^r is relative earnings ratio; * indicates significance at the 5% level, ** at the 1% level.

At the aggregate level, our estimates imply rather small values of the substitution elasticity between unskilled and skilled labour. In fact, the substitution elasticity seems to be not statistically significantly different from zero for both males and females. However, as the regression results for the various sectors show, this is mainly due to the high level of aggregation. For some sectors, we obtain quite large and statistically significant substitution elasticities. For men working in the manufacturing sector we replicate the estimate reported by Steiner and Wagner (1998a) of a substitution elasticity of approximately –0.3, which is somewhat below the other estimates reported in Section 8.3.[9] However, most of these studies are based on highly aggregated data, do not differentiate between males and females and rely on a rather different grouping of employees by type of qualification. These estimates are, therefore, not directly comparable to the ones reported here.

We also find a rather large substitution elasticity of about –1.4 for males in construction and transportation, which roughly corresponds to the estimate reported by Falk and Koebel (1997a) for construction alone, but is smaller than the estimate obtained by Fitzenberger and Franz (1997) for that sector.[10] This sector traditionally employs a large share of all male workers with little or no vocational qualification.

For women, the estimated substitution elasticity for the manufacturing sector as well as for construction and transportation turned out to be insignificant. For women, the non-manufacturing sector that accounted for the largest portion of employment is personal services. The estimated elasticity of substitution for this sector is approximately –0.8. Thus, it again appears that, although the overall elasticity of substitution is small, in precisely the sector which traditionally employs women the elasticity of substitution is relatively large. The remaining results for women show either insignificant or, in the case of business services, a positive and marginally significant coefficient on relative earnings.

Disaggregated Analysis for the Manufacturing Sector

In order to shed some light on sectoral differences with respect to the degree of import competition and technological change, we have estimated the relative labour demand function for the respective subsamples of manufacturing industries in Table 8.3. These subsamples were constructed by splitting the sample according to the quartile into which an industry's import share or rate of productivity growth falls. Here, we differentiate between industries with low, middle and high import intensity and rate of total factor productivity growth respectively.[11] By differentiating this sector along these two dimensions, we hope to obtain some additional evidence to discriminate between the trade and technological change hypotheses of the trend decline in the skills ratio. Since there would be too many cells with only a few observations for women in quite a few manufacturing industries, we restrict this analysis to men.

As the differences in estimated coefficients on the time trend show, the autonomous decline of unskilled labour of 3 per cent per year was rather uniform across industries with different import intensities. Thus, this more disaggregated analysis confirms the previous results that there is little evidence for the hypothesis of negative trade effects on the employment of unskilled labour in German manufacturing.

However, estimated substitution elasticities seem to differ by import share. Its value of about –0.5 is above average in industries with relatively low import shares, compared to about –0.37 in industries with high import competition. However, the latter elasticity seems rather imprecisely estimated (with a standard error of 0.206),[12] and it is thus not clear whether there is in fact a statistically significant difference between these two sectors. In industries with import shares falling in between the two categories the coefficient on the earnings ratio is also only marginally significant.

Table 8.3

Fixed effects estimates of the relative labour demand function by import intensity and rate of productivity growth, 1975–90 (men)

	Import intensity			Rate of productivity growth		
	low	middle	high	low	middle	high
constant	−0.721**	−0.475**	−0.291**	−0.382	−0.547**	−0.507
	(0.037)	(0.023)	(.041)	(0.052)	(0.022)	(0.032)
trend	−0.030**	−0.029**	−0.033**	−0.023**	−0.028**	−0.038**
	(0.002)	(0.001)	(0.002)	(0.003)	(0.001)	(0.002)
$\ln w_{t-1}^r$ [a]	−0.542**	−0.221	−0.365	−0.348	−0.616**	0.161
	(0.190)	(0.130)	(0.206)	(0.257)	(0.124)	(0.172)
observations	412	908	239	185	969	405
R^2adj.	0.935	0.936	0.937	0.931	0.937	0.939

Note: w^r is the relative earnings ratio, which is instrumented by its one-period lagged value
Standard errors in parentheses below parameter estimates; * 5% level significance, ** 1% level.

The estimation results for the subsamples of industries defined by the rate of total factor productivity growth show that the autonomous decline of the skill ratio in industries with high growth rates in the observation period was markedly higher than in the other sectors. In the former sector, the trend decline in the relative demand of unskilled labour was about 4 per cent per year, almost double the rate experienced in industries characterised by low rates of technological change. Assuming that the difference between the trend decline of the skills ratio in industries with a high (low) growth rate of total factor productivity proxies the effect of skill-biased technological change, this factor would explain at most half of the overall observed decline of the skills ratio in industries characterised by strong productivity growth.

The importance of relative earnings for determining the relative demand for skilled and unskilled labour at the industry level also depends on the rate of technological change. The substitution elasticity obtains its highest absolute value in industries where the rate of technological change is neither particularly high nor low. In the latter industries this elasticity is very imprecisely estimated, which is probably due to the small number of remaining observations in this sector. On the other hand, in industries with high rates of productivity growth changes in relative earnings seem to have no statistically significant effect on the relative demand for unskilled labour (the point estimate is even positive).

The results presented in Table 8.3 are rather insensitive to changes in the specification of the relative labour demand equation. Including the level of real output and the real capital stock or, alternatively, the capital–output ratio, the user costs of capital or the relative price of intermediate inputs has very little effect on the estimated trend decline in the skills ratio and the substitution elasticity (see also Steiner and Wagner 1997, Table 8.1).

8.5 SUMMARY AND CONCLUSIONS

Our empirical analysis has shown that the dramatic decline of the employment of unskilled labour occurred in all industries within West German manufacturing, but to a varying degree. Although the reduction in the relative supply of unskilled labour has certainly contributed to this development, it is only part of the story. The decline in the relative demand for unskilled labour has also played an important role. We find that the substitution elasticity between unskilled and skilled labour is rather low in most sectors of the economy, except for the construction sector and personal services. In these sectors, the earnings of unskilled workers have even increased relative to skilled workers in the observation period. In these sectors too, cuts in the relative earnings of unskilled workers could have contributed to a stabilisation of their relative employment level. However, the wages of unskilled women in personal services are still at a relatively low level, and an increase in wage inequality in this sector may therefore not be politically feasible. In other sectors of the economy, the decline in the employment share of unskilled workers attributable to an inflexible earnings structure therefore seems to have been modest compared to the trend decline in the skills ratio.

From the quite uniform decline of the skills ratio across broad sectors of the economy and within the manufacturing sector between industries with different levels of trade integration we conclude that increased international competition had little direct effects on the relative employment of unskilled labour. On the other hand, the rather uniform decline of the skills ratio across all sectors of the West German economy and the much stronger trend decline of the skills ratio in manufacturing industries characterised by a relatively high growth rate of total factor productivity seems compatible with the alternative hypothesis of unskilled-labour-biased technological change. This is also the hypothesis supported by most other studies for various countries (Berman et al. 1997; Machin and van Reenen 1997). However, technological change, too, can only explain part of the overall decline in the skills ratio in Germany. In particular, it does not explain the fact that the skills ratio has declined at a much faster rate for women than for men across all sectors of the German economy. This suggests that supply-side factors, in particular the general upgrading of the level of educational and vocational qualification has also played an important role for the trend decline of the skills ratio. These supply-side factors which could not be adequately taken into account in this study certainly merit to be more systematically explored in future studies on the relationship between structural chance, the adjustment of relative earnings and the substitution of unskilled labour in Germany.

NOTES

1. Here and in the following, Germany always refers to West Germany prior to unification in 1990.
2. For econometric studies on substitution elasticities in Germany, Kugler et al.(1988), Fitzroy and Funke (1995), Entorf (1996), Falk and Koebel (1997a, 1997b), Fitzenberger and Franz (1997), Steiner and Wagner (1998a), and Beissinger and Möller (1998).
3. These and, if not otherwise stated, the following facts are documented in Steiner and Wagner (1998a).
4. The differentiation between, respectively, production/non-production or blue-/white-collar workers often found in the US literature is, in our opinion, not a useful one, at least for the German situation. Another possible differentiation used in German studies is based on the qualification grouping ('Leistungsgruppen') found in collective bargaining agreements, which differentiates between three blue-collar and four white-collar groups (Entorf 1996 for a recent study). However, this classification does not differentiate workers by their level of labour market experience.
5. Note the lower real wage scale for women.
6. For the more general case without this strong separability assumption and with four factors of production see Shadma-Mehta and Sneesens (1995).
7. Due to the relatively small number of observations, separate estimation of the model for each experience group yielded mostly insignificant parameter estimates.
8. Both for males and females, an F-test cannot reject, at the 5 per cent level, the hypothesis that the trend coefficients for manufacturing, construction and transportation, wholesale and retail trade, and personal services are equal. The relevant test statistics are 0.54 for men and 2.43 for women.
9. Steiner and Wagner (1998a, Table 8.1) report a value of -0.321 for their specification (5) which also includes the lagged relative wage as an instrument and also the capital/output ratio as additional regressor. When they use the contemporaneous instead of the lagged earnings ratio in their specifications of the relative labour demand model they obtain a somewhat higher substitution elasticity of about -0.5.
10. These authors do not directly report substitution elasticities between unskilled and skilled labour, but they can be derived from the reported cross-price $\varepsilon_{x,u}$ and own-price elasticities $\varepsilon_{u,u}$ according to the formulae $\sigma_{u,s} = \varepsilon_{x,u} - \varepsilon_{u,u}$ (see Fitzenberger and Franz 1997, Table 3, Falk and Koebel, 1997a, Table 8.4). The results of Fitzenberger and Franz (1997) refer to males only, whereas Falk and Koebel (1997a) use aggregate data and thus cannot differentiate by gender.
11. The 'middle' category aggregates industries falling into the second and third quartile. We divided the observation period into three sub-periods (1975–79, 1980–84, 1985–90) and compared the relative position of each industry over time. It turned out that there was very little change in the industry ranking of import ratios in the observation period. The same also holds for the rate of total factor productivity growth which was obtained for each industry on the basis of a modified growth accounting procedure (see Steiner and Wagner 1998a).
12. The large standard error can be explained by the relatively small number of observations

remaining in this sector.

REFERENCES

Abraham, Katherine and Susan N. Houseman (1995), 'Earnings Inequality in Germany', in Richard B. Freeman and Lawrence F. Katz (eds), *Differences and Changes in Wage Structure*, University of Chicago Press.

Beissinger, Thomas and Joachim Möller (1998), 'Wage Flexibility and Employment Performance: A Microdata Analysis of Different Age-Education Groups for Germany', *Regensburger Diskussionsbeitraege* 307, Regensburg.

Berman, Eli, John Bound and Stephen Machin (1997), 'Implications of Skill-Biased Technological Change: International Evidence, Institute of Economics and Statistics', Discussion Paper Series *The Labour Market Consequences of Technical and Structural Change*, No. 25, University of Oxford.

Borghans, Lex, Andres de Grip and Peter J. Sloane (1998), 'Underutilisation of Skills, Bumping Down and Low Wages', in Claudio Lucifora and Wiemer Salverda (eds), *Policies for Low Wage Employment an Social Exclusion*, Franco Angeli, Milan.

Blau, Francine D. and Lawrence M. Kahn (1996), 'International Differences in Male Wage Inequality: Institutions versus Market Forces', *Journal of Political Economy*, **104**, 791–837.

Bound, John and George Johnson (1992), 'Changes in the Structure of Wages in the 1980s: An Evaluation of Alternative Explanations', *American Economic Review*, **82**, 371–92.

Card, David, Francis Kramarz and Thomas Lemieux (1996), *Changes in the Relative Structure of Wages and Employment: A Comparison of the United States, Canada and France*, NBER Working Paper, 5487.

Entorf, Horst (1996), 'Strukturelle Arbeitslosigkeit in Deutschland: Mismatch, Mobilität und Technischer Wandel', in Bernhard Gahlen et al. (eds), '*Arbeitslosigkeit und Möglichkeiten ihrer Überwindung*', Wirtschaftswissenschaftliches Seminar Ottobeuren, J.C.B. Mohr (Paul Siebeck) Tübingen (1996), 139–70.

Falk, Martin and Bertrand Koebel (1997a), *The Demand for Heterogeneous Labour in Germany*, ZEW Discussion Paper No. 97-28, Mannheim.

Falk, Martin and Bertrand Koebel (1997b), 'Determinanten der qualifikatorischen Arbeitsnachfrage in der westdeutschen Industrie 1978–90: FuE-intensive versus nicht FuE-intensive Industrien, in Friedhelm Pfeiffer and Winfried Pohlmeier (eds) (1997), *Qualifikation, Weiterbildung und Arbeitsmarkterfolg* ZEW Wirtschaftsanalysen,Vol. **31** Nomos Verlagsgesellschaft.

Fitzenberger, Bernd and Wolfgang Franz (1997), 'Flexibilität der qualifikatorischen Lohnstruktur und Lastverteilung der Arbeitslosigkeit: Eine ökonometrische Analyse für Westdeutschland', ZEW Discussion Paper No. 97-32, Mannheim.

Fitzroy, Felix and Michael Funke (1994), 'Capital-Skill Complementarity in West German Manufacturing', Empirical Economics, **20**, 651–65.

Gottschalk, Peter and Timothy M. Smeeding (1997), 'Cross National Comparisons of Earnings and Income Inequality', *Journal of Economic Literature*, **35**, 633–87.

Greene, William H. (1993), *Econometric Analysis*, Macmillan, New York.

Goux, Dominique and Eric Maurin (1997), 'The Decline in Demand for Unskilled Labour: An Empirical Analysis Method and its Application to France', INSEE Working Paper, Paris.

Hamermesh, Daniel S. (1993), *Labour Demand*, Princeton University Press.
Katz, Lawrence and Kevin Murphy (1992), 'Changes in Relative Wages 1963–1987: Supply and Demand Factors', *Quarterly Journal of Economics*, February 1992, 35–78.
Krueger, Alan B. and Jörn-Steffen Pischke (1997), 'Observations and Conjectures on the USA Employment Miracle', NBER Working Paper No. 6146, Cambridge, Mass.
Kugler, Peter, Urs Müller and George Sheldon (1988), 'Struktur der Arbeitsfrage im technologischen Wandel – Eine empirische Analyse für die Bundesrepublik Deutschland', Weltwirtschaftliches Archiv, 124, 490–500.
Machin Stephen and John van Reenen, 'Technology and Changes in Skill Structure: Evidence from Seven OECD Countries', Institute of Economics and Statistics, Discussion Paper Series, *The Labour Market Consequences of Technical and Structural Change*, No. 24, University of Oxford.
Möller, Joachim (1996), 'Technological Change, Unemployment, and Recent Trends in Human Capital Formation – Did the German Wage Structure Respond to these Impulses?', *Regensburger Diskussionsbeiträge*, No. 280, Universität Regensburg.
Nickell, Stephen (1997), 'Unemployment and Labour Market Rigidities: Europe versus North America', *Journal of Economic Perspectives*, **11**, 55–74.
Nickell, Stephen and Brian Bell (1995), 'The Collapse in Demand for the Unskilled and Unemployment Across the OECD', *Oxford Review of Economic Policy*, **11**, 40–62.
Nickell, Stephen and Brian Bell (1997), 'Would Cutting Payroll Taxes on the Unskilled have a Significant Impact on Unemployment?', in Dennis J. Snower and Guillermo de la Dehesa (eds), *Unemployment Policy. Government Options for the Labour Market*, Cambridge University Press.
OECD (1996), *Employment Outlook*, Chapter 3, Paris.
Sachverständigenrat (German Council of Economic Experts) (1994), *Jahresgutachten 1994/95 des Sachverständigenrates zur Begutachtung der gesamtwirtschaftlichen Entwicklung*.
Shadman-Mehta, Fatemeh and Henri Sneesens (1995), 'Skill Demand and Factor Stubstitution', CEPR Discusssion Paper No. 1279, London.
Siebert, Horst (1997), 'Labour Market Rigidities and Unemployment in Europe', *Journal of Economic Perspectives*, **11**, 37–54.
Steiner, Viktor and Kersten Wagner (1998a), 'Relative Earnings and the Demand for Unskilled Labour in West German Manufacturing', in Stanley Black (ed.), *Globalization, Technological Change, and the Welfare State*, Kluwer Academic Publisher, Boston/Dordrecht/London.
Steiner, Viktor and Kersten Wagner (1998b), 'Has Earnings Inequality in Germany Changed in the 1980s?', *Zeitschrift für Wirtschafts- und Sozialwissenschaften*, **118**, 29–59.

DATA APPENDIX

We match sectoral information from the disaggregated national accounts and individual-level employment as well as earnings information from the Employment Register of the Federal Labour Office, the so-called '*IAB-Beschäftigtenstichprobe*', IABS for short (for details see Steiner and Wagner

1998a, 1998b). The IABS is a 1 per cent random sample of all dependently employed persons living in Germany who are covered by the social security system. The database from which the IABS is drawn includes about 80 per cent of all employed people in Germany. In each of these years, about 200,000 individuals were randomly sampled from the population. For our empirical analysis, the sample is restricted to full-time employed males and females, apprentices are excluded.

Table 8.A1
Industry classifications in the IABS

IABS Code(s)	Description	Sector/subsector
00–08	agriculture, forestry, fishing, energy and mining	agriculture, mining
09–13	chemical products, oil products, rubber	manufacturing
14–24	stone, clay, glass, primary metals, fabricated metals	manufacturing
25–32	mechanical machinery	manufacturing
33–39	data processing, office and electrical machinery	manufacturing
40–58	lumber, furniture, paper, printing, leather, textiles, food, tobacco	manufacturing
59–61	construction	construction
	wholesale and retail trade	trade
63–68	transportation	transportation
	credit and insurance	business services
70–71	restaurants, hotels and accommodations	personal services
72–73, 86	barbers, cleaning services and other services	personal services
74–75	educational services	public services
	art and theatre	public services
	publication and literature	business services
79–81	law, financial consulting, architecture, engineering and real estate	business services
82–83	marketing and photography	business services
78, 84	hygiene, medicine and veterinary services	personal services
	auction houses	business services
87–89	NGOs, politics and churches	public services
	private homes	personal services
91, 93	General public administration and social	public services
	security defense and public safety	public services
	representation of foreign nations	public services

Aside from the very large sample size, the greatest advantage of the IABS is its supposedly reliable earnings data, although there are some shortcomings as described in Steiner and Wagner (1998b). The IABS also contains information on an individual's vocational/educational qualification and age which can be used to construct skill groups as defined by the level of formal qualification and labour market experience. Following Steiner and Wagner (1998a, 1998b), we use the following three vocational/educational groups: no vocational/education degree, vocational degree/higher education, and university/polytechnical degree. Following usual practice, we define an individual's potential labour market experience as: age – years of schooling – six years. Years of schooling are derived from the highest vocational/ educational degree as described in Steiner and Wagner (1998a, Table 5.A1).

The IABS contains information on an individual's industry affiliation at the two digit-level. For the sectoral analysis in Section 8.4 industries were aggregated as described in Table 8.A1. For the more detailed analysis of the manufacturing sector, industries were aggregated into 30 two-digit industries as described in Steiner and Wagner (1998a, Table 5.A2), where the classification of industries by quartile of import share and growth rate of total factor productivity, respectively, is also given.

9. Recent Findings on Trade, Technology and Wage Inequality

Jonathan E. Haskel[1]

9.1 INTRODUCTION

Figure 9.1 shows the United Kingdom skilled/unskilled wage differential in manufacturing since 1958 (with the comparable data for the US shown as well).[2] The relative wage fell more or less continuously from the end of the war to the late 1970s. Since then, it has risen very sharply; indeed the proportional rise exceeding the widely-discussed US figure.[3]

Figure 9.1
UK and US skilled/unskilled wage differentials (W_s/W_u)

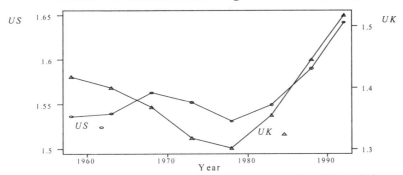

Note: UK differential is the manufacturing non-manual/manual wage ratio and the US is the non-production/production ratio.

Sources: UK Census of Manufacturing and US NBER productivity data set.

Three main theories have been advanced to explain these trends: (a) changes in world trading conditions that have had Stolper–Samuelson (SS) effects lowering the wage of the unskilled, (b) changes in technology that have lowered labour demand for the unskilled[4] and (c) changes in institutions, for example minimum wages or unionisation, that have disadvantaged the unskilled.[5] Our focus here is on SS effects.

Understanding the contributions of these effects is important for understanding the situation of low-wage workers and policy. It is clearly desirable to have increased information on the way that trade might have affected the labour market and the Heckscher–Ohlin model set out in this chapter is a way of addressing this issue. Equally, if the model that is based on market clearing and has no explicit role for institutions does not account well for labour market changes, then it is important to develop other models of non-market-clearing and institutions that incorporate trade. As for policy, if, for example, foreign trade has raised inequality then protectionism might be a policy to reverse it (although even those who argue that foreign trade is important have been cautious about protectionism, for example, Wood 1994). Even if protectionism is ruled out, estimating the magnitudes of these effects is important in forecasting the consequences of future policy, for example the reduction of trade barriers.

A number of recent empirical UK studies have looked for SS effects, see for example Desjonqueres et al. (1997) and Neven and Wyplosz (1996) (see Wood 1994, for a factor content study). The SS effect arises in the (production side of the) Heckscher–Ohlin (HO) model.[6] It arises from the assumption that each sector in the economy makes zero profits, so that when prices change, relative wages have to change to restore zero-profit equilibrium. SS-induced increases in wage inequality arise when prices fall for goods produced in industries that employ unskilled workers relatively intensively. When prices change differently across sectors of different skill-intensity, price changes are said to be 'sector biased'. To detect the sector bias of price changes, empirical analysis therefore regresses changes in prices on industry skilled–unskilled employment ratios for a cross-section of industries. A positive coefficient suggests that prices have risen relatively more in skilled-employment-intensive industries (or equivalently have fallen in unskilled-employment-intensive industries). This is referred to as a skilled sector bias price change. In fact this work typically finds that prices did *not* seem to have fallen relatively in the unskilled-intensive industries in the 1980s. Rather the coefficient tends to be insignificant, indicating no strong sector bias of price changes. This has led to the conclusion that there is little evidence for SS effects in the 1980s.

There are, however, number of difficulties with these studies. First, the type of regression described immediately above is misspecified relative to HO theory. The zero-profit relation links the level of prices and levels of factor inputs. Yet the coefficient estimated is from a regression of the change in prices on the level of factor inputs. In addition, the regression is for the ratio of just two inputs, and so does not account for other inputs. Second, a number of details of the studies may be criticised: Desjonqueres et al. (1997) for example have only 17 sectors on which they base their cross-industry studies.

This chapter therefore looks again for SS effects on UK skill premia. We follow Leamer's (1998) approach to estimating SS effects, using an analogous data set to Leamer's for the UK (his was based on the US *Census of Production* industry data, ours is based on the UK *Census of Production*). Hence our work is of interest for comparative purposes. It is also of interest since our findings are different to other studies for the UK and to Leamer's for the US: we do find SS effects on UK skill premia for the 1980s.

As well as SS effects we can also look at the effects of technology. Just as changes in prices require a sector bias to change skill premia, so do changes in technology, that is technical progress has to be faster in the skilled-employment-intensive industries. We find that UK technical change in the 1980s had no clear sector bias and hence did not contribute to wage inequality.

The next section of this chapter begins by reviewing the theory of technical and price change in two-sector models. We then outline the Leamer (1998) approach to measuring sector bias. Section 9.3 discusses the UK data and presents our results. Section 9.4 concludes.

9.2   ESTIMATING STOLPER–SAMUELSON EFFECTS

The Labour and Trade Approaches to Wage Inequality[7]

The standard labour approach to estimating the effects of wage inequality is based on supply and demand. There are two typical empirical implementations of this. First, relative (skilled/unskilled) labour supply is calculated from aggregate population data. Then, using a CES-type production function to generate relative labour demand and assuming relative wages are determined by supply and demand, aggregate relative demand is calculated as a residual from changes in relative wages net of supplies, see for example Johnson (1997). As Katz and Autor (1999) are careful to point out, such changes in aggregate relative demand change could come from skill-biased technical change, trade, changes in taste or any other factor that might have caused intersectoral demand changes.

The second empirical route is to use industry data to estimate relative labour demand functions and see if there is evidence that technical progress is skill-biased. Typically, skill-biased technical change (SBTC) is found in many industries. With the supply/demand intuition the presence of SBTC in many sectors seems strong evidence that technology has caused the skill premium to rise. However, trade theory suggests that the finding is not as conclusive as first thought. Suppose that there is SBTC (or indeed product price changes) in sector A but not in sector B. Does this mean there is no change in relative wages in sector B? The answer critically depends on whether workers can move between sectors A and B. In the long run, it seems reasonable to suppose they can: a cleaner in industry A can be a cleaner in industry B. Now, if relative wages are increased in sector A then presumably skilled workers will migrate to that sector unless relative wages rise in sector B. Hence relative wages must change in sector B, even though there is no SBTC there. But this means that if workers can move between sectors, it is perfectly possible that relative wages might change in a sector even with *no* SBTC in that sector. Put another way, the supply/demand partial equilibrium intuition breaks down in general equilibrium.

Can one then make any conclusions about the connection between technical change and relative wages in multi-sector models when workers are mobile between sectors? The (production side) of the standard trade literature, the 2 × 2 HO model, assumes two sectors (of unequal skill-intensity), two factors (skilled and unskilled labour) and mobile labour between sectors. Now, the model has mostly been used to look at the SS effects, that is the effect of exogenous changes in prices on relative wages (see, for example Slaughter 1999). Here the effects are well-known. As set out in the introduction, the model starts with zero profits in both sectors. Any change in product prices induces changes in factor prices to restore zero profits. A rise in prices in the skill-intensive sector raises profits there and skilled/unskilled wages must rise to restore general equilibrium (to show this, note that any *fall* in relative skilled wages merely raises the relative profitability in the skilled sector and so exacerbates the disequilibrium). It can be shown that the effect of price changes on relative wages depends on the 'sector bias' of those price changes: if they are in the skilled (unskilled) intensive sectors, then relative wages rise (fall).

Analysis of technical change in this model is, however, comparatively sparse. In an early paper, Findlay and Grubert (1958) considered technical change in one sector. They showed that the intuition of sector bias held as well. If technical change lowers costs, then it too raises sector profits, just as changes in prices do. Such changes in profits cause changes in wages to restore zero-profit equilibrium. Hence technical change that reduces costs more in the skilled (unskilled) sector raises (lowers) wage inequality.[8]

A more recent literature, summarised in Haskel and Slaughter (1998) and Johnson and Stafford (1998), considers the case of technical change that then influences sector product prices. Hence there are two effects: the 'direct' effect on profits (via costs) at given product prices (as analysed by Findlay and Grubert 1959) and the additional 'indirect' effect on profits from the change in product prices. Davis (1997) and Krugman (1995) consider these two effects in a model with technical change in one sector. As Haskel and Slaughter (1998) show, these effects oppose each other, but if the indirect effects are small then the sector bias intuition still holds.[9] Berman et al. (1998) consider (skill-biased) technical change in *both* sectors that influences product prices, and claim that this raises relative wages. Once again, however, there is a direct and indirect effect, but Berman et al. (1998) look at the special case where there is no direct effect as the changes in both sectors exactly offset each other.[10] As Haskel and Slaughter (1998) show the results critically depend on this assumption.

It is worth noting that the type of technical change matters in these models. Hicks-neutral technical change unambiguously raises the productivity of all factors and so lowers costs and raises profits. The effect of SBTC depends on its exact form. If it raises the productivity of skilled workers *ceteris paribus* (intensive SBTC, Johnson and Stafford 1998) it lowers costs. But if it raises the productivity of skilled workers *and also* lowers that of unskilled workers (extensive SBTC, Johnson and Stafford 1998), it may not lower costs.[11] See Haskel and Slaughter (1998) and Johnson and Stafford (1998) for more discussion.

The empirical implications of this are therefore that in a multi-sector model with labour mobility one should look for the sector bias of changes in prices and all types of technology. The contribution of Leamer (1998) is to set out a formal framework in which this may be done.

Leamer's Approach to Measuring Sector Bias

Following the production side of HO theory assume that competition ensures that price equals average cost in all tradable industries in a country and that labour is mobile across industries. For any sector i this condition can be written as

$$p_I = a_{si}w_s + a_{ui}w_u \tag{9.1}$$

where p_i is the domestic gross-output price in sector i; w_s and w_u, are the domestic prices for skilled and unskilled labour and a_{ji} is the quantity of factor j required to produce one unit of product i and for the moment we ignore intermediate inputs and capital (see the appendix for the algebra when they are included). Note that w_s and w_u are not indexed by i, since free mobility ensures equal wage across sectors for given skill types. Differentiating (9.1) for sufficiently small time periods gives (Leamer 1998)

$$\Delta\log p_{it} + \Delta\log TFP_{it} = (\Delta\log w_{st} \times V_{s,it}) + (\Delta\log w_{ut} \times V_{u,it}) \tag{9.2}$$

where $V_{s,it}$ and $V_{u,it}$ are the skilled and unskilled wage bill shares in total costs and $\Delta \log TFP_{it}$ is total factor productivity growth (real output growth less cost share-weighted real input growth).

Equation (9.2) shows how skilled and unskilled wages adjust to the sector bias of changes in prices ($\Delta \log p_{it}$) and technology ($\Delta \log TFP_{it}$) at initial cost shares. To recap, if such changes are in the skilled or unskilled-intensive sectors, defined by cost shares, they change relative sectoral profitability (note that cost shares are appropriate, since they determine how profits are affected by changes in factor prices). This induces changes in economy-wide factor prices to restore zero-profit general equilibrium. Such changes depend on the sector bias of changes in prices and TFP. Note that changes in TFP, which of course include neutral and biased technical change (Berndt and Wood 1982) matter, since any type of technical change might change costs and so relative sectoral profits.

Leamer (1998) partitions out the effects on relative wages due to trade and technology as follows. Suppose the technology effect on wages (denoted $\Delta \log w_{st}(t)$ and $\Delta \log w_{ut}(t)$) is that arising from TFP growth and the portion of changes in prices due to technology (denoted $\Delta \log p_{it}(t)$). This gives

$$\Delta \log p_{it}(t) + \Delta \log TFP_{it} = [\Delta \log w_{st}(t) \times V_{s,it}) + (\Delta \log w_{ut}(t) \times V_{u,it}] \qquad (9.3)$$

Analogously, the SS or globalisation effect is defined as

$$\Delta \log p_{it}(g) = [\Delta \log w_{st}(g) \times V_{s,it}) + (\Delta \log w_{ut}(g) \times V_{u,it}] \qquad (9.4)$$

where actual price changes are an amalgam of prices changes due to technology and globalisation

$$\Delta \log p_{it} = \Delta \log p_{it}(t) + \Delta \log p_{it}(g) \qquad (9.5)$$

Define the price change induced by technology, $\Delta \log p_{it}$ as

$$\Delta \log p_{it}(t) = \lambda \Delta \log TFP_{it} \qquad (9.6)$$

where λ is the pass-through from changes in TFP to prices. Combining (9.3), (9.5) and (9.6) gives that the effect of technology on wages is

$$(1 - \lambda) \Delta \log TFP_{it} = [\Delta \log w_{st}(t) \times V_{s,it}] + [\Delta \log w_{ut}(t) \times V_{u,it}] \qquad (9.7)$$

and the effect of globalisation on wages is

$$\Delta \log p_{it}(g) + \lambda \Delta \log TFP_{it} = [\Delta \log w_{ut}(g) \times V_{s,it}] + [\Delta \log w_{ut}(g) \times V_{u,it}] \qquad (9.8)$$

With different assumptions on λ, the effects of globalisation and technology can be estimated from (9.7) and (9.8). Suppose, for example, that the UK is a small open economy so that $\Delta \log p_{it}$ is exogenously determined by international forces, and that $\Delta \log TFP_{it}$ is exogenous. Then $\lambda = 0$ and the SS effects can be written

$$\Delta \log p_{it} = [\Delta \log w_{st}(g) \times V_{s,it}] + [\Delta \log w_{ut}(g) \times V_{u,it}] \qquad (9.9)$$

In (9.9), we can use data on prices, outputs and inputs to construct $\Delta\log p_{it}$, $V_{s,it}$ and $V_{u,\,it}$. The terms $\Delta\log w_s$ and $\Delta\log w_u$ are of course unknown since they are the changes in economy-wide factor prices required to maintain zero profits in the face of price changes. To find them, Leamer (1998) estimates

$$\Delta\log p_{it} = \beta_s V_{s,it} + \beta_u V_{u,\,it} + \varepsilon_{1it} \tag{9.10}$$

here β_s and β_u are coefficients to be estimated and ε_{1it} is a random error arising from measurement error, the failure of zero profits to hold exactly etc. Comparing (9.9) and (9.10), β_s and β_u estimate changes in skilled and unskilled wages, consistent with zero profits, in response to changes in prices, that is SS effects. These coefficients summarise the sector bias of $\Delta\log p_{it}$. If $\beta_s > \beta_u$ ($\beta_u > \beta_s$) then price changes are concentrated in skilled-intensive (unskilled-intensive) sectors, in which case relative skilled wages rise (fall).

Similarly the effects of technology when $\lambda = 0$ are

$$\Delta\log TFP_{it} = [\Delta\log w_{st}(t) \times V_{s,it}] + [\Delta\log w_{ut}(t) \times V_{u,it}] \tag{9.11}$$

in which case we construct $\Delta\log TFP_{it}$, $V_{s,it}$ and $V_{u,it}$ and estimate the regression, where ε_{2it} is an iid error

$$\Delta\log TFP_{it} = \gamma_s V_{s,it} + \gamma_u V_{u,it} + \varepsilon_{2it} \tag{9.12}$$

where comparing (9.11) and (9.12), γ_s and γ_u estimate the changes in skilled and unskilled wages consistent with zero profits in response to changes in TFP. Finally, the total estimated change in log w_s, $\beta_s + \gamma_s$, and in $\log w_u$, $\beta_u + \gamma_u$ can of course be compared with actual changes to gauge the accuracy of the model.[12]

Discussion of the HO Framework

Regarding the HO model above, the following points are worth noting. First, the regressions performed for the UK by Neven and Wyplosz (1996) and Desjonqueres et al. (1997) (and earlier for the US by Lawrence and Slaughter, 1993) are of the form

$$\Delta\log p_{it} = \alpha + \beta (N_s/N_u)_{it} + \varepsilon_{it} \tag{9.13}$$

Whilst N_s/N_u is a readily available measure, (9.10) shows that the theoretically appropriate specification is in terms of cost shares.

Second, the production side of HO theory seems more appropriate in the long run for it assumes competition works to bid profits to zero and the workers are mobile enough to equalise wages. What then if these assumptions do not hold? As for the zero (normal) profits assumption, the method still follows with positive profits so long as they are constant over time.[13] As for labour immobility, this would presumably enable workers to earn sector-specific rents. Such rents (and unobserved quality) might be part of the explanation as to why skilled and unskilled wages differ across industries (Katz and Summers 1989). To the extent rents exist, then part of the change in inequality could be due to changes in the ability of skilled and unskilled to capture rents due, for example, to changes in unionisation.

There are two issues here, theoretical and empirical. On the theory side, Davidson et al. (1999) examine SS effects in a model where there is immobility between sectors due to imperfect matching and wages are determined by means of a Nash bargain between employers and matched skilled and unskilled workers. In the short to medium run, the (expected) wages of currently unmatched workers in the face of sector biased price changes depend on their skill, as predicted by SS theory, since they are mobile between sectors. The wages of matched workers depend instead on their sector (for example, wages of the matched skilled in the skill-intensive sector rise if prices rise in the wage-intensive sector). In the long run matched workers face an increased chance of being unmatched and hence wage changes depend on skills rather than sectoral attachments. Thus theory suggests that our empirical analysis should be conducted over sufficient time to enable workers to flow between sectors.

On the empirical side, Borjas and Ramey (1995) find little effect on US skill premia from changes in industry rents.[14] Overall, then, it seems reasonable, at a first pass, to fit an institution-free model, but based on a well worked out general equilibrium model, and see how accurately it predicts wages. If its predictions are poor, this suggests incorporating instititions and/or monopoly rents in future work.

Third, in the HO model labour supply affects relative wages if changes in labour supply affect the range of products being made and hence lead to a new set of zero-profit conditions, or if supply changes lead to output changes which affect relative prices. The model we estimate looks only at the demand side and assumes that the range of products remains the same. Once again, we feel that a pragmatic approach is therefore to compare our estimated wages with actual wages: if they do not match, then supply might be important. We return to this issue below.

9.3   DATA AND RESULTS

Since the 1980s are of such interest, we look at two data sets both based on the UK Census of Production which covers manufacturing.[15] The first is the Oulton and O'Mahony (OO) panel comprising 123 three-digit industries 1979–86 (Oulton and O'Mahony 1994).[16] These data cross a major change in the SIC industry definition in 1980 and are matched to the 1968 classification (OO, Appendix C). The data set contains information on prices and quantities of output, labour, capital and intermediate goods. The labour data is divided into manual and non-manual employees, and we use this as our measure of unskilled and skilled workers, respectively. Whilst this is not ideal, it is correlated with industry education differences (Haskel and Heden 1999) and it is the only skill measure consistently available with disaggregated trade and technology indicators. The second data set is also drawn from the Census but covers 67 three-digit industrial sectors, 1980–89 (on the 1980 SIC classification, see Haskel (1999a). Hence it covers the whole of the 1980s and does not cross any change in SIC definition. Details of data construction are set out in the data appendix.

Results

We start by estimating the Lawrence–Slaughter equation (9.13). Table 9.1 shows the results.

Table 9.1
Regression estimates of equation (9.13)
dependent variable $\Delta \log p_{it}$

	1979–86	1980–89
$(N_s/N_u)_{I, t-1}$	0.18	0.04
	(1.99)	(0.40)
R^2	0.13	0.01
Number of observations	123	68

Note: Each column reports estimations of (9.13) for different years. Independent variable dated at start of year shown. Equations weighted by average-period employment. Absolute heteroscedastic-robust t statistics in parentheses.

These regressions suggest that prices rose mostly in the skill-intensive industries which would suggest a role for price in the rise in wage inequality in that time. One should, however, be cautious since the equation is not consistent with (9.10).[17]

Turning to the Leamer (1998) method, Table 9.2 reports estimates of (9.10) and (9.12) (plus capital share, see A6 and A7 in the Appendix) using three different data sets. To read this table, consider the top left-hand cell. This shows that between 1979 and 1986 TFP changes were such that skilled wages would have to have risen 6 per cent to maintain zero profits across sectors. The cell underneath shows unskilled wages would have to have risen by 49 per cent. Hence the rise in inequality over this period mandated by technology is (6–49) = –43 per cent. This says that technical change was mainly in the unskilled-intensive sector.

The next two columns show the same regression using different data sets. The second column uses the 1980–89 three-digit *Census* data, and shows that the sector bias of $\Delta\log TFP_{it}$ is slightly concentrated in the unskilled-intensive sector. Column 3 shows the results obtained by Gregory and Zissimos (1998). Their data consists of 87 sectors based on the UK input/output tables. They include the service sector and their skill categories are high-, medium- and low-educated workers (measured by average industry educational attainment). As the table shows, $\Delta\log TFP_{it}$ is concentrated in the unskilled-intensive sectors.

Table 9.2

Sector bias of prices and technology in the 1980s:

estimates of equations (9.10) and (9.12) plus capital

(dependent variables: $\Delta\log p_{it}$ and $\Delta\log TFP_{it}$ for each indicated year interval)

	$\Delta\log TFP_{it}$			$\Delta\log p_{it}$		
study	HS	HS	GZ	HS	HS	GZ
years	1979–86	1980–89	1981–91	1979–86	1980–89	1981–91
data	3-digit	3-digit	IO	3-digit	3-digit	IO
V_s	0.06	0.22	−0.47	0.92	0.77	2.50
	(0.13)	(0.41)	(0.16)	(2.11)	(1.40)	(5.38)
V_u	0.49	0.29	3.65	−0.16	0.08	−0.31
	(3.18)	(1.47)	(1.37)	(0.96)	(0.40)	(0.74)
V_k	−0.49	0.21	−1.39	0.94	0.16	1.55
	(1.67)	(0.40)	(0.84)	(3.37)	(0.27)	(6.00)
$\beta_s \neq \beta_u$ (p val)						
	0.42	0.92	–	0.05	0.36	–
R^2	0.16	0.05	0.95	0.30	0.15	0.95
Observations	123	67	87	123	67	87

Notes: Absolute heteroscedastic-robust t statistics in parentheses. Capital share of total costs included as a regressor: coefficients not reported. Studies are HS (Haskel and Slaughter 1999), GZ (Gregory and Zissimos 1998) using, respectively, 3-digit industry and input/output data. V_s and V_u are shares in total costs of: non-manual and manuals (HS) and high and medium-educated workers (GZ). GZ also include the share of low-educated workers (not reported). – indicates p not available.

Sources: Gregory and Zissimos (1998, Tables 4 and 5); Haskel and Slaughter (1999, Table 2).

In sum, these point estimates consistently find that $\Delta\log TFP_{it}$ was concentrated in the unskilled-intensive sector. The key test is, however, whether $\Delta\log TFP_{it}$ was significantly concentrated in the skilled or unskilled sectors, or neither. To test this formally, the fourth row shows the p value for the probability of accepting the hypothesis that the coefficient on V_s equals that on V_u (this was not reported in GZ). In both cases one can accept the hypothesis, at conventional levels of significance, confirming that $\Delta\log TFP_{it}$

was not significantly concentrated in either the skilled or unskilled sector. The *t* statistics on the coefficients for the GZ case suggest this is also likely to be the case, but without the appropriate covariances this cannot be tested formally from the data given.

The picture for prices, set out in the right-hand panel, is rather different. All point estimates suggest price rises were concentrated in the skilled-intensive sector. Looking at the *p* values, the 1979–86 price changes were significantly concentrated in the skill-intensive sector. The 1980–89 significance test shows no statistically significant concentration over those years (although when we reran the regression for 1980–88 we obtained a *p* value of 0.07 for $\Delta \log p_{it}$ and 0.48 for $\Delta \log TFP_{it}$). Once again we cannot compute a p value for the GZ data, but the point estimates suggest a significant difference between V_s and V_u. Thus we conclude there is suggestive evidence for significant SS effects in the UK in the 1980s.

A number of issues arise from these findings. First, how do these results relate to other work? Haskel and Slaughter (1998) examine the sector bias of SBTC and find that SBTC was concentrated in the skill-intensive industries during the 1980s. The different sector biases of SBTC and TFP highlight the fact that TFP is a combination of factor-biased and factor-neutral technical change. For the US, Leamer estimates that TFP growth and product prices changes had no clear sector bias during the 1980s. At the very least, this evidence suggests that advanced economies do not all share common trade shocks (though they may share common technology shocks).

Second, a consistent result from Table 9.2 is that the actual unskilled wage increase exceeds the one predicted by the zero profit conditions.[18] This suggests that there may be institutional forces, not modelled, that are maintaining unskilled wages above what they would otherwise be.

Third, our work begs the question of what causes $\Delta \log TFP_{it}$ and $\Delta \log p_{it}$. In a small open economy prices are exogenous. Haskel and Slaughter (1999) examine this by regressing $\Delta \log p_{it}$ on foreign prices and trade barriers and find that both caused a significant rise in wage inequality in the 1980s.

9.4   CONCLUSION

This chapter estimates Stolper–Samuelson effects on UK relative wages for the 1980s to see if prices have fallen in relatively unskilled-intensive sectors (where factor-intensity is measured by factor cost shares). We find significant Stolper–Samuelson effects that raised UK wage inequality over the 1980s. We also find, consistently across different datasets, that technical change had no clear sector bias, suggesting the technical change did not contribute to increased wage inequality over the period.

We see two particular avenues for further work. On the theory side, developing tractable, empirically-orientated general equilibrium models that relax some of the assumptions, such as free mobility, and incorporates institutions, seems to be important. On the empirical side, developing a better understanding of what drives industry product price changes seems to be vital in understanding the behaviour of wage inequality. As for policy, to the extent that price changes are driven by policies such as tariffs (Haskel and Slaughter, 1999) future falls in tariffs are likely to raise wage inequality. This suggests that inequality is likely to remain on the policy agenda and could explain some of the opposition to tariff reform. Also, giving citizens subsidised computers is, of itself, unlikely to narrow the wage gap.

NOTES

1. This chapter reports some of the empirical results contained in Haskel and Slaughter (1999). For financial support Haskel thanks the U.K. Economic and Social Research Council for grants R000236653 and R000222730 and Slaughter thanks the Russell Sage Foundation for grants #85-96-18 and #85-97-18. We particularly thank an anonymous referee for very useful comments and participants at the 1998 LoWER meeting. Thanks to Ylva Heden for excellent research assistance. Errors are our own.
2. The UK differential is measured by the non-manual/manual wage differential. This is correlated with the differential as measured by years of schooling, see Haskel and Heden (1999).
3. The UK data is used in the regressions below. The non-manual/manual relative wage fell in the 1970s and then rose in the 1980s in many OECD countries, although the 1980s increases were rather less in Scandinavian countries than in the UK or US (Haskel and Slaughter 1998). We do not show other countries to avoid clutter.
4. Wood (1994) argues that changes in technology have been caused, at least in part, by changes in trade.
5. For institutional work see, for example, Blau and Khan (1996), Card (1998), DiNardo et al. (1996), Fortin and Lemieux (1997), Freeman (1993, 1996), OECD (1996).
6. The 'production side' of HO theory assumes (i) different technologies across sectors leading to different factor intensities; (ii) zero profits in each sector and (iii) factor mobility. Additional assumptions (for example countries having the same tastes and technology, free trade and so on) are necessary to make predictions about specialisation, international factor-price equalisation and so on. Those additional assumptions are *not* made here and so Stolper–Samuelson effects are not dependent on these additional assumptions. Assuming zero profits and factor mobility suggests applying the model to the long run when firms have sufficient time to compete profiable opportunities away and workers to move. The consequences of relaxing these assumptions are set out below.
7. This section draws on Haskel (1999b) which has further discussion.
8. In the light of this, consider the finding that many industries have had rises in both skill-intensity and relative wages (Berman et al. 1994). It is theoretically possible that SBTC might be raising the skill-intensity of various sectors with no effect on relative wages. As argued above, what drives relative wages is the sector bias of technical change. It is not enough to know that SBTC is occurring in many sectors to know what is happening to relative wages, rather one needs to know its sector bias and whether SBTC has lowered costs in a sector, see below and note 10.
9. Krugman (1995) claims that SBTC in either sector raises relative wages. This claim is only true, however, if one ignores the direct effect and assumes Leontief production functions

(Haskel and Slaughter 1998).

10. They assume that technical change lowers costs in both skilled and unskilled-intensive sectors, but the cost changes are equal so that relative sector profits do not change. Hence there is no direct effect on relative wages arising from changes in intersectoral profitability, but an indirect effect as SBTC induces price changes.

11. Consider the cost function $C=\{[\alpha^{\sigma}(w_s/\lambda_s)^{1-\sigma}+ (1-\alpha)^{\sigma}(w_u/\lambda_u)^{1-\sigma}]\}^{1/(1-\sigma)} A^{-1} Y$ where λ_s and λ_u are intensive skilled and unskilled labour biased technical progress, α is extensive skilled labour biased technical progress and A is neutral technical progress. The intuition behind extensive and intensive is that a rise in λ_i can be thought of as an increase in the ability of each type of worker to perform the job they currently do, whereas a rise in α is that skilled workers improve their potential ability to preform the tasks that unskilled workers do (Johnson and Stafford 1998, Section 4.6). Straightforward differentiation shows that neutral technical change (a rise in A) lowers C, intensive biased technical change (a rise in λ) lowers C but extensive biased technical change (a rise in α) lowers C if the wage bill share of the skilled in total costs exceeds α. The intuition here is that the skilled have to be sufficiently important in total costs for an increase in their efficiency to lower costs.

12. Leamer also considers $\lambda = 1$ in which case one regresses the sum of $\Delta\log TFP_{it}$ and $\Delta\log p_{it}$ on the cost shares. The coefficients from this regression are simply the sums of the coefficients from the regressions (9.10) and (9.12).

13. Evaluating this assumption is hard since it is difficult to compute normal returns to capital. Leamer (1998) subsumes profits into the return to capital by defining capital payments as gross output less the wage bill less material costs since he argues that capital measures are inadequate to measure capital's payments independently.

14. Gosling and Machin (1996) find evidence that unions are not important in explaining the variance of UK wages. The work referenced in note 5 suggest that institutions are important but such work does not look at industry rents in a general equilibrium model. One possibility is that institutions work in other ways besides rent-sharing.

15. Haskel and Slaughter (1999a) find that TFP growth was significantly skilled-sector biased in the 1960s but neither price nor TFP growth were significantly sector biased in the 1970s.

16. We are extremely grateful to Nicholas Oulton for kindly providing us with these data.

17. Our finding is qualitatively similar to Neven and Wyplosz (1996), who find an insignificantly positive relationship, as do Desjonqueres et al. (1997). It is difficult to relate these different studies, however, because of differences in timing and in industry coverage (for example, Desjonqueres et al., 1997, have data for only 17 industries).

18. For the 1979–86 data the mandated skilled wage rise is 0.97 (with 95 per cent confidence intervals 0.63 and 1.32) and the actual rise 0.77, whereas the mandated unskilled rise is 0.32 (0.17 and 0.48) and the actual 0.68.

REFERENCES

Berman, Eli, John Bound and Zvi Griliches (1994), 'Changes in the Demand for Skilled Labour within U.S. Manufacturing: Evidence from the Annual Survey of Manufactures', *Quarterly Journal of Economics*, May, 367–97.

Berman, Eli, John Bound and Stephen Machin (1998), 'Implications of Skill-Biased Technological Change: International Evidence', *Quarterly Journal of Economics*, November, 1245–80.

Berndt, Ernst R. and David O. Wood (1982), 'The Specification and Measurement of Technical Change in U.S. Manufacturing', *Advances in the Economics of Energy and Resources*, **4**, JAI Press, 199–221.

Blau, F.D. and L.M. Kahn (1996), 'International Differences in Male Wage Inequality: Institutions Versus Market Forces', *Journal of Political Economy*, **104** (4), 791–836.

Borjas, George and Valerie Ramey (1995), 'Foreign Competition, Market Power and Wage Inequality', *Quarterly Journal of Economics*, **110** (4), 246–51.

Card, D. (1998), 'The Impact of Declining Unionisation on Wage Inequality', *National Bureau of Economic Research*, WP. 5520.

Davidson, Carl, Lawrence Martin and Steven Matusz (1999), 'Trade and Search-Generated Unemployment,' *Journal of International Economics*, **48**, 271–99.

Davis, Donald R. (1997), 'Technology, Unemployment and Relative Wages in a Global Economy', *European Economic Review*, **42**, 9, 1613–33.

Desjonqueres, Thibaut, Stephen Machin and John van Reenen (1997), 'Another Nail in the Coffin? Or Can the Trade Based Explanation of Changing Skill Structures be Resurrected?' mimeo (December 1997).

DiNardo, J., N. Fortin and T. Lemieux (1996), 'Labor Market Institutions and The Distribution of Wages, 1973–1992: A Semi-Parametric Approach', *Econometrica*, **64** (5), 1001–44.

Feenstra, Robert C. and Gordon H. Hanson (1999), 'Productivity Measurement and the Impact of Trade and Technology on Wages: Estimates For the U.S., 1972–1990', National Bureau of Economic Research Working Paper #6052, (June 1997), *Quarterly Journal of Economics*, forthcoming.

Findlay, Ronald and Harry Grubert (1959), 'Factor Intensities, Technological Progress, and the Terms of Trade', *Oxford Economic Papers*, **11**, 111–21.

Fortin, N. and T. Lemieux (1997), Institutional Change and Rising Wage Inequality, *Journal of Economic Perspectives*, **11** (2), 75–96.

Freeman, R.B. (1993), 'How Much Has De-Unionization Contributed to the Rise in Male Earnings Inequality?', in S. Danziger and P. Gottschalk (eds), *Uneven Tides: Rising Inequality in America*, Russell Sage Foundation, New York, 99–164.

Freeman, R.B. (1996), 'Labor Market Institutions and Earnings Inequality', *England Economic Review*, May–June, 157–72.

Gosling, A. and S. Machin (1993), 'Trade Unions and the Dispersion of Earnings in British Establishments, 1980–1990', *Oxford Bullitin of Economics and Statistics*, **57** (2), 167–84.

Gregory, Mary and Ben Zissimos (1998), 'In Search of Stolper–Samuelson Effects: A Review of Methodological Issues and some Illustrative Results using UK Wages', mimeo.

Haskel, Jonathan (1999a), 'Small Firms, Contracting Out, Computers and Wage Inequality: Evidence from the UK', *Economica*, **53** (3), 265–80.

Haskel, Jonathan (1999b), 'The Trade and Labour Approaches to Wage Inequality', Queen Mary and Westfield College, Discussion Paper.

Haskel, Jonathan E. and Ylva Heden (1999), 'Computers and the Demand for Skilled Labour: Industry and Establishment Panel Evidence for the UK', *Economic Journal*, **109**, 454, C68–C79.

Haskel, Jonathan E. and Matthew J. Slaughter, (1998), 'Does the Sector Bias of Skill-Biased Technical Change Explain Changing Wage Inequality?', National Bureau of Economic Research Working Paper #6565, May 1998.

Haskel, Jonathan E. and Matthew J. Slaughter (1999), 'Trade, Technology and UK Wage Inequality', National Bureau of Economic Research Working Paper # 6978, revised.

Johnson, George (1997), 'Changes in Earnings Inequality: The Role of Demand Shifts', *Journal of Economic Perspectives*, **11** (2), Spring, 41–54.

Johnson, George and Stafford Frank (1998), 'The Labour Market Implications of

International Trade', forthcoming in O. Ashenfelter and A.D. Card (eds), *Handbook of Labour Economics*, North Holland.

Katz, Lawrence and David Autor (1999), 'Wage Inequality', forthcoming in O. Ashenfelter and A.D. Card (eds), *Handbook of Labour Economics*, North Holland.

Katz, Lawrence F. and Lawrence H. Summers (1989), 'Industry Rents: Evidence and Implications', *Brookings Papers on Economic Activity*, 209–75.

Krugman, Paul R. (1995), 'Technology, Trade, and Factor Prices', National Bureau of Economic Research Working Paper #5355, November.

Lawrence, Robert Z. and Matthew J. Slaughter (1993), 'International Trade and American Wages in the 1980s: Giant Sucking Sound or Small Hiccup?' in Martin Neil Baily and Clifford Winston (eds), *Brookings Papers on Economic Activity: Microeconomics 2*, 161–211.

Leamer, Edward E. (1998), 'In Search of Stolper–Samuelson Effects on U.S. Wages', in Susan Collins (ed.), *Imports, Exports and the American Worker*, The Brookings Institution, Washington, DC.

Neven, Damien and Charles Wyplosz (1996), 'Relative Prices, Trade and Restructuring in European Industry', Centre for Economic Policy Discussion Paper #1451, August 1996.

OECD (1996), *Employment Outlook*, Paris.

Oulton, Nicholas and Mary O'Mahony (1994), *Productivity and Growth: A Study of British Industry 1954–1986*, Cambridge University Press, Cambridge.

Slaughter, Matthew (1999), 'What are the Results of Product Price Studies and What can we Learn from their Differences?', forthcoming in Robert C. Feenstra (ed.), *International Trade and Wages*, National Bureau of Economic Research, Cambridge, MA.

Wood, Adrian (1994), *North–South Trade, Employment and Inequality: Changing Fortunes in a Skill Driven World*, Clarendon Press, Oxford.

10. Strategies to Promote Regular Employment in Services to Private Households: Current Policy Experience

Claudia Weinkopf

10.1 INTRODUCTION

At both national and European level, domestic services to private households are regarded as having a great deal of employment potential. The growing importance of such services can be attributed to a number of factors:

- rising rates of female labour market participation;
- a more or less unchanged distribution of social roles in household, family and childcare responsibilities between men and women;
- difficulties in reconciling paid employment and family responsibilities, in particular because of inadequate public childcare provision and lack of support for housework in the broadest sense of the term (canteens, washing and shopping services);
- the growing number of single parents;
- the increasing number of elderly people living alone (more and more of whom are comfortably off).

However, any discussion of the additional employment potential of services to private households must take account of the fact that they are already very prevalent. Services to private households already constitute a large employment market, which unlike most others is virtually unregulated. Legally binding employment contracts, dismissal protection, social security cover, collective bargaining and health and safety protection are virtually non-existent; in many ways, the labour market in this area is still a grey or even a black market.

The purpose of this chapter is to investigate how employment in the provision of services to private households can be promoted. Particular attention will be paid to those approaches that seem likely to increase the quality of services and of employment equally, since without such qualitative improvements it will, in our view, be scarcely possible to force back the boundaries of the black economy in favour of regular employment.

The chapter is structured as follows. In Section 10.2, the specifics of services to private households are outlined. Section 10.3 focuses on the strategies adopted in various countries to promote employment in the provision of services to private households. Particular attention will be paid to the Federal Republic of Germany, where demand-side subsidies and a kind of service voucher scheme, as well as new forms of service companies (pools and agencies), have been introduced in this field. On this empirical basis, it will be shown in Section 10.4 why the promotion of regular employment in services to households tends to be rather problematic. Furthermore, preliminary policy implications and recommendations to improve the efficiency and the employment effects of schemes to promote services to private households will be worked out.

10.2   SERVICES TO PRIVATE HOUSEHOLDS

The provision of services to private households can be organised in various ways. A high proportion of domestic work is done within households, often for other family members outside the person's own family as well.[1] Responsibility for domestic work has traditionally been assigned to women, and even today women still do the greatest share of such work. There are also service firms that make it possible to delegate certain domestic tasks, for example, laundries and ironing services. And, not least, there is always the option of having some or all of the housework done by domestic employees or cleaners who work in the household in question and have to be paid.

The trends outlined above indicate that the need for household support services has already risen and is likely to rise further. To date, however, this has hardly been reflected in any increase in regular employment in the provision of services to private households. Why is this?

In comparison with other services, domestic work has certain specific characteristics that impact adversely on market demand. Households can substitute own production for consumption of such services. The decision on whether or not to consume services depends on prices, the value placed on family members' time and the flexibility of the time budget. The consumption of services may be attractive if specialist skills are required or if it is more efficient or productive to hire a professional (if special machines are required, for example). If this is not the case, the demand for such services will depend to a large extent on the difference between an individual's net wage and the cost of the service. If the difference is small and is further reduced by taxes and other deductions, then there is little scope for demand to develop (Appelbaum and Schettkat 1996).

At least this is true of 'official' demand. However, the black market is booming, which may be illustrated by some facts on the German situation. For Germany, socio-economic panel data show that in 1994 the share of households that regularly employ domestic help or cleaners was 9 per cent, which equated to 2.65 million households. In addition, there were a further 1.4 million households (4.6 per cent) that made at least occasional use of domestic help or cleaners (Munz 1996, 39f.). These figures far outstrip the number of regular employees in private households, which official estimates put at a mere 38,000 in 1998. Even the number of employees in marginal, non-insurable part-time jobs working in private households is significantly lower than might be expected from the above-mentioned number of households employing domestic help. In 1997, private households accounted for the largest share (28 per cent, or 1.3 million people) of employees in Western Germany working very short hours and not liable for social security contributions (the so-called *'geringfügige Beschäftigung'*) (Institut für Sozialforschung und Gesellschaftspolitik 1997).[2]

This suggests that a considerable proportion of services to households must be provided in the black economy. It is true that households are obliged to register any domestic help they employ for statutory accident insurance, but the same does not apply in other areas; for example, there is no obligation to notify health insurers. It can be assumed that many people are ignorant of such minimum regulations, but it is equally likely that only few people, the employing households as well as the persons being employed, consider wrongdoing in this area to be a very serious offence.

Thus services to private households already constitute a major area of employment, albeit one that can be more or less clearly distinguished from other spheres of work. It is subject to very little regulation. Binding employment contracts, dismissal protection, social protection, regulation through collective agreements, health and safety at work and job security have virtually no meaning. In many areas, the labour market in private households remains a grey or even a black market.

10.3   NATIONAL SCHEMES TO PROMOTE SERVICES TO PRIVATE HOUSEHOLDS

Since the choice between 'do-it-yourself' and buying services provided by a third party is particularly relevant in the sphere of household services, the cost of such services is obviously of special significance. This makes it more difficult to draw up strategies for creating officially registered jobs and providing proper social security cover, since non-wage costs, such as social security contributions, and the granting of other benefits, such as paid holidays, sick pay and bonus payments, will inevitably raise the cost of the services. Thus it is reasonable to assume that state support will be required if the employment potential of services to private households is to be more fully exploited.

Table 10.1
Approaches to the promotion of services to private households

Country	Supply-side promotion	Demand-side promotion	Form of support	Specific features
France	–	Service vouchers (*chèques emploi-service*)	Simplifying administration and tax concessions	Cleaning and childcare; costs offset against tax liability
Netherlands	Subsidies for employment of long-term unemployed	–	Subsidies for up to 2 years	Cleaning jobs only
Denmark	Subsidies to companies and initiatives	–	Permanent subsidies (50 % of the customer's bill)	Cleaning and domestic support
Germany	Service agencies/pools	–	Subsidies for a certain period (1–3 years)	Regular jobs or placement
	–	Service vouchers (*Haushalts-schecks*)	Simplifying administration and tax concessions	Only jobs in private households; costs deducted from taxable income

Source: compiled by author.

Essentially what is required is the targeted promotion of services to private households, which could be achieved by subsidising both the demand and the supply sides. Such subsidies could be implemented in a variety of ways. They could be either permanent or paid for a limited period (in order to stimulate the development of new services and/or markets), and they could be made subject to certain conditions. The cost, the potential employment effect and, where applicable, the distributive effects of such subsidies are likely to vary according to the form they take.

In the following, we will describe and compare the approaches to promote services to private households in France, the Netherlands, Denmark and Germany and the implications arising from them. Table 10.1 gives a brief overview of some aspects of the different approaches.

France

Since the end of the 1980s, there have been initiatives in France to stimulate the demand for services to private households through the introduction of tax concessions and measures to simplify administrative costs. In 1994, so-called 'chèques emploi-service' (service job vouchers) were introduced which can be used by private individuals to pay the wages and social security contributions of a worker hired to do domestic work. Such work includes all household and family tasks, such as housework, childcare, gardening, care of the elderly, private tutoring for children and so on. The vouchers cannot be used to pay for any support services the employer might need in his or her professional life, such as secretarial services. The purpose of the cheques is to make life much simpler for both employer and employee when the work in question is occasional or involves only a few hours per week: no employment contract is required, salary statements do not have to be drawn up and social security contributions do not have to be calculated.

Normally, employers in France have to make no fewer than nine different social security contributions, all at different rates.[3] The introduction of service job vouchers has considerably reduced the time and effort required; books of cheques can be obtained from banks, savings banks and post offices. Each cheque is made up of two sheets of paper – one for the payment of wages and one on which the number of hours worked and the hourly rate of pay are entered – and then sent to the collecting agency for social security contributions in St Etienne. Here, the social security contributions payable are calculated and a bill is sent to the employing household. The individual worker is responsible for income-tax payments; France has no PAYE system for deducting income tax at source.

Households can use vouchers for more than one employee, provided that the weekly working time for each does not exceed eight hours per week. The working-time limit was repealed at the beginning of 1996. Employees may work for more than one household; their total weekly working time, however, must not exceed 39 hours. The service voucher is also intended to give a series of 'small jobs' the status of an 'occupation', thereby enabling those who depend on such employment to work full time and enjoy the same social advantages as other employees.[4]

The service voucher system is of value to private households not only because it simplifies the administration involved in employing people but also, and more particularly, because of the tax advantages associated with it. Private households employing domestic workers are entitled to a tax reduction of 50 per cent on the costs incurred, up to a maximum saving of 45,000 FF. The tax relief covers the additional expenditure on social security contributions that would not have been incurred if illicit workers or moonlighters had been employed. Since the costs are deducted from the overall tax liability, low-income and high-income households benefit to the same extent.

There are also so-called local placement agencies that match the supply and demand for jobs in private households and make it possible for workers to hold several different jobs at the same time. As far as potential employers are concerned, these agencies have the advantage of allowing them to select employees on the basis of their occupational skills. Their services are also available to both sides after the placement has been made. The agencies can also offer additional services, such as issuing books of service vouchers or filling in the social security sections of the vouchers. In addition, the agencies make it their business to try to reintegrate certain target groups into the labour market.

According to data published by the French Ministry of Labour, in the summer of 1996 some 202,000 households per month made use of service job checks for an average of five hours' work per week, which is equivalent to about 30,000 full-time jobs (Beck 1996).

The French experience with service vouchers is being observed with interest abroad. However, the French system is not without problems, as has been shown by recent reports that suggest that the main winners are the employing households and that the situation of those they employ has not been significantly improved. This can probably be attributed largely to the fact that the voucher system does nothing to alleviate the high level of dependency that exists between the employing households and those they employ. The employees are still dependent on one or more employers and are still working very much in isolation. Household services have not been professionalised, nor has there been any perceptible improvement in the level of social security cover provided.[5]

For this reason, the French trade unions and welfare organisations in particular have demanded that the role of the placement agencies be strengthened. This has been translated into action as far as householders now are also allowed to use the vouchers for domestic services provided by professional companies (inforMISEP, 9).[6] This is reminiscent of the Dutch and Danish approaches, which aim to subsidise demand rather than supply. It is not employment by private households that is encouraged, but rather the provision of services by employees of professional companies.

The Netherlands

In the Netherlands, initiatives or firms providing services to private households and employing workers on a basis that makes them liable for social security contributions have been able since June 1996 to claim wage subsidies up to a maximum of 18,000 guilders for a period of up to two years, provided that they employ long-term unemployed people with an entitlement to social assistance ('SchoonmaakSter'). The costs are met by the Dutch Ministry of Labour. The employers' association in the commercial cleaning business also pays an annual subsidy of up to 5000 guilders per worker. Part of this is financed by wage moderation for this purpose according to the collective agreement. This enables programmes or firms to provide their services at prices that very closely match those that might be charged by illicit workers or moonlighters. Customers are spared the cost and effort of recruiting workers and the firm or programme employing the workers guarantees their reliability and qualifications for the job in question.

According to initial reports, the scheme has got off to a very shaky start in the three cities, where the programme has been started. Firms have been being frightened off by the relatively high administrative costs involved. Even the unemployed have shown little interest in the scheme, since the domestic services sector has a poor image and rates of pay are low as well as the only jobs on offer are often fixed-term, with a very short weekly working time. Nevertheless, the scheme has been transferred (with marginal changes) to the national level in January 1998.

Denmark

In Denmark, existing or newly established firms providing services to private households have been receiving government subsidies of about 50 per cent since the beginning of the year 1994 – up to 1997 on an experimental basis and since January 1998 as a permanent 'HomeService scheme'. The services are provided to households at a subsidised price which is set at roughly the level of a similar service in the black economy. The purposes of the scheme are

- to assist families and elderly with their household work;
- to eliminate black-market work; and
- to create 10,000 full-time jobs in professional business.

Subsidies are only paid for services performed by approved private HomeService companies. Criteria for approval are, for example, VAT registration, liability insurance covering any damages occurring on the job, proper working conditions for all employees, and environmental guidelines. Furthermore, the company may not have debts of more than 50,000 DKK (approximately 6700 EURO) to any public agency and the owner may not have a criminal record (Schlegel 1999, 5f.). The HomeService scheme covers the following services:

- grocery shopping,
- cleaning,
- window cleaning and cleaning of gutters,
- cooking, dishwashing, jam making,
- laundry, ironing,
- snow removal, sweeping, ordinary garden work,
- packing and unpacking related to moving,
- dog-walking,
- other types of ordinary housework.

Construction, repair and maintenance works as well as nursing and other types of personal care are excluded. The subsidies amount to 50 per cent of the customer's bill.

According to the available information, in 1998, about 4000 companies were involved in the scheme.

10.4   CONCLUSIONS AND POLICY RECOMMENDATIONS

Taken as a whole, experiences to date show that it is very difficult to promote services to private households and that the anticipated, or at least hoped-for, employment effects have not yet been achieved. There seem to be two main reasons for that. First, there is a lack of willingness on the part of households to pay for the services on offer. It has so far proved virtually impossible to gain acceptance for prices considerably in excess of those prevailing in the black market. Second, on the employees' side, there seems to be little interest in working in this field. Services to private households have a poor image, and rates of pay tend to be low.

However, these problems should not, in our view, be used as an excuse to abandon attempts to create additional jobs in this field. Further experiments are needed in order to ascertain which approaches are the most suitable. A number of other countries, including Belgium, Finland, Austria and Italy, have now developed or are about to implement schemes for promoting services to private households. Even though differences in societal conditions mean that experiences in other countries are not immediately transferable, those experiences can, nevertheless, provide interesting food for thought.

One of the most important questions is how to improve the low regard in which services to private households are held by both customers and workers. The societal regard of housework suffers among other things from the fact that the need for formal qualifications is denied – often following the motto 'everyone can do it' (at least every woman!). It is underestimated that the required qualifications for doing housework in another household on a professional basis are completely different from those needed to manage one's own household. Furthermore it should be taken into account that the estimation of work in households is still shaped by societal value judgements which are based on the traditional character of housework as the unpaid work of women. There can be no doubt that these attitudes cannot be changed overnight. But in our view the effort to change them is worthwhile, although it may be regarded as an attempt to overcome a vicious circle. The image of household-related services can hardly be improved without professional-isation and the creation of more legal and regular jobs in this field, but this can hardly be realised without improving the image.

Nevertheless, in the following we present some provisional conclusions and policy recommendations which can be drawn from the attempts and experiences made to date to promote employment in the provision of services to private households and which may be helpful in order to make progress.

First, significant employment effects can be achieved only by professionalising services to private households and establishing new forms of organisation. It is our view that delivering such services through properly constituted companies is the most promising way of professionalising them and improving their quality, thereby increasing demand for them and improving their image.

Second, there is also every reason to believe that the chances of producing acceptable working conditions and of minimising abuse will be greater if the available support is channelled towards professional service providers rather than towards private households seeking to hire workers themselves. Companies are obliged to report and document many of their activities and to provide opportunities for work force representation, while the regulations governing personal privacy act against the establishment of effective controls in private households. The isolation of domestic workers further aggravates the situation.

In order to make jobs in the provision of services to private households more attractive to potential employees, professionalisation is very important as well. Furthermore, it might perhaps seem sensible to introduce measures to raise the income that can be earned from low-paid activities, for example by granting tax relief and/or reducing social security contributions.[7]

In principle, professional service provision can be supported through supply-side and demand-side subsidies. A combination of the two may also be sensible. In the case of demand-side subsidies, the potential employment effects will be greater the wider the circle of recipients. Tax concessions seem to us to be less advantageous than vouchers that can be redeemed in exchange for services offered by professional providers. In contrast to tax concessions, which only take effect retrospectively (and often with a considerable time lag), a voucher system ensures that customers benefit from subsidised prices without delay. If necessary, the subsidies can also be varied according to income and/or neediness.

Attention should also be paid to the societal framework. The tax and social insurance systems have a substantial impact on the willingness of people to participate in the official labour market on the one hand or to work in the black economy on the other. This does not only affect the total level of deductions but also particular arrangements for married couples which impact adversely on the labour market participation of both partners. This is, for example, the case in tax systems with progressive marginal taxation rates in which the two partners each pay income tax on half the total of their combined income. The lowest taxes will have to be paid by households with a single earner.

Not least, it would seem essential to put in place more effective controls to combat illicit work and to initiate a concerted public relations campaign to improve the image of domestic work.

Finally, it behoves me to mention one difficulty that is frequently overlooked. Services to private households are often regarded as an area in which new employment opportunities for low-skill workers can be opened up. This seems to be questionable in at least two respects. On the one hand, the frequent claims of household-related services being low-skill jobs counteract efforts to improve their image. On the other hand, it should not be ignored that even if technical skills required for such jobs tends to be low (which is questionable as well) a relatively high level of social skills is required. All approaches to promoting employment in this area require the services to be provided in individual households on a decentralised and 'itinerant' basis. Therefore, workers must be able to react flexibly to customer expectations and to work with minimum supervision. This may also be one of the reasons for difficulties in the recruitment of suitable staff. Against this background, I am convinced that all efforts to promote employment in services to private households have to take into account the need for training in this area.

Since some low-skill workers are unable, are no longer able or are not immediately in a position to fulfil these requirements, other forms of work organisation are additionally required that will make it possible to provide more guidance and to exercise greater supervision. How this could be achieved in the area of services to private households is a matter for further discussion.

NOTES

1. According to the results of the time-budget surveys carried out by the Federal Statistical Office, 77 billion hours of unpaid work are performed every year in 36 million private households in Germany, 76 per cent of which relate to domestic services (see Stiegler 1997, 6).
2. Since April 1999, the regulation of this marginal part-time work has been changed. Now employers have to pay social insurance contributions even for jobs with monthly earnings up to 630 DM whereas the exemption of the employees remains unchanged. But up to now, it is not clear whether private households as employers observe their obligations.
3. Unemployment, pension and sickness insurance, supplementary pension scheme for domestic employees, family and accident insurance, the CSG (a general social security contribution), the RDS (a contribution to the repayment of the social insurance debt), the national housing fund and the widows' pension fund (see Beck 1996).
4. In addition, there are special provisions for unemployed people. They are allowed to do paid work within the voucher system to the value of 70 per cent of their last wage without losing their benefits completely. This special provision applies for a maximum period of 18 months, and the hours worked and paid for by means of service job vouchers are used to build up new entitlement to unemployment benefit.
5. Although social insurance contributions have to be paid for every working hour in France, employees are only entitled to receive social insurance payments if they have worked at least 16 hours per week respectively 800 hours per year (see Bittner et al. 1998).
6. A similar strategy to that adopted in France is also being pursued in Belgium, although here some long-term unemployed people are also being employed, with compensation being paid for the extra costs involved. Trials are also being conducted with the use of vouchers in partial payment of employees' wages. As far as we know these trials have not yet been evaluated, but this could be an interesting way of avoiding competition from the black economy. The vouchers can be claimed only for certain forms of service provision, whereas cash payments can also be used to pay for illicit work.
7. There is a vivacious debate in Germany about the chances and risks of such approaches (see Weinkopf 1999). Some *Länder* are now about to implement experimental schemes to find out the employment effects, costs and potential negative impacts on the labour market.

REFERENCES

Appelbaum, E. and R. Schettkat (1996), *Das Beschäftigungsproblem der Industrieländer. Eine Neuinterpretation.* Statement zur 1. Internationalen Wirtschaftstagung der Sozialdemokratischen Partei Deutschlands 'Neue Beschäftigungspolitik für Deutschland' am 28 August 1996 in Bonn-Bad Godesberg. Vervielfältigtes Manuskript. O.O.

Beck, D. (1996), 'Ann-Marie ist mit dem System nicht zufrieden. Der französische Dienstleistungsscheck und die Realität', *Frankfurter Rundschau,* 3 August 1996.

Bittner, S., I. Dingeldey, S. Strauf and C. Weinkopf (1998), *Für eine Reform der geringfügigen Beschäftigung,* Projektbericht des Instituts Arbeit und Technik 1998-02, Gelsenkirchen.

inforMISEP, Frankreich, Ausweitung des Dienstleistungsschecks', Nr. 54, Summer

1996, 9–11.

Institut für Sozialforschung und Gesellschaftspolitik (1997), *Sozialversicherungsfreie Beschäftigung,* Untersuchung im Auftrag des Bundesministeriums für Arbeit und Sozialordnung, 2, Wiederholungsuntersuchung, Köln.

Munz, S. (1996), 'Beschäftigungspotentiale im Bereich privater Haushalte', *IFO-Schnelldienst* 17–18, 38–45.

Schlegel, J. (1999), *The Danish HomeService Scheme.* Paper presented to the Seminar of the European Commission 'Employment in Services', Brussels, 17 February 1999.

Stiegler, B. (1997), *Das 654-Milliarden-Paket,* Vervielfältigtes Manuskript, Friedrich-Ebert-Stiftung, Bonn.

Weinkopf, C. (1996a), *Arbeitskräftepools – Überbetriebliche Beschäftigung im Spannungsfeld von Flexibilität, Mobilität und sozialer Sicherheit,* München/Mering.

Weinkopf, C. (1996b), 'Dienstleistungspools – ein Ansatz zur Professionalisierung von Dienstleistungen in Privathaushalten?', *WSI-Mitteilungen* 1, 36–43.

Weinkopf, C. (1996c), *Personal services: trends, problems and employment prospects,* Report for the European Commission/DG V. Vervielfältigtes Manuskript, Bad Honnef.

Weinkopf, C. (1998), 'Möglichkeiten zur Beschäftigungsförderung im Dienstleistungssektor. Das Beispiel haushaltsbezogener Dienstleistungen', in G. Bosch (ed.), *Zukunft der Erwerbsarbeit. Strategien für Arbeit und Umwelt,* Frankfurt/New York: 458–482.

Weinkopf, C. (1999), *Schaffung von zusätzlichen Arbeitsplätzen für Geringqualifizierte,* Revised and updated version of a Memorandum for the of von Schleswig-Holstein, Graue Reihe of the Institut Arbeit und Technik 1999-06, Gelsenkirchen.

11. Job Satisfaction and Labour Turnover in the Retail and Hotel Sectors

Donna Brown and Steven McIntosh

11.1 INTRODUCTION

In this chapter we look at the link between satisfaction and separations of workers in two national service sector companies, one in retail trade and one a hotel chain. We selected the service sector because it has been characterised as low wage. The *OECD Employment Outlook* (OECD 1996) reports that 36.1 per cent of workers in the British wholesale/retail trade were low-paid in 1995, compared to a national average of 19.6 per cent.[1] Similarly, Metcalf (1998), in his study of the effects of the introduction of the UK national minimum wage, reports that in 1998 private services accounted for two-thirds of the total number of employees to be affected (that is, earning less than the minimum wage prior to its introduction), while almost one-third of the total number affected worked in the retail and hospitality industries alone. As many traditional manufacturing-based jobs disappear, the service sector firms considered increasingly represent the principal employment opportunity for low-skilled individuals, and hence it is important to understand the employment relation in such jobs. Who works in this sector, how happy are they with their employment, and are such matches stable or suspect to high turnover? Is the choice of turnover unconstrained?

Evidence from the Labour Force Survey (LFS) suggests that turnover in our two sectors is high. In 1996, average job tenure was 96 months. However, in the retail trade sector, this figure was 72 months, and in the hotels and restaurants sector it was only 57 months. Given the costs associated with low tenure, and hence high turnover, it is important to investigate its causes. We initially examine the link between job satisfaction and separation probability, and then consider further causes of labour turnover.

The issue of the link between satisfaction and quits is important for individuals' welfare and also of interest to employers. The firms studied experience relatively high labour turnover and spend substantial amounts, up to 12 per cent of a median starter's total pay packet, on induction and training of new recruits. Therefore establishing a clear link between satisfaction and quits might encourage them to address low satisfaction before workers quit. Alternatively employers who rely on workers' quits as a means of reducing head count and of removing less productive staff will be concerned by any apparent disruption to this mechanism. In the absence of a clear progression from dissatisfaction to quitting, workers who would ceteris paribus quit are forced to stay in a job which they would prefer to leave. Workers trapped in unsatisfying jobs may receive a lower than optimal level of utility. Therefore we also seek to identify whether this end of the labour market is competitive or monopsonistic, by examining whether workers in the sectors we consider tend to have demographic characteristics that might lead to constraints on their labour market mobility.

In the next section we examine the existing literature on the link between satisfaction and quits. In Section 11.3 we develop our model using existing theory linking satisfaction and turnover and outline the empirical specification. Section 11.4 presents the data, and Section 11.5 reports the results of our empirical work. We offer conclusions and inferences for policymakers in Section 11.6.

11.2   LITERATURE

Initially the literature on job satisfaction approached the issue using a psychological framework but economists have increasingly shown an interest in both the determinants and implications of job satisfaction.

Locke (1976) provided an extensive discussion and analysis of the existing literature on satisfaction, including discussion of the links between job satisfaction and outcomes such as turnover. Following on from the work of Locke, other authors have chosen to rely on a relatively consistent group of independent variables in their job satisfaction equations. In general, studies focus on the relationship between job satisfaction and one particular independent variable, for example gender (Clark 1997), age (Clark et al. 1996), race (Bartel 1981), education (Tsang et al. 1991), wages (Cappelli and Sherer 1988; Clark and Oswald 1996; Sloane and Williams 1996; and Watson et al. 1996), trade union status (Gordon and Denisi 1995; Meng 1990; Miller 1990; and Schwochau 1987), or establishment size (Idson 1990). In this chapter our literature review concentrates on studies which have looked at the relationship between satisfaction and quits, following our examination of the demographic determinants of satisfaction in an earlier work (Brown and McIntosh 1998).

Freeman (1978) defended the use of satisfaction as an economic variable, concluding that despite its subjective nature, consistency of results across studies into the influence of independent variables made it a valid area for economic investigation. In the same paper he examined its relationship with job turnover and so established the analysis of the implications of low job satisfaction as a legitimate area for economists' study. However, in his analysis of the existing literature, Locke (1976) argued that as studies have consistently found a significant link between job satisfaction and turnover further research in the area is warranted only if the link is disproved, in which case alternative causes of turnover should be identified. Most work that has followed has continued to find a positive effect of job satisfaction on quits.

Most of the more recent studies have been performed by psychologists, concentrating not just on the links between job satisfaction and quits but also the role of alternative job opportunities, the intention to search for other work and the intention to quit the current job in determining worker turnover. Mobley et al. (1978) argued that existing studies were inadequate. Along with most psychological approaches they separate out turnover into the decision to quit and the actual departure from the job. Their decision to examine intention to quit was motivated by the assessment of Schneider (1976) who argued that the existence of alternative options was an important determinant in the formation of an intention to quit. Whilst their sample was similar to ours, consisting of hospital workers of varying low to intermediate skill levels, they found that the best indicator of quitting was the decision to seek alternative work. Unfortunately this is not possible to examine with our data set. Neither satisfaction nor the availability of other jobs proved to be significant determinants of intention or final decision to quit.

Arnold and Feldman (1982) looked at another distinct group of employees – accountants – whose greater labour market power may make them a non-comparable group. Satisfaction and the alternatives available in the labour market affected intention to search and to quit rather than the actual quit decision. More closely related to our work is the study of Carsten and Spector (1987). They modelled quits as a function of economic opportunity factors, individual factors, and work-related characteristics. They argued for the inclusion of economic opportunity factors on the grounds that during a slump both the dissatisfied and the satisfied considered carefully whether to move or not (Hulin et al. 1985). During a boom it was the least satisfied who chose to move, as good economic conditions meant that workers were more able and likely to give weight to their satisfaction in deciding whether to move.

Work from an economist's perspective includes that of Weiss (1984). Weiss examined how satisfaction, alternative opportunities and the costs of quitting affect the decision to quit. Some results are rather different to our own, presumably reflecting the different time periods and type of workers under study, Weiss considering 1977–79 and relatively well-paid manufacturing workers respectively. Results for new starters showed that those previously unemployed were more likely to quit, as were those performing more complex tasks. However, those with a higher level of education were less likely to leave the job, having corrected for their enhanced opportunities elsewhere. He also found that those with family responsibilities had a lower rate of turnover. He does not explicitly include job satisfaction in his equation, but interprets many variables' results as working through satisfaction, thus assuming the latter to have an effect on quits, as predicted by his model.

Related developments in the linking of satisfaction and turnover emerged from the seminal work of Hirschman (1970), who examined the relationship between loyalty to an organisation and the decision of whether to exercise voice or to leave the organisation following a deterioration in that organisation's performance. Freeman (1980) extended the analysis of dissatisfied workers in relation to a choice of whether to use voice or quit the job. In this model firms may benefit if workers decide to exercise voice as they will retain their firm-specific human capital and save on hiring and training costs. This decision on the part of workers will probably reflect their earlier satisfaction with the job. Freeman's study of 1980 was the first to take individual data and examine whether this theoretical voice effect could actually be detected in workers' quit rates. However here we are not concerned with the impact of institutional mechanisms on turnover.

Developing the theme of these works, Boroff and Lewin (1997) argued that the Hirschman model is ill thought out, as its basis is a tautology. They do identify a negative relationship between satisfaction and the probability of exit, although they ignore questions of mobility.

11.3   MODEL

The theoretical underpinnings of the current chapter will be based on both economists' and psychologists' models of labour turnover, outlined in the literature review above. If workers are unsatisfied with their current job, then they will begin to search for alternatives, and consider quitting the firm. Intention to quit the firm will differ from actual quitting behaviour, however, according to how the alternatives compare with the current employment. Only those individuals for whom the alternatives yield a utility level which exceeds that derived from their current position and covers the costs of changing jobs, will actually quit the firm. The remainder will choose to stay with their current employer. While employers might consider the latter to be a good outcome, in terms of removing the need to incur turnover costs, it is unlikely to be in the long-term interests of firms to employ dissatisfied workers who would rather be working elsewhere given the chance.

This picture of trapped and discontented labour implicitly assumes a model of the labour market that differs from the world of perfect competition. In perfect competition, all firms face a supply of labour curve that is perfectly elastic at the going market wage, and so all firms offer this rate. If any firm paid even fractionally below this rate, then all of its employees would immediately leave to earn the going rate elsewhere. Our description of the theoretical underpinnings is therefore more at home in a world of dynamic monopsony. Such a model of the labour market does not assume a single employer, as in the classic textbook model of monopsony, but argues that imperfections in the labour market mean that if a single firm offers less than the going rate its quit rate will rise, but it will not lose all of its workers. Because of these imperfections, such as incomplete information on job matches or job mobility costs, not all workers quit the firm, even if they are dissatisfied with what is on offer. This theory fits our picture of the possible outcome of an individual's quit decision-making process. Similarly, if a firm in this world was to increase its wage above the going rate, it would not face an infinite number of applicants, but could slightly increase its application and recruitment rates and reduce its quit rate. The dynamic monopsonist therefore faces an upward-sloping supply of labour curve, exactly as in the classic case of a single-employer monopsonist. They will behave in the same way, paying a wage below the marginal product of labour.[2]

Many analyses of labour turnover have found quit rates to be positively related to measures of job dissatisfaction; the more dissatisfied are employees with their jobs, the more likely they are to quit. The aim of this chapter is to examine whether this is also typical of the low-wage service sector, or whether restrictions on mobility prevent such turnover, and provide employers in this sector with some monopsonistic power.

The underlying equation that we want to estimate is:

$$S_i = \beta^s X_i + \gamma^s J_i + \delta^s F_i + \varepsilon_i^s \tag{11.1}$$

where S_i is a measure of individual i's underlying likelihood of separating from his or her job, X_i is a vector of observed individual characteristics, J_i is a vector of observed job characteristics, F_i is an unobserved characteristic of the individual, such as his or her commitment, and ε_i^s is a normally distributed disturbance term. If the unobserved characteristic is correlated with the observed characteristics, then estimating equation (11.1) with F_i excluded will lead to biased estimates of the β^s and γ^s coefficients.

Almost all empirical studies of labour turnover include individuals' tenure with the firm at the point of survey as an explanatory variable. The problem with doing so is that tenure is an endogenous variable, with the factors that affect an individual's current length of service likely to be similar to those that affect whether or not they remain in the job in the future. We could therefore specify a tenure equation:

$$T_i = \beta^t X_i + \gamma^t J_i + \delta^t F_i + \varepsilon_i^t \tag{11.2}$$

where T_i is individual i's elapsed tenure with the firm, and X_i, J_i and F_i are defined as above.

Miller and Mulvey (1991) offer a theoretical rationale for including tenure in the separation equation, that the unobserved characteristic can be substituted out of the separation equation through the inclusion of the tenure variable. If equation 11.2 is used to substitute in for the unobserved characteristic in equation 11.1, the result is:

$$S_i = \left(\beta^s - \beta^t \frac{\delta^s}{\delta^t} \right) X_i + \left(\gamma^s - \gamma^t \frac{\delta^s}{\delta^t} \right) J_i + \frac{\delta^s}{\delta^t} T_i - \frac{\delta^s}{\delta^t} \varepsilon_i^t + \varepsilon_i^s \tag{11.3}$$

All variables are observed in equation (11.3), and it can be estimated without suffering from omitted variable bias. Intuitively, the tenure variable picks up the effect of the unobservable variable, commitment, on separations. However, the coefficient on any X variable is now $\beta^s - \beta^t \delta^s / \delta^t$, rather than the pure effect of that variable on separations, as measured by β^s. It is reasonable to assume that any variable that has a positive effect on tenure will have a negative effect on separations, and vice versa, so that β^s and β^t will have opposite signs, as will δ^s and δ^t. From the coefficient formula in equation (11.3), it can therefore be seen that the effect of any variable will be biased towards zero, relative to its true effect, β^s. The coefficients on the J variables, representing job characteristics, are similarly affected. Any statistically significant coefficients we find when we estimate equation (11.3) can therefore be considered to be particularly strong results.

An issue arising when estimating equation (11.3) is that an endogeneity problem is introduced, since the tenure variable will be correlated with the unobserved disturbance term ε_i^t, resulting in inconsistent estimated coefficients. In the absence of any suitable instruments for tenure in our data set, we could not test for or allow for such endogeneity, and so we simply estimated our equation with tenure included. However, we also estimated a specification with tenure excluded, to obtain information about the possible effects of any endogeneity bias.

A final estimation issue concerns the fact that we do not observe the continuous likelihood of the separating variable, S_i, but only the dichotomous variable, S_i^*, which equals 1 if individual i separates from his or her job, and zero otherwise. Assuming that $S_i^* = 1$ when $S_I > 0$ and $S_i^* = 0$ when $S_I \leq 0$, and that ε_i^t and ε_i^s are jointly normally distributed, then we can write:

$$\text{prob}\,(S_i^* = 1) = \Phi\,(\,\beta^* \, X_i + \gamma^* \, J_i + \delta^* \, T_i) \tag{11.4}$$

$$\text{prob}\,(S_i^* = 0) = 1 - \Phi\,(\,\beta^* \, X_i + \gamma^* \, J_i + \delta^* T_i) \tag{11.5}$$

where $\beta^* = \beta^s - \beta^t \delta^s / \delta^t$, $\gamma^* = \gamma^s - \gamma^t \delta^s / \delta^t$, $\delta^* = \delta^s / \delta^t$, and Φ is the cumulative normal distribution. The probit estimation of the coefficients then involves maximising the following log likelihood function:

$$\ln l = \sum_i \left\{ S_i^* \ln \Phi(\beta^* X_i + \gamma^* j_i + \delta^* T_i \text{sub})_i + (1 - S_i^*) \ln \left[1 - \Phi(\beta^* X_i + \gamma^* J_i + \delta^* T_i) \right] \right\} \tag{11.6}$$

11.4   DATA

The data we use are derived from staff questionnaires, distributed in late 1996 and early 1997, which have then been matched to two instalments of payroll information covering the initial survey period and early 1998. Two national service sector companies are involved, a supermarket chain and a hotel group, providing us with information on around 800 individuals over a total of 18 sites. Given the growth in the service sector over the last two decades, the proportion of the employed labour force covered by these two sectors is around 15 per cent. These companies were also chosen because they represent differing degrees of low-paying employment. The median hourly wage for hospitality is £3.35, approximately the same as that of our hotel chain, illustrating that it will be affected by the new British national minimum wage. The national median in the retail sector is slightly higher, at £3.88, which falls below that for our retail chain. Examining annual turnover rates shows that the hotel chain has annual turnover of 182 per cent whereas for the retail chain it is 60 per cent.

The payroll information provides details of starting dates, job grade, hourly pay rates, weekly working hours and various other employer characteristics. Staff questionnaires provide us with personal information about household status, educational qualifications, and previous labour market attachments. The questionnaire also elicits workers' satisfaction with eleven different aspects of the position as well as questioning them about their overall satisfaction with the job. For this chapter we chose to use the question relating to overall satisfaction with the job.

The sites were chosen as regional clusters around the West Midlands, Yorkshire, the Southeast, Southwest and Northwest. The travel-to-work area of each site was identified, which enables us to map in the median wage for each travel-to-work area using the April 1996 New Earnings Survey. Dividing the actual hourly rate by the local median provides us with a measure of the relative wage received by workers. We have also mapped in the unemployment rate for each travel-to-work area as this is likely to shape workers' expectations about the ease of finding alternative work.

The response rates varied from an average of 50 per cent for the hotel chain to 23 per cent at the supermarket chain. If we examine whether the survey respondents were representative of each company's workforce we find some variation. At both firms, women and older workers were more likely to respond than young male employees with short tenure. If we compare the achieved sample in each firm to that of their industry's average using the 1997 Labour Force Survey we find that the hotel chain is fairly representative of hospitality, save that in our sample tenure is only half as long as the industry average. Looking at the retail chain, it employs more women and slightly younger staff than the retail industry as a whole.

There is the possibility that by focussing on two sectors in particular, our results may be affected by sample selection issues. In particular, if the factors that influence the allocation of employees to this sector are correlated with the unobservables in the estimated separation equation, then the results will suffer from sample selection bias. For example, the jobs observed in our sample, which do not require a large investment in human capital, may attract individuals with a lower attachment to the labour force, who are not looking for a long career and who do not want to undergo extensive training. If individuals with a low labour market attachment are also more likely to quit, then the sample selection rule is linked to the separation decision, and biased results can emerge. However, our survey did not include additional variables with which we could model the decision to work in these sectors, and so we could not test for or remove this potential bias, a fact which should be borne in mind when the results are considered.

Turning now to the variables used in our analysis, we could identify any individual who had left their job from the second round of payroll data that we received. The dependent variable is then simply a dummy variable indicating whether the individual has left their job between the time of the original survey date and the time of the second round of payroll data being delivered, approximately eighteen months later. If an individual had indeed separated from their job, we were given the reason for this. Although the theory outlined above is related to voluntary quits, we decided not to distinguish between voluntary and involuntary separations, since, as argued by Freeman (1980), the distinction in empirical work is not necessarily as clear-cut as supposed. For example, there is unlikely to be a great deal of difference between an individual who quits because they are dissatisfied with a job, and one who loses all interest in their work because they are dissatisfied, and are dismissed as a result. Similarly, a firm could dismiss unwanted workers, or harass them into quitting. In addition, the turnover costs to a firm are the same whether the individual quits or is dismissed. In this sense, firms will be most interested in total separations. We did, however, re-run our equations with only voluntary quits as the dependent variable, but the results were largely unchanged. This is due to that fact that 80 per cent of all separations were voluntary quits.

The explanatory variables can be grouped under various headings. First are the satisfaction variables. Respondents were asked to rate their overall satisfaction with their jobs, on a scale going from 1 (highly unsatisfied) to 5 (highly satisfied). The responses cannot be treated as a continuous cardinal variable, so instead we enter four dummy variables indicating rising levels of job satisfaction. Individuals who are highly unsatisfied form the reference category.

Next we have the personal and family characteristics of the respondents; gender, age, race, marital status, existence of children (plus an interaction term between the last two, representing single parents) and education. It is hypothesised that an individual's characteristics can affect his or her alternative job opportunities, as well as the costs of undertaking a job move. We also include amongst the characteristics of the individuals, dummy variables to indicate their previous economic state, prior to accepting the job in the survey firm. The possibilities are that the respondent was employed in another firm, unemployed, looking after a home, studying, or 'other'. The first of these groups forms the reference category.

It is important to include indicators of the current job, as well as of the individual performing the job, as such job conditions can influence an individual's desire to leave. Thus, variables measuring an individual's hourly wage rate, hours of work and occupation grade are included. As described above, tenure with the firm at the time of interview is also included as an explanatory variable in some specifications. In addition, we include a dummy variable indicating in which of the two companies the individual works. Of course there may also be unobserved workplace characteristics which can influence the decision to quit. Our sample allows us to examine separation decisions for groups of workers at the same site, so that unobserved workplace characteristics can be controlled for through the inclusion of workplace dummies. These were found not to be statistically significant, however, and so were excluded.

The final group of variables represents outside opportunities open to the respondents. We know the travel-to-work region of each surveyed establishment, allowing us to map into our data set the unemployment rate at the time of the survey in the individual's local labour markets. We also experimented with average wage levels in the local labour market, as an additional measure of alternative opportunities open to the individual. Finally, other interests are measured by dummy variables indicating whether the individual has another job elsewhere, or whether he or she is still studying at college, at the time of interview. An individual in either of these situations is expected to have lower commitment to the firm.

The mean values of all variables can be found in column 3 of Table 11.1.

11.5 RESULTS

The foot of Table 11.1 reveals that the (18 month) separation rate in the sample was 22.6 per cent. Therefore, just over one in five of the original respondents to the survey had left their jobs when the firms were recontacted about eighteen months later. The main body of the table uses non-parametric techniques to show how this separation rate differs across the discrete explanatory variables, and reports whether these differences are statistically significant using either a t-test or F-test.

The first row of Table 11.1 suggests that there is no link between satisfaction and labour turnover. The separation rates by different satisfaction levels are very similar and a Spearman rank-order correlation coefficient of −0.03 between job satisfaction and job separation, which is also highly insignificant, reinforces this finding. It appears that dissatisfied workers in low-wage service sector jobs are no more likely than satisfied workers to quit their jobs. However, looking at the other results in the table, it appears as though we can go some way to explaining the determinants of turnover in this sector.

The education results are quite striking, in that there is virtually a monotonic increase in the separation rate as individuals become better qualified.[3] One in two of the respondents in our sample who hold a degree, and more than one in three with A levels, have left the firm eighteen months later. On the assumption that there are a greater number of alternative employment opportunities open to the more highly qualified, this would tend to suggest that such alternatives are an important determinant of turnover in this sector. It could be argued that labour market discrimination reduces job opportunities for females, which would also make the significantly higher separation rate of males in our sample consistent with such a story about outside alternatives.

The availability of another source of employment is not the only deter- minant of turnover, however, as individuals must be sufficiently mobile to be able to make the change. It is interesting to note that both single and childless individuals have higher separation rates than married individuals and parents, 18 and 11 percentage points respectively, both differences being statistically significant. Therefore family commitments seem to reduce mobility. Conversely, the lower half of the table reveals that those who are currently

Table 11.1
Variable means and separation rates by characteristics

Variable	Categories	Means	Separation rate	T-/F-test
job satisfaction	highly dissatisfied	0.045	0.211	0.24
	dissatisfied	0.097	0.241	
	indifferent	0.335	0.218	
	satisfied	0.331	0.205	
	highly satisfied	0.192	0.191	
sex	female	0.746	0.191	2.47**
	male	0.254	0.272	
age		33.7 yrs		
race	white	0.912	0.215	0.95
	non-white	0.088	0.169	
marital status	single	0.361	0.33	6.40***
	married (or living as)	0.639	0.146	
family status	children	0.44	0.151	3.90***
	no children	0.56	0.26	
highest educ. level	no qualifications	0.299	0.133	8.85***
	CSEs	0.075	0.19	
	vocational qualifications	0.178	0.133	
	O-levels/GCSEs	0.332	0.274	
	A-levels	0.081	0.362	
	degree	0.034	0.48	
previous econ. state	employed	0.367	0.177	14.38***
	looking after the home	0.232	0.11	
	studying	0.22	0.345	
	unemployed	0.142	0.184	
	other	0.039	0.556	
tenure		61.3 mths		
hourly wages		£4.13		
occupation	unskilled & trainee	0.151	0.244	0.43
	semi-skilled	0.485	0.211	
	semi-skilled with junior responsibility	0.141	0.18	
	skilled worker/ supervisor	0.124	0.196	
	low level management and professional	0.099	0.224	
weekly hours		25.4 hrs		
firm	hotel chain	0.425	0.323	6.48**
	supermarket chain	0.575	0.14	
local unempl. rate		6.92%		
other job	yes	0.081	0.22	0.12
	no	0.919	0.214	
currently at college	yes	0.269	0.335	5.24***
	no	0.731	0.167	
all			0.226	

Notes: ***, **, * indicate statistical significance at the 1%, 5% and 10% levels respectively.

studying, or were studying prior to taking the current job, have higher separation rates. Their recently acquired skills presumably make it easier for them to gain alternative employment. Finally, the rate of turnover is higher in the hotel chain than in the supermarket chain.

The results discussed so far are simple correlations between the separation rate and each of our explanatory variables. Table (11.2) moves on to a more formal multivariate analysis of the determinants of job separations, by estimating the probit equation suggested by equation (11.6). All coefficients in Table 11.2 are the marginal effects associated with the (unreported) probit results, calculated at the mean of all variables.[4] The majority of the explanatory variables are dummy variables, and their associated marginal effects show the change in the probability of a separation for a discrete change in the dummy from 0 to 1. The marginal effects for the continuous variables can be interpreted as the change in the separation probability for a unit deviation from the mean of the explanatory variable.

Our first examination is of the unadulterated effect of job satisfaction on separations. The first column of Table 11.2 includes only the dummy variables for the various satisfaction levels. The marginal effects are very small, and are highly statistically insignificant, as suggested by the separation rates in Table 11.1. Column 2 of Table 11.2 adds in all of the explanatory variables discussed above. Controlling for all of these influences, there is still no evidence of a relationship between job satisfaction and job separations. The marginal effects remain very small, and the Z-score for each satisfaction coefficient is less than 0.3 in absolute value. It does not appear as though the dissatisfied in the low-wage service sector are any more likely to separate from their jobs than the satisfied.

Who then, is more likely to leave? Column 2 shows that quite a few of the correlations found in the raw data survive in the multivariate analysis, and continue to tell a story that outside alternatives and ease of mobility are important determinants of turnover in this sector. Some of the largest marginal effects are found on the two highest qualification levels. Individuals with A-levels or a degree have a separation probability almost 20 percentage points higher than the unqualified. Those who have the best chance of finding good alternative employment are the most likely to leave the companies under analysis here. The relationship between education and separations is no longer monotonic in the multivariate analysis, in that individuals with CSEs, but not those with GCSEs are more likely than the unqualified to exit. It is not immediately obvious why this is the case, although it does not affect the underlying result that the more qualified are more likely to leave the two companies studied.

Considering previous economic state, it can be seen that individuals working in this sector after a spell of unemployment are eight percentage

Table 11.2
Probit estimates of the determinants of separations – marginal effects

Variable	Marg. effect	(s.e.)	Marg. effect	(s.e.)	Marg. effect	(s.e.)
Job satisfaction						
dissatisfied	0.030	(0.085)	0.002	(0.090)	0.038	(0.109)
indifferent	0.007	(0.071)	−0.015	(0.080)	0.035	(0.094)
satisfied	−0.006	(0.070)	−0.023	(0.079)	0.017	(0.092)
highly satisfied	−0.020	(0.071)	0.026	(0.091)	0.123	(0.114)
Iindividual characteristics						
female			0.041	(0.032)	0.026	(0.038)
age			−0.034***	(0.011)	−0.046***	(0.011)
age-squared			0.040***	(0.013)	0.051***	(0.014)
ethnic minority			0.052	(0.060)	0.040	(0.063)
single			0.091**	(0.044)	0.104**	(0.048)
has children			0.005	(0.051)	0.027	(0.055)
single parent			−0.062	(0.051)	−0.086	(0.054)
CSE			0.139*	(0.090)	0.149*	(0.091)
vocational qualifications			−0.001	(0.050)	0.027	(0.059)
O-levels/GCSEs			0.037	(0.048)	0.060	(0.054)
A-levels			0.186**	(0.090)	0.226***	(0.094)
degree			0.193*	(0.125)	0.268**	(0.131)
Previous economic state						
looking after home			0.029	(0.053)	−0.017	(0.051)
studying			−0.062	(0.045)	−0.122**	(0.042)
unemployed			−0.078*	(0.036)	−0.082*	(0.043)
other			0.283***	(0.124)	0.268***	(0.116)
Job characteristics						
tenure			−0.003***	(0.000)	−	
wage rate			0.013	(0.023)	0.004	(0.025)
semi-skilled			−0.057	(0.042)	−0.080*	(0.047)
semi-skilled/junior responsibility			−0.088*	(0.039)	−0.126**	(0.039)
skilled workers/supervisors			−0.060	(0.050)	−0.089	(0.051)
low management/supervisors			−0.035	(0.071)	−0.075	(0.067
hours of work			0.002	(0.002)	0.001	(0.002)
hotel chain			0.050	(0.038)	0.084**	(0.041)
Outside factors						
local unemployment rate			−0.009	(0.011)	−0.020*	(0.012)
holds other job			−0.008	(0.053)	0.002	(0.061)
currently at college			0.002	(0.041)	0.003	(0.045)
number of observations	834		668		668	
log likelihood	−428		−268.2		−284.7	
pseudo R^2	0.001		0.249		0.203	

Notes: Estimation is by probit. The numbers given are the marginal effects associated with the unreported underlying coefficients, calculated at the mean values of all variables. Standard errors are reported in parentheses. ***, **, * indicate statistical significance at the 1%, 5% and 10% levels respectively.

points less likely to leave than those who moved straight into our companies from a different job, this difference being statistically significant at the 10 per cent level. It may be that employment in these firms does not fully remove the scarring effect, real or supposed, of a period of unemployment. Individuals who have made this transition may therefore have fewer alternative opportunities, with the consequence that they are less likely to leave their current employment. So this result is consistent with the idea of outside alternatives determining separations. There may also be a lesson for firms fearful of hiring individuals from the unemployment pool, in that such individuals may be less likely to quit in the future, resulting in lower firm turnover costs. Table 11.2 also reveals that respondents who were previously in an 'other' economic state are more likely to exit than those previously in employment. This result is difficult to interpret, however, since we do not know what these individuals were doing. They are not a numerically important group, however, Table 11.1 revealing that only 4 per cent of our respondents answered in this way.

Not only must there be reasonable alternatives before individuals leave the service sector companies under analysis, but they must also be mobile. Table 11.2 shows that single employees have a separation probability that is nine percentage points higher than similar married employees, consistent with such a mobility story. However, if the single person also has children, then a large part of this 'single effect' is wiped out, as revealed by the negative coefficient on the single parent interaction coefficient (although this interaction coefficient fails to achieve statistical significance). These results suggest that family commitments, in terms of either a partner or children, can reduce mobility, and therefore the likelihood of such individuals exiting.[5]

The finding of a statistically significant, U-shaped relationship between age and separations is also consistent with a mobility story. The implication is that the prime-aged are the least likely to exit. Holding their family commitments constant, the prime-aged could have other commitments that reduce their mobility, particularly financial commitments. For example, it is plausible that the prime-aged are more likely than both the young and the old to have recently bought a house, with mortgage repayments reducing the likelihood that they will want to leave their jobs.

The overall picture, then, is that, in these low-wage service sector companies, it is not the most dissatisfied who are most likely to leave, but those who have the best outside opportunities and the easiest mobility. Those in favour of the satisfaction motive for turnover could point out that the control variables in the estimated equation are picking up the effects of job satisfaction on turnover.[6] However, in reply we can point to column 1 of Table 11.2, which shows that having removed all controls we still fail to find a significant correlation between job satisfaction and job separations. Of course, there remains the possibility that satisfaction is jointly determined with separation behaviour in a multi-equation model, so that satisfaction would be correlated with the unobservables in the separation equation, leading to endogeneity bias. In the absence of suitable instruments, we cannot control for this endogeneity of the satisfaction variable, however we suggest that the extremely small coefficients on the satisfaction variables are unlikely to be significantly altered even if we could do so.

A criticism that we can more easily deal with is the time lapse between the satisfaction surveys and the second round of payroll data, which highlights those who have left. It may be that feelings of dissatisfaction do not affect behaviour eighteen months later. However, we also have information on the timing of separations so we can examine whether this is an issue. In fact 75 per cent of separations had occurred within twelve months of the original survey (which is the period of time usually considered in turnover studies). We duplicated the analysis, using a dependent variable indicating only those who had separated within 12 months of the original survey, with no change in the qualitative results.

Even when we narrowed the sample to cover only those who exited within six months of the original survey, there was very little difference in the results.[7] In particular, there was still no relationship whatsoever between self-reported job satisfaction and exiting behaviour in the following six months. The Spearman rank-order correlation coefficients between job satisfaction and job separations within twelve months and six months were -0.03 and -0.01 respectively, neither of which even vaguely approached statistical significance. Finally, we estimated a hazard model, with the time to a separation as the dependent variable, but still found no evidence that job satisfaction is a statistically significant influence on separations.

Briefly considering the other coefficients in column 2 of Table 11.2, it is interesting to note that, in contrast to most turnover studies, we find no evidence of a statistically significant influence of wages on separations. This would suggest that labour turnover in the low-wage service sector is unresponsive to the wage rate, which is also consistent with the picture that we are building of this sector, in which imperfections such as mobility costs and lack of alternatives make worker behaviour sluggish in response to market signals. Such evidence points to the existence of monopsony power in this sector. However, it may be that employees consider not the absolute value of the wage rate, but its value relative to some alternative. We investigated this possibility by mapping into our data set the average wage in the individual's local labour market, taken from the 1996 New Earnings Survey. Defining an individual's relative wage rate to be the ratio of their actual wage to the local average, we included this relative wage measure in our estimated equation, but still could find no statistically significant influence on separations.

Turning to the occupation dummy variables, the only one to attract a statistically significant coefficient is that representing semi-skilled employees with junior responsibility, which is ranked in the middle of our five-point occupational scale. Such individuals are nine percentage points less likely to exit than the unskilled, although why only this group show a statistically significant difference is not obvious.

Finally in column 2, a highly statistically significant coefficient on tenure is obtained, with the marginal effect suggesting a 0.3 percentage point fall in the probability of a separation, for every additional month of prior tenure. Such a result is typically found in labour turnover research, with the interpretation being that tenure measures unobserved characteristics of individuals, related to their perseverance, or 'stick-with-it-ness'. Thus employees who have already worked in a firm for a long time are less likely to leave in the future. As explained earlier, however, tenure should properly be treated as endogenous, and its presence in the separation equation, while controlling for unobserved characteristics, can also lead to endogeneity bias on the estimated coefficients. Column 3 therefore repeats the analysis, omitting the tenure variable.

It was suggested previously that the coefficients in column 2 could be biased towards zero by the presence of tenure in the estimated equation, and indeed the marginal effects displayed in column 3 are almost all larger in absolute value than their counterparts in the previous column. However, the substance of the results remains unchanged, in that satisfaction still has no effect on separations, while the variables reflecting ease of mobility and alternative opportunities all continue to have statistically significant effects. The initial findings therefore do not appear to have been simply the result of any endogeneity bias.

In addition, some new statistically significant effects are obtained in column 3. In particular, the local unemployment rate is now negatively related to separations, with a point increase in unemployment reducing the probability of a separation by two percentage points. Insofar as the level of local unemployment is related to outside opportunities, this result is consistent with the previous findings that fewer such opportunities leads to a reduction in separations.

The firm dummy variable also gains a statistically significant coefficient in column 3, suggesting a probability of separation that is 8.4 percentage points higher in the hotel chain than in the supermarket chain. It is tempting to point to the fact that most of the hotels are in urban or inner city areas, while the supermarkets are typically found in out-of-town sites, and so to claim that hotel employees have more potential alternatives open to them, being based in cities already. However, place of residence, rather than place of work, is probably the key location variable for determining outside alternatives available to individuals. The company result obtained here is more likely to be due to a whole range of differences between the two companies, ranging from the type of work undertaken to company personnel policies, that are not controlled for in this analysis.

The other additional effects obtained in column 3 suggest that semi-skilled employees are less likely to separate than unskilled workers, and that individuals who were studying prior to working in the low-wage service sector are less likely to separate than those who were previously in alternative employment.

11.6   CONCLUSION

This chapter has used survey data to look at the determinants of job turnover in two national companies in the British low-wage service sector. Previous analyses of labour turnover, with a more general focus, have repeatedly found that the more dissatisfied an individual, the more likely he or she is to leave their job. Such a finding sits easily with intuition, and so could be thought of as an established fact. However, no evidence whatsoever of such a relationship was found in this analysis: the dissatisfied seem no more likely to leave their jobs than the satisfied. Instead, ease of exit, in terms of both ease of mobility and availability of outside alternatives, seems to be the key determinant of turnover.

We acknowledge that our results are specific to the sector studied, and are not representative of the economy as a whole. However, they suggest the following policy interventions. At the national level, average utility will be reduced if mobility problems are hindering job turnover, leaving individuals in jobs with which they are dissatisfied. Thus government policy needs to look at ways to increase mobility, for example by improving the skills of employees in order that they can compete for other work. Alternatively it may be a lack of affordable childcare which forces people to remain in jobs which provide them with little satisfaction. Another characteristic of our results is that they are consistent with the possibility of dynamic monopsony existing within the low-wage service sector. Looking in particular at the effect of the wage rate, turnover seems very unresponsive to the level of wages, suggesting that the labour supply curve could be quite steep. It is interesting to note that monopsony has been advanced (for example, by Machin and Manning 1994) as a possible explanation for research findings that suggest a zero or even positive effect of minimum wage increases on employment. Card and Krueger have been responsible for much of this empirical research in the US, and indeed it is in exactly the type of low-wage service sector companies that we consider here, that they found rising employment levels following an increase in minimum wages (see Card and Krueger 1995). Thus, the raising of minimum wage levels could be a welfare-enhancing policy that is at least employment-neutral, in the low-wage service sector.

Turning to policies for individual firms within this sector, these will need to address dissatisfaction levels, as our results show that immobile dissatisfied workers do not exit the firm, leaving a discontented workforce and possibly causing low morale and a poor working climate. Even amongst the mobile, if dissatisfaction leads to exit, firms are faced with potentially avoidable hiring and training costs. Overall, our data suggest that employers must be realistic when matching applicants to vacancies. Accepting applicants with education levels which exceed that required for the job seems to lead to low levels of satisfaction and thence to high turnover rates. Our results are therefore consistent with those of Tsang et al. (1991), who showed that overeducation significantly reduces job satisfaction, and McEvoy and Cascio (1985), who found that quits are higher where workers have unrealistic job expectations.

Our results also suggest that, provided that the initial job–applicant match is good, then employing applicants who were previously unemployed seems to benefit our firms in terms of future turnover, since they will retain experienced staff for longer periods of time and save on advertising vacancies, as well as the costs of training and inducting new recruits. In line with the British government's policy of combating social exclusion by encouraging disadvantaged groups back into the labour market, our results suggest that employers in the sectors studied should seriously consider using long-term unemployed individuals.

NOTES

1. Low-paid workers are defined as full-time workers who earn less than two-thirds of median earnings for all full-time workers.
2. See Green et al. (1996) for a full discussion of dynamic monopsony.
3. Individuals are categorised according to the highest level of qualification which they possess. The level of vocational qualifications held by respondents cannot be determined from the available data, and so we have arbitrarily ranked them between CSEs and GCSEs, on the assumption that individuals working in this sector will in general have quite low level vocational qualifications. Had we ranked this group below CSEs, the relationship between education level and separation rate would have been perfectly monotonic.
4. Full results are available from the authors upon request.
5. We investigated whether the presence of a partner affected men and women differently. In the raw data, married women had a lower separation rate than married men, 0.131 versus 0.214, the difference being statistically significant at the 5 per cent level. This suggested that the mobility of married women is more constrained than that of married men. However, when we introduced a gender, marital status interaction term into our estimated equation, its

coefficient was statistically insignificant, possibly reflecting the quite small number of married men in the sample.

6. Indeed, many of the variables included in the separation equation were included by us in an earlier study of job satisfaction, using the same data set (see Brown and McIntosh 1998).

7. The only changes in statistical significance were the coefficient on the degree variable becoming statistically insignificant, possibly because of the smaller number of six-month separators and the small number of degree holders making the coefficient unstable, and the gaining of a negative, statistically significant coefficient on the single parent variable, in line with the mobility story.

REFERENCES

Arnold, H. and D. Feldman (1982), 'A Multivariate Analysis of the Determinants of Job Turnover', *Journal of Applied Psychology*, **67** (3), 350–60.

Bartel, A.P. (1981), 'Race Differences in Job Satisfaction: a Reappraisal', *Journal of Human Resources*, **16**, 294–303.

Boroff, K.E. and D. Lewin (1997), 'Loyalty, Voice and Intent to Exit a Union Firm: a Conceptual and Empirical Analysis', *Industrial and Labor Relations Review*, **51** (1), 50–63.

Brown, D. and S. McIntosh (1998), *If You're Happy and You Know It....Job Satisfaction in the Low Wage Service Sector*, Centre for Economic Performance Discussion Paper 405.

Cappelli, P. and P.D. Sherer (1988), 'Satisfaction, Market Wages, and Labor Relations: an Airline Study', *Industrial Relations*, **27**, 56–73.

Card, D. and A.B. Krueger (1995), *Myth and Measurement: The New Economics of the Minimum Wage*, Princeton University Press, Princeton.

Carsten, J. and P. Spector (1987), 'Unemployment, Job Satisfaction and Employee Turnover: A Meta-analytic Test of the Muchinsky Model', *Journal of Applied Psychology*, **72** (3), 374–81.

Clark, A.E. (1997), 'Job Satisfaction and Gender: Why are Women so Happy at Work?', *Labour Economics*, **4**, 341–72.

Clark, A.E. and A.J. Oswald (1996), 'Satisfaction and Comparison Income', *Journal of Public Economics*, **61**, 359–81.

Clark, A.E., A.J. Oswald and P.B. Warr (1996), 'Is Job Satisfaction U-shaped in Age?', *Journal of Occupational and Organizational Psychology*, **69**, 57–81.

Freeman, R.B. (1978), 'Job Satisfaction as an Economic Variable', *American Economic Review*, **68**, 135–41.

Freeman, R. (1980), 'The Exit-Voice Tradeoff in the Labor Market: Unionism, Job Tenure, Quits and Separations', *Quarterly Journal of Economics*, **94** (4), 643–73.

Green, F., S. Machin and A. Manning (1996), 'The Employer Size-Wage Effect: Can Dynamic Monopsony Provide an Explanation', *Oxford Economic Papers*, **48**, 433–55.

Gordon, M.E. and A.S. Denisi (1995), 'A Re-examination of the Relationship Between Union Membership and Job Satisfaction', *Industrial and Labor Relations Review*, **48**, 222–36.

Hirschman, A. (1970), *Exit, Voice and Loyalty*, Harvard University Press, Cambridge.

Hulin, C., M. Roznowski and D. Hachiya (1985), 'Alternative Opportunities and Withdrawal Decisions: Empirical and Theoretical Discrepancies and An Integration', *Psychology Bulletin*, **97**, 233–50.

Idson, T.L. (1990), 'Establishment Size, Job Satisfaction and the Structure of Work', *Applied Economics*, **22**, 1007–18.

Locke, E.A. (1976), 'The Nature and Causes of Job Satisfaction', in M.D. Dunnette (ed.), *Handbook of Industrial and Organizational Psychology*, Rand McNally College Publishing Company, Chicago.

Machin, S. and A. Manning (1994), 'The Effects of Minimum Wages on Wage Dispersion and Employment: Evidence from the UK Wages Council', *Industrial and Labor Relations Review*, **47** (2), 319–29.

McEvoy, G. and W. Cascio (1985), 'Strategies for Reducing Employee Turnover: a Meta-Analysis', *Journal of Applied Psychology*, **70** (2), 342–53.

Meng, R. (1990), 'The Relationship Between Unions and Job Satisfaction', *Applied Economics*, **22**, 1635–48.

Metcalf, D. (1998), 'The National Minimum Wage in Private Services', Centre for Economic Performance Working Paper 1000.

Miller, P. (1990), 'Trade Unions and Job Satisfaction', *Australian Economic Papers*, **29**, 226–48.

Miller, P. and C. Mulvey (1991), 'Australian Evidence on the Exit/Voice Model of the Labor Market', *Industrial and Labor Relations Review*, **45** (1), 44–57.

Mobley, W., S. Horner and A. Hollingsworth (1978), 'An Evaluation of Precursors of Hospital Employee Turnover', *Journal of Applied Psychology*, **63** (4), 408–14.

OECD (1996), *Employment Outlook*, OECD, Paris.

Schneider, J. (1976), 'The Greener Grass Phenomenon: Differential Effects of A Work Context Alternative on Organisational Participation and Withdrawal Intentions', *Organisational Behaviour and Human Performance*, **16**, 408–33.

Schwochau, S. (1987), 'Union Effects on Job Attitudes', *Industrial and Labor Relations Review*, **40**, 209–24.

Sloane, P.J. and H. Williams (1996), 'Are Overpaid Workers Really Unhappy? A Test of the Theory of Cognitive Dissonance', *Labour*, **10**, 3–15.

Tsang, M.C., R.W. Rumberger and H.M. Levin (1991), 'The Impact of Surplus Schooling on Work Productivity', *Industrial Relations,* 30, 209–28.

Watson, R., D. Storey, P. Wynarczyk, K. Keasey and H. Short (1996), 'The Relationship Between Job Satisfaction and Managerial Remuneration in Small and Medium-sized Enterprises: an Empirical Test of Comparison Income and Equity Theory Hypotheses', *Applied Economics*, **28**, 567–76.

Weiss, A. (1984), 'Determinants of Quit Behaviour', *Journal of Labour Economics*, **2** (3), 371–87.

Index